HEALING WITH WORDS SERIES

D0391725

When a Lifemate Dies

STORIES OF LOVE, LOSS, AND HEALING

Edited by Susan Heinlein,
Grace Brumett, and Jane-Ellen Tibbals

Fairview Press
Minneapolis

Published by Fairview Press, 2450 Riverside Avenue South, Minneapolis, MN 55454.

Library of Congress Cataloging-in-Publication Data
When a lifemate dies: stories of love, loss, and healing / edited by Susan
    Heinlein, Grace Brumett, and Jane-Ellen Tibbals. -- 1st ed.
        p.   cm. -- (Healing with words series)
    ISBN 1-57749-056-8 (pbk.: alk. paper)
    1. Grief. 2. Bereavement--Psychological aspects. 3. Loss
    (Psychology) 4. Widows--Psychology. 5. Widowers--Psychology.
    I. Heinlein, Susan, 1950–   . II. Brumett, Grace, 1946–   .
    III. Tibbals, Jane-Ellen, 1943–   . IV. Series.
BF575.G7W47   1997
155.9'37--dc21   97–33609
                                                                                        CIP

FIRST EDITION
First Printing: September 1997

Printed in the United States of America
01 00 99 98 97   7 6 5 4 3 2 1

Cover design: Laurie Duren
Cover photo: Dale Matlock. "Shadows" captures Dale and his wife, Nancy, shortly before her death on March 7, 1994.
Author photo: Paul Schraub Photography, Santa Cruz, California.

Publisher's Note: Fairview Press publishes books and other materials related to the subjects of social and family issues. Its publications, including *When a Lifemate Dies,* do not necessarily reflect the philosophy of the Fairview Health System or its treatment programs.

For a free current catalog of Fairview Press titles, please call 1-800-544-8207, or visit our web site at www.press.fairview.org.

Acknowledgments for previously published work:
"Attending to Details" © 1993 by Ruth Coughlin (excerpt from *Grieving: A Love Story,* Random House), used by permission. "Angel Wing" © 1995 by S. K. Duff (first published in *Blue Violin),* used by permission. Excerpt © by T. S. Eliot (Harcourt Brace & Co.), used by permission. Excerpt © by Robert Frost (Hyperion Books), used by permission. Excerpts from *Safe Passages* © 1992 by Molly Fumia (Conari Press), used by permission. "Recuerdo" © 1995 by David Garnes (first published in *A Loving Testimony: Remembering Loved Ones Lost to AIDS,* Crossing Press), used by permission. "In the Moment," "Stories," and excerpt © 1996 by Fenton Johnson (excerpt from *Geography of the Heart,* Scribner), used by permission. Excerpt from *Crow and Weasel* © 1990 by Barry Lopez (North Point Press), used by permison. "Summons" © Amber Coverdale Sumrall (first published in *Sonoma Mandala Review,* volume 16), used by permission. "Wingspan" © by Amber Coverdale Sumrall (first published in *Porter Gulch Review),* used by permission.

When all the ceremonies
of death are done
The eulogies said
The flowers gone
When there are
no more offerings
of food
When the mail
returns to mostly junk
Then the true mourning
will begin—
the quiet grief.

—Betty Peckinpah, 1994

CONTENTS

DEDICATION

For our soulmates, Michael, Don, and Merrill.
Guiding us still.

FOREWORD

Thomas Moore

The most unsettling mystery in a life full of mysteries is the loss of a person who has completed your life in some way, who has appeared miraculously to make up for all the misunderstanding, misinterpreting, and misreading of your life that may have gone on for years. It may take a long search to find such a person who is truly a soulmate, and then, when that rare companion is taken from you, you wonder what arcane and heartless law of the universe is at play, and you wonder how you can continue to live with the raw emptiness that is achingly slow to fill again with life.

I write not as one who has known this mystery firsthand, although I have had my fill of death and separation, but as a counselor who has sat with many a person in the still, vertical waters of grief, and I write in response to the chilling and poignant stories told in this volume of despair and hope. Almost every tale of accident, cancer, suicide, and murder reminds me of a face, someone I have sat with over weeks, months, and years, as grief has gradually worked itself, through an alchemy of dreams, conversations, inner dialogues, life changes, and spiritual discoveries, into a fixed element of character. Grief provides us with the necessary loss of innocence and an acquaintance with the rule of death, which contributes as much to our humanity as does the largesse of life.

Hidden in these tales of mourning is some elusive wisdom, some of it revealed immediately in the presence of death, some of it learned painfully over years of questing for peace and continuing life. "Don't tell me to get on with life, don't tell me to get a life," many of these courageous people say. Americans deal well with progress, advances, and success—at least we're good at accomplishment and creativity, but we seem to have been absent when the lessons were given on dealing with the past, with loss, and with death. We know how to be strong, but we're not terribly skilled at acknowledging and living fruitfully with weakness and loss. Many of the voices in this collection tell of the loneliness involved in finding one's way through the thicket of emotions and fantasies that appears as soon as death makes an appearance.

These stories also articulate nuances in the anger that sometimes unexpectedly rises, directed against fate, the universe, God, and the much loved person who has gone. On the surface, the anger may appear irrational and misplaced, nevertheless it comes through strong and clear. Old traditional tales describe anger as a signal of fortitude and inner strength, as having a role to play, even if it doesn't seem to make sense, in the continuance of life. It can co-exist with acceptance and surrender as an expression of the soul filling out these other more spiritual emotional achievements. The stories here tell of the red-hot anger needed so as not to be talked out of necessary feelings and honest reactions. The soul has its own ways of constructing and reconstructing itself, ways that are often idiosyncratic and highly individual and may bear little relation to conventional wisdom.

As I read these stories, I felt my own anger rising: at a society that loves its efficient bureaucracy and doesn't understand the importance of compassion, a society that continues to fiddle with nature for financial profit and ignores the extreme physical and emotional pain entailed in diseases that its own sciences tell us are caused by thoughtless and self-serving manipulation of nature and food products, and a society that refuses to put its resources wholeheartedly into treating the causes of violence. We have created a social machine, including a medical establishment, that too often lacks a heart, and this book is all about broken and wounded hearts looking for warm comfort in a cool social environment. Thank God for the generosity of hospice workers and for physicians and nurses who refuse to hide the colors of their humanity behind the blank white of their professional frocks.

This book on loss is also a collection of love stories. Who said that romance is dead and that the family no longer holds together? These are not naive, unrealistic tales of uncomplicated passion, they are stories of human loves, clearly made more vivid by death. The ordinariness of the people and their circumstances contributes to the humanity of their ordeals and to the lessons they have to offer the reader who is open to the depth and substance of their emotion. Here you find neither avoidance of emotional complexity nor lukewarm sentimentality.

Children appear frequently in these stories, the sons and daughters who are left behind showing the muffled signs of their feelings of loss. A nation's soul is alive only to the extent that it cares for its children, but a lifemate's death may also complicate feelings toward the children. Life begs to be lived simply and directly, without deals and manipulations, but the directions the heart takes in its feelings may be unpredictable and confusing. It seems we care for the soul best, even in the presence of death, by being fully present to our children, amid all the confusion, denial, and exasperating complexity of their feelings and expressions.

These stories confirm for me the importance, in dealing with life's deepest challenges, of a spiritual sensibility, and especially of rituals that come from or at least address the individual heart and imagination. Why not ignore the agnosticism and rationalism of our time and speak trustingly with our departed friends and mates? Why not pray for them and to them and ask for their forgiveness and their leave eventually to go on with life? Why not hope unrealistically in the face of medicine's cocksureness, and why not transgress as many rules as necessary in the quest for life, understanding, peace, and the eternal continuance of love?

Death can restore to us a sense of religion—not an institution or a doctrine, but an attitude characterized by faithfulness to life itself, the ability to make rituals that touch the heart, the capacity to forgive and let go, a feeling for family and community that has no bounds, and a corresponding commitment to justice. Our feelings of loss may then slowly open up, like the wings of spirit itself, into a wider, less self-oriented love.

The authors of the stories collected here don't talk about the broadening of their hearts through loss, but their generosity in telling their stories so vividly, with artfulness and candor, reveals an element in their story that hides between the lines. Their loss has given them the courage and the imagination to make a story of their experience, to turn their wounded hearts inside out in narrative form. This is the beginning of what we call community, a tired and often hollow word that needs restoration. We all need to tell our stories of pain and survival, and we all need to read and listen to the stories that are told. This exchange of hearts could warm up our society, so that our essential loneliness, felt so keenly in times of loss, might at least have a source of containment.

If it's true that those who have lost a mate can recognize each other's torment in a few minutes and with few words, then when a community, even a nation, has a soul, it should have a similar effect. No one should feel utterly alone or be treated as an object without a heart and a life. This definition of community is not unrealistic; it simply calls for a revolution in the way we treat each other.

How do we reach that goal? Encourage friends to read these stories and others like them, stories that educate us in our humanity. Get these stories into the schools, especially into the graduate schools and medical schools, where the heart is as important to education as the mind and the hands. Tell your stories. Keep them honest, like those in this book. Don't let the clever mind take control of the heart and the imagination. I'm less worried about the dumbing of society than the numbing of our people, who have good reason to become irrational with the overwhelming challenges of life and death. Live your life fully, as well as the death that comes into it like an enemy. Nothing less will keep your humanity intact.

INTRODUCTION

Carol Staudacher

The memory is clear: the Vietnam veteran sits in my study, wearing a shirt with a bright floral print, the vibrancy of the colors contrasting sharply with the tone of our interview. Quietly, meticulously, he makes his way through the labyrinth of his grief experiences, recounting how he suffered—not the loss of one person, but of many.

Finally, he clasps his hands together, tears rising in his eyes, and tells me in a strong, sure voice: "Writing saved my life. It did. The whole time I was in Vietnam, then after I came back, writing saved my life. I would have died if I could not have written about what I was experiencing."

This wide-ranging collection evokes his words. I am sure that writing similarly helped some of these survivors, at least in little ways—saved them from the unanticipated pain of the moment, or from the jagged hole created by another new, seemingly endless day to endure. It gave them a lifeline to hold throughout the confusing first few years, as they sought new footing in a drastically changed personal landscape.

Writing often delivers survivors from the pressure that builds in the throat when words won't allow themselves to be spoken; though the writing hand may tremble, as the voice surely would, it will not be witnessed. "Sometimes," said one survivor, "it seems that paper is the only thing you can trust, the only thing that you can depend on to hear you."

The writers in this collection have put their trust in paper. Their stories illuminate the major work of the grieving process. Coping with feelings of isolation and vulnerability, for instance, and the sense that the wounds of loss will never heal. Experiencing new and daunting surges of emotion. Struggling to accept that the loved one's death was beyond the survivor's control; that they neither caused, nor could have prevented it. Grappling with the realization that death means the loved one is permanently gone—a seemingly obvious fact that in reality is assimilated only painfully and over time.

These personal accounts also illustrate that to resolve their loss fully, survivors must grieve the loss of the whole person—not an idealized remembrance. Moreover, they must express themselves and discuss their emotions, because unreleased grief will go underground and ultimately harm survivors.

As these selections also show, grieving people often find unrecognized, untapped resources within themselves. Eventually survivors integrate loss into their lives. They incorporate what the experience has taught them: in many ways they will never be the same, yet many changes that happen will enrich the rest of their lives. But it will not be easy, as Maude Meehan tells us in her poem, "For This Journey": "Now it is time. We gather round this man, / the hub of all our lives. Hands joined, we sing, / speak final words. Leave with a last caress. / Now he is ready for this journey. We are not."

We travel with these writers, none ready for their journeys, but all having moved forward in one creative, courageous way or another. And even though they are bound by their common experience and their voices combine in a chorus of authenticity, each one is unique. Some of the stories and poems here are raw and evolving. They are not designed as much as they are delivered, as one would deliver a newborn. Others are like archaeological finds from hallowed, sacred sites, simultaneously presenting a mystery as well as unveiling it. *Here is this artifact I hold in my hand,* the writer observes. *What do I make of it? How does it fit into my life?* Still other writers in this collection have come to their contributions as to works of art, their writings honed and polished until they are finely, precisely wrought.

Ruth Coughlin tells us, in "Attending to Details": "I have now learned, am continuing to learn, another language, the language of loss. Like the language of music and love, it is universal. You don't need a dictionary, you don't need a translator, you don't need a thesaurus. All you need to do is go through it once, just once, to get it."

These writers do undoubtedly speak the same language. Thrust into the most devastating, wrenching experience of their lives, they have, against their wishes, "gotten it."

Ginny Stanford tells us what all survivors experience in one way or another—that shocking moment when they think the death is all a mistake, that their loved one has returned, and then they discover that they have tricked themselves again, perhaps for the thousandth time.

The reader slips alongside Nancy Wambach in "The Anniversary Waltz," and as she wraps her arms around her dying husband, she also wraps them around our hearts and takes us with her, each dogged, determined step of the way through the challenging early hours of her twentieth wedding anniversary.

In "Night-Blooming Jasmine and Summer Sheets," Mary Schultz offers another powerful slice of reality, as she acknowledges both the positive and negative aspects of marriage to a beloved partner: "Together he and I were on our way to forging a next-generation dysfunctional family to rival those from which we'd come. Now, I'd have to complete the task alone. Alone."

Grace Brumett's "Bless This House" combines reminiscences, laments, and blessings as she takes the reader through one of the most taxing and disorienting challenges a surviving mate may face: moving from the home that was shared with her mate. There is no easy way to do this.

"Going in Circles," Susan Heinlein's poignant work, explores both the burden and relief of letting go, the necessary letting go of a mate's material possessions so that they may be replaced by indelible memories.

Regardless of how hard survivors work at getting through it, sometimes there are elements of grief that are unrelenting. They linger longer, so long, in fact, that it seems they will never go away. Amber Coverdale Sumrall addresses this dilemma as she tells us in her quiet, meditative poem, "I want to tear open thin tissue, / expose what refuses to heal."

And survivors who had no opportunity to say goodbye to loved ones understand the need that moved Jane-Ellen Tibbals to write "Letter to a Murdered Mate." This wrenching farewell to her mate, however, also recounts her course through shock, disorientation, and despair into a state of loving remembrance and gratitude.

So finally, blessedly, healing does occur, a well-earned reward after an almost unbearable journey. Maureen Cannon's "Where Tunnels End" puts the experience in profound perspective: "pain keeps one alive / As much as joy does." But when later she asks, "Ah, has / The world grown round again, and is the night / Less long?" we know the answer: Yes.

The world indeed has regained its shape. Surviving mates are getting through the night; it is no longer their enemy. And like the victims of fire and flood, the writers in this volume have collectively broken through the devastation that accompanies tragedy, the estrangement that naturally affixes itself to grief. These writers bond together to pay tribute to their loved ones, and to their own human spirit—and to the spirit of many survivors they never will meet. They form the voice for those who have not spoken.

In the most delightful of outcomes, they may even motivate a survivor who reads this collection to take up a pen to join in the illumination of grief's long journey, or to memorialize a beloved partner. And there, at the table or desk, during some stolen morning hours, or in a tale told long into the darkness, will emerge a story no one else can tell, a poem no other person on this planet can write any more than one individual can breathe for another. And, if so, the world will be that much richer for the telling.

THE JOURNEY

The Editors

When a mate dies, there is no possible preparation for the onslaught of feeling. Disbelief hits like a thunderbolt. The ache of loneliness and utter disorientation shift to anger, despair, anguish, and back again. The sense of emptiness is beyond imagination.

In the starkness of this unfamiliar landscape, each uncertain step is an initiation. What signposts can help us through our grief? What refuge can ease the aching heart of our mourning? Although we each must find our own way through sorrow, we can find solace in others.

As three younger widows who lost our mates to death in the past few years—one to cancer after years of caregiving; another to cancer after only a few short months of illness; and the last, suddenly and violently, to murder—we know this journey. In October 1994, when our grief was new, we met at a hospice-sponsored spousal grief group. We were all "widow/ers"—the term used loosely here to signify one who has lost a lifemate, husband or wife, lover, male or female. A glimmer of healing emerged that night, when we warily began to open our lives and hearts to one another with our stories and tears. We had found a refuge.

We learned the powerful healing that comes with the simple telling of, and listening to, a story. Those stories, told from our bones, are authentic, and only the authentic count in the midst of grief. These stories become the signposts beckoning through the dark tunnel of grief with a small ray of connection we humans desperately need. They don't promise anything—no happy endings, no solutions, no "fix-its"—just a story.

The tales we told one another on those nights wove a strong fabric to warm us in a way that was found nowhere else. Knowing so many others, each in his or her own way, were walking the same path, we found we could go on. Once again, we even found moments of laughter.

The idea for this book was conceived out of our group. We wanted to collect authentic stories and poems told from the heart by widows and widowers. Indeed, we found widow/ers wanting to speak and connect everywhere. Death, after all, is a given for each of us. It is all around us. Built into every relationship is an end.

We are reminded of death's inevitable presence with a small and very old story. It goes like this:

> *There was once a young woman who lived in a village with her husband. Though the two of them were considered poor, they*

had all that they needed because of their deep love for one another. But one day, without any warning, her husband died. The poor woman was overcome with grief. She ran from neighbor to neighbor, begging them for medicine to bring back her husband. People thought she had lost her senses. They took her, shrieking and wailing, to the wise old man who lived at the edge of the forest.

"Old wise one, I beg you, give me the medicine that will bring back my husband."

He nodded his head slowly. "I will help you, but first I need a handful of mustard seed. It must be mustard seed taken from a house where no one has lost a husband, a child, a parent, or a friend; where death is not known."

The woman joyfully raced from house to house in the village to find the mustard seed. The people, pitying her, were ready to give her what she wanted.

But when she asked, "Did a husband or wife, a son or daughter, a father or mother die in your family?" they answered her, "Alas, the living are few; but the dead are many. Do not remind us of our deepest grief."

After some time the woman, weary and hopeless, stopped her search and sat at the edge of the roadside, watching the lights of the village as they flickered and died. At last, the darkness of the night reigned everywhere, and she sat contemplating the ever-changing fate of humanity.

On her return, the wise old man saw that her understanding was complete. "The life of mortals in this world is troubled, brief, and combined with pain. For there are no means by which those who have been born can avoid dying," he told her.

Allowing the pain to be as it was, the woman buried her husband in the forest and went on.

Our stories have come from people of many different backgrounds, places, and beliefs. They touch on many different kinds of raw and ragged emotions. They reveal inner feelings sometimes unacceptable to the outer world. They avoid easy sentiments. In their telling is much sadness, anger, and tenderness. They speak brutal truths of mourning. Yet they bring tremendous hope and healing, too. They ring of courage, honesty, and compassion.

Someone once asked us, "But where is the hope in these stories?"

Our answer was simple: hope is found in the truth. When we hear a surviving mate's story, our hearts resonate with understanding; grieving mates want only the truth, not false hope. Hope is the story itself. If we have learned nothing else from our pain, we know that a powerful healing comes from the simple exchange with another who has traveled the same path. With this honesty comes relief. Our compassion is awakened, and out of this awakening comes real hope—the human connection—the first step toward healing.

Consider the simple words of another wise storyteller, Barry Lopez, in the preface to his book *Crow and Weasel*:

> *"I would ask you to remember only this one thing," said Badger. "The stories people tell have a way of taking care of them. If stories come to you, care for them. And learn to give them away where they are needed. Sometimes a person needs a story more than food to stay alive. That is why we put these stories in each other's memory. This is how people care for themselves."*

When all is said and done, what we really have is our stories—around the campfire, around the kitchen table, at the end of a long day, at the end of a life.

We imagine if you are reading this book, it is likely you already know the pain and transformation embedded in each voice. You will recognize the absolute authenticity in these stories. So as you, or one you know, moves through the crossing points, the unfinished conversations, the shattered remnants of a broken mirror, the aloneness of solo flying, and the heart's composting, just know that sharing our stories is an important part of the metamorphosis to healing.

Chapter One
Crossing Points

I find myself going over and over the details of your death with everyone I know. To speak and speak again of this event proclaims its awful truth to me, perhaps not yet quite convinced, perhaps not sure of my place in its unfolding.

—Molly Fumia, *Safe Passage*

Death is a profound threshold. No matter how a loved one dies, for those left behind, the parting becomes a reference point. One's world view is irrevocably altered. Now the wholeness of life includes death.

Each of these stories and poems tells of death's crossing point. They describe, literally and metaphorically, the steps taken with one's mate to the very borderline of death and the initial effect of that final separation.

There are as many ways to move through sorrow as there are ways to die. The voices here show how differently individuals move through this passage. They describe the ways we say good-bye, and the ways we don't. They tell of rituals and memorials that come through the dying.

Several speak of the agony of witnessing a slow dying. There are so many small deaths along the way for everyone. As caretakers, these writers express the helplessness and ache of hanging on, and then finally letting go.

Dying severs so much. Even with a lengthy dying, there is that moment when our mate is physically gone. Ask any widow/er—he or she can vividly recount the exact details of the moment of crossing, whether or not he or she was at their mate's side. In truth, it was their crossing, too.

In each of these pieces you will find that the writer, even in the midst of this crossing and before the separation of death, is feeling a sense of continuing connection.

You will find phrases such as "still leading the way" and "break free through all barriers" and "the magical key to everything" that refer to this connectedness. Others honestly state another sentiment, telling one of grief's seeming contradictions: "He is ready for this journey. We are not." These stories and poems recognize the undeniable impact of our mate's death—that unforgettable moment in time. Each story shows that death is a significant crossing point not only for the dead who cross on, but for their mates who must cross back.

LEADING THE WAY

Carl Stancil

You are slipping away.
I feel your weakness each day.
Your body is still pink and soft as a child.
The electronic machine still stupidly grinds away its
        electrochemistry attempting to make life bearable.
Your consciousness rises and falls like the tides.
I feel closer to you now than ever.

I hold your puffy feet.
The feet that carried you through the deep Sierra
        snows after your skis had long given up.
They walked in the muddy streets of Ernesto Acuna with
        Contra gunfire in the background.
They flew through the air at the Aikido dojo.
Oh! The fear of flying.
I remember how they led the way on the path to
        Muktinath as Anapurna watched.
Now they carry you up the stairs to your room this one
        last time.

Still you are leading the way.

PISSING UPWIND

Susan Heinlein

All around me, I hear the sounds of life: Start living again. It's been nearly a year. You're not the one who died, go out and have some fun!

I try to explain the problem I have with these (get-a-life) recommendations. "This is my life," I tell my concerned friends, but I know they're worried about me anyway. They can't understand. I sense their relief when I tell them that I'm busy, working; okay. How can I explain that this is the only life I can live?

"Go get laid," another suggests. Their prescription for the good life has a problem since the two main ingredients are the ones most dead: Merrill. And passion.

They just shake their heads. But I know what they are feeling: I am not thinking straight. They're wrong. I've never been so awake. I'd give anything to be ignorant again. And innocent; that was the best.

When did my life go bad? Just under a decade after it went good. Diagnosis: lung cancer. Grade IV. Non-small cell. Inoperable. The doc is not sympathetic (*you brought it on yourself* is what he thinks-but-doesn't-say). A death-numbed man who relates to the world with a pat on the shoulder: no cure; no hope; no future; get-your-life-in-order; dead, dead, gone. After less than thirty minutes, the doctor smiles sadly and squeezes a slumped, defeated shoulder. *So-sorry, gotta go now. Other people are waiting.*

I wanted 3600 seconds. I wanted 90 minutes. I wanted a lifetime.

I got six months. Merrill got less. He didn't die when he took his last breath; he died when he was told he was dying. He died his little deaths each time the pain swept through his body in its relentless destruction. I can only imagine the torture. Eradicating the pain became our trip itinerary. We weren't very successful; bumbling tourists dressed in loud, flowery shirts; cameras hanging around our necks while we squinted through life's viewfinder. Shooting everything. Seeing nothing.

Every day we tried to defeat the pain. But nothing worked, not until three weeks before he died when relief was administered through a surgical hole in his chest with a portable, shoulder-strapped, radio-sized digital druggist so he could move freely while under the influence (too bad he could no longer walk).

Timing is everything.

Until then, it was morphine-on-a-clock. Time-released promises. I used to wonder when all that morphine would be liberated. Could all those hundreds of milligrams be lying in wait for a single second to rush through his arteries like a speeding train? Would I suddenly come upon Merrill dancing a jig, stoned out of his mind? I wish I had. The morphine sure as hell didn't seem to work when a pill was swallowed, a patch slapped on his chest, or liquid squirted down his throat by a rodent-sized eye dropper, so he'd swallow/slap/squirt more and more.

"What was the worst thing that could happen?" the doctor queried. Addiction? Overdose? Good point.

Pain was the first order of business when we arrived for his weekly, multi-minute audience. It was about all he could treat, but we didn't believe that at the time (read my lips: no cure; no hope; no future; get-your-life-in-order; dead, dead, gone). We still believed in miracles.

So where was the pain this week? the doc would ask.

I can hear it now, Merrill dutifully reciting every excruciating moment. Without the distraction of death, Merrill-the-scientist/engineer would have developed a comprehensive pain presentation with formulas and schematics that should birth a product, not kill a man. If he had felt even better, he would have provided his specialty: a flow chart, arrows and lines noting each metastasis, aberrant cell, and tumor. I still have all his notes—written by tremoring hands, once steady enough to fix anything—as he tried to troubleshoot his body's technical difficulties. These scribbles are precious; a documentary detailing six months of comprehensive, high-performance dying.

Then there were the treatments. The chemotherapy room had a big, comfy, cold-leather recliner, a metal table, and a tall, rolling drug holder tree with plastic bags hanging from its branches. The procedure tried our patience—one drop every minute or so—like we had all the time in the world. We'd sit and talk while the poison snaked through his veins.

In the beginning we tread carefully among the verb tenses. Tell no lies; tell no truths. I became the information officer, spinning tomorrows in bite-sized inducements, thinking, I suppose, that if I came up with some things he wouldn't want to miss, he'd reschedule his departure.

I avoided sentences that depicted all he'd miss. He never learned about his future step-grandchild and great-nephew—most notable for their lousy timing—who would arrive seven months too late. We didn't talk about his early retirement, begun only a few months before he was diagnosed. Or our book collaboration with the wild, techno-thriller plot only he could conjure. Or the sauna he wanted to build. Or the inventions he would create. Or our trips to the warm, breezy islands he loved to visit. Or our summer BBQs where he controlled the grill like a picnic terrorist. Sometimes, I wished he had future-amnesia.

Ah, my friends are back. They are concerned. I must try to explain again. "Please listen, this is important: Losing a mate is different from other deaths; I know—I've done those, too. This is too big to fantasize by day. It's too big to dream at night. It's too big for your small repairs (no cure; no hope; no future; dead, dead, gone)."

But thank you for caring. Your concern keeps me sane. Sometimes.

Sometimes during chemo my mind twisted with surreal visions. There was a Kevorkian-style recipe for two: To end pain, empty large drug bag (the one with the toxic warning icon) into urine cups. Add contents of saline solution for taste. Mix with tongue depressor.

But I must not forget the good times—like the first chemo treatment. The doctor asked Merrill if he wanted steroids with his Carboplatin-Itoposide (pickles and onions with your burger, sir?), a special sauce guaranteed to add spice. He did, and when we got home that first night, Merrill felt better than he had in weeks. He had energy. Tomorrow held promise. He wanted to mow the lawn.

No doubt about it: Hope had arrived at our doorstep.

"It'll be okay. Really," he said with a lopsided steroid grin. I believed him. Had to. Those smiles were precious—a mother lode of promises.

But Hope was only a brief houseguest. It took her only four days to pack her bags and flee. She didn't even say goodbye.

Hope's replacement came in the guise of constant, agonizing, chemo-induced pain, which seemed to bring on the cancer, full-strength—a degree of sickness that would never once leave him during the 165 or so days left. The pain became more than physical. It's true what they say: Cancer destroys the spirit long before it takes out the body.

While he was awake, I did what I could to make him comfortable, but mostly I just stood and watched. Looking stupid. However, when he napped, I got to work. I'd continue my negotiations with all the cosmic possibilities: God, Goddess, Buddha, Mohammed, Zeus. My desperation was flexible.

I tried the switch maneuver: Take me, dammit!

I added bait: I'll go to church regularly. I'll become: Nun/Minister/Rabbi. I will/will not . . . (fill in the blank).

Friends called; stopped by. "What can I do? Just name it," they'd ask, poised to promise me their world; that strange, wonderful, innocent place I once inhabited if I could only find my way back. But I couldn't. I could barely remember those days.

Stop this death! I would tell them. They would have done so if they could.

Without any sign of divine intervention or medical miracle, I decided it was up to me to end this pandemonium. When Merrill could sleep (of what does a dying man dream?), I'd dash to the library, read medical books, make calls, or go on the "net." I was out of my mind to find a way through this madness. I studied fish cartilage, vegetable soup, the alphabet of vitamins, beta carotene, roots, berries, and tree bark. Baggies of unpronounceable teas were everywhere. I even found an interesting concoction—guaranteed to revitalize damaged cells, the write-up said—including a mashed Asian beetle. I became conversational in dosages, contra-indications, Megace, H2 blockers, Taxol, carbo-this and carbo-that, Navelbine, Sensimide, chemosensitivity testing, and the FDA. I knew the phone number of every third-world clinic that promised salvation, and every U.S. hospital that did not. I knew the PDR like an evangelist, the New Testament.

I was an expert on everything but dying.

If Merrill believed in anything, it was his doctor's medicine. He was polite to my proselytizing of the communion of body and mind, but never a participant. I became a devout follower of the Church of Hope (or as one friend said, the Cult of Denial). I thought that if we laughed, visualized, and really, really believed that we could beat it, we would. I was the quixotic engineer on the-little-train-that-could. Merrill rode in the caboose. I thought we could. Thought we could. We could.

Couldn't. We never even made it to the top of the hill.

I was clearly missing the point. I never learned the difference between the twin sisters, Hope and Denial. I still cannot tell them apart. Did I not hear the doctor when he said, no cure, no hope, no future?

But how can you live without hope? I never had the courage to ask Merrill this question. Even as he sat in his beloved, tattered, mahogany-colored recliner with its shredding arms and Merrill-imprinted seat, he—down from 220 pounds to 150, no hair; sunken, dilated eyes; bones pressing outward from his six-foot-two-inch body—was trying to protect me. While he experienced closed-loop suffering: weakness, nausea, constipation, diarrhea, knife-sharp pains, dull-throbbing pains, hearing loss, vision loss, a golfball-sized tumor in his armpit, pain, pain, and refrain, I went for the gold. He was solicitous of my endless drivel of a magical mystery tour that would save him, and he never stopped nurturing my hope, no matter how exhausting the hyperbole or excruciating his pain. I never understood his silence; I was too busy searching for the antidotal grail.

I was the bane of his doctor. As if he had waltzed out of medical school yesterday, I faxed him every odd elixir and treatment I stumbled on. And like the priestly principal at a parochial school, he'd call me into his office for the sermon: Be a team player (Father, what team would that be?) and stop sending those damn faxes.

He was a busy man.

And I was a busy woman. I would go home and shoot off another cure. While my fax machine buzzed with optimism, Merrill continued to die. Together, we were spinning completely out of control.

We both cried alone. I was weak; I didn't want him to see my anguish. He was strong; he didn't want me to see his anguish. In this we agreed. Our emotions orbited close together, but never collided. I didn't know how to ask him to talk to me. He didn't know what to say. Life's last stand-off.

I learned to give him daily shots of some drugs. One would increase his white cell count; the other his red. He watched as I practiced on an orange, plunging the needle into the juicy fruit like Freddie Kruger to his teenage victim. Merrill was wary, suggesting that I be less enthusiastic: "My good arm is not the enemy." After all, he reminded me, it was one of his few body parts that still worked according to manufacturer's warranty.

He never complained when the needle missed its mark, bounced off his skin, or penetrated too deep. He was always so grateful, even when I added to the pain. Wham, bam, thank you ma'am. Every so often I was able to push the needle in like a sensitive and gentle lover, but overall, my success was dubious. He told me once that he was sure his name had become, "So-sorry."

Oh God, I can't remember . . . Did I tell him I was so-sorry more than how precious he was to me? That I loved him more than life? Had it all degenerated to apologies?

Oh, sweet, gentle, Merrill, I ache at the thought of the pain I put you through in my desperation. I did it for love; the doctors for money, but in the end, the reasons didn't matter. It was agony, every day of the 24-1/2 weeks that you suffered.

Did I do it all wrong? Did I push for a triple-strength treatment; the trinity of bad medicine that destroyed your cells, your spirit, and what little time you had left? You resisted; but I was stronger; the rapist, forcing my shaft of hope into your body. Thrusting for time; forgetful of quality.

I know I'm supposed to remember all the wonderful years we had together and not focus on the dying. Most of the time, I do. But I don't always control my mind anymore. It goes where it pleases into dark, damp corners without concern for my feelings or your memory.

How, I wonder, do I exorcise those last snapshots? You are lying on the rented hospital bed in our family room; one eye open and bright; the other half-closed and out-of-focus, unable to see out the window the land you loved so with its ancient redwoods towering above, and the gently flowing river below. How can I ever forgive my ignorance when I cheered you on, thinking that you were finally clearing the blockage in your throat, but were actually taking your final breath? How can I release myself from the picture of your body, cooled and hardened, as I sat for hours caressing it; searching your beloved face for the you I knew, long after death had shoplifted your memories?

Please, somebody tell me. What do I do with these pictures?

My friends, they are back now. Persistent. They mean well, I know. They want me to be the person they once knew, but I can't be; I know too much. Each time the wind changes, I don't turn my back as I used to, as my friends still do. Even when I yearn for their innocence—and I do—I'll never trust it again. I face forward, no longer pretending that I don't know the outcome of death's uncompromising physics. Life is just a matter of pissing upwind.

FOR THIS JOURNEY

Maude Meehan

We are not supposed to be here
where they speak only euphemese,
here in this room of stainless sinks,
strange instruments and acrid chemicals
for preservation, but have persuaded them
to let this husband, father, lover, dear companion
be bathed and dressed by known, loved hands.

We are not prepared, who could be, for this,
this silent stranger, sheet draped,
refrigerator cold, skin mottled bluish-grey.
I warm your face between my hands, your lips with mine.
Folds of your neck are pink, soft, partly thawed.
Their living texture shocks. I know this skin,
these folds, stroke them, shut out the room, pretend.

You are made ready as you would have wished.
A favorite sweatshirt, worn khakis,
two-for-one-price sneaks (you called them "spiffy")
and in your hands the battered, stained safari hat
that traveled with you on each new adventure.

We drape the muted fabric of your Balinese sarong
over the satin lining of the coffin,
surround your stillness with mementos, smile, weep,
at shared stories of your well-lived, well-loved life,
strew petals on the strong and perfect body
that hid its fatal flaw from you, from us.

Now it is time. We gather round this man,
the hub of all our lives. Hands joined, we sing,
speak final words. Leave with a last caress.
Now he is ready for this journey. We are not.

MEAL TIME

Nancy Gotter Gates

It was seven in the morning, and I could hear the food cart clattering its way down the hall, the aides banging the covers on the trays as they carried them into each room. George's room was at the end, which meant his tray was always delivered last.

I had been awake for some time, aroused as usual by the sounds of hospital routine. The new shift of nurses and aides were making their rounds, efficiently monitoring pulses and blood pressure as though they were garage mechanics checking under the hoods of malfunctioning cars. I realized that they had to maintain a shield of brisk detachment on the oncology floor. How else could they survive it?

George was lying with his back to me, revealing the few wisps of remaining hair that looked like craze lines in the glaze of old china. It reminded me of our daughter when she was born, for she had been much balder than either of the boys. I had been surprised and moved by the baby softness of George's pink scalp in contrast to his ruddy face and neck, permanently darkened by the sun.

I picked up the mattress from the floor where I had slept and stowed it behind the green imitation leather chair. This unlovely piece of furniture had developed a permanent imprint from my backside over the past seven weeks, and although it was not especially comfortable, it had assumed a significant role in my greatly diminished world. It was where I spent each day, flanked by George's bed and the large window overlooking the new wing of the hospital that was half completed. I was glad for the view. Although the annoying sounds of construction were only partially muffled by the thick glass panes, the activity gave me something to do during the day when George slept and I grew tired of reading. I would watch the men, their tanned, robust bodies glistening with sweat, as they placed the forms for the massive concrete pillars that would support each of the ten floors.

George had been admitted to the hospital again seven weeks earlier. He had spent eight weeks here in the spring, when the leukemia was first discovered, undergoing chemotherapy and fighting pneumonia. When he left, his disease was in remission, but throughout the summer he returned twice a week for blood tests and brief chemotherapy treatments, precautionary measures.

It had been a perfect August day when we arrived for a routine checkup. As we walked from the parking garage to the clinic, George was upbeat.

"I feel so good today for a change. I can't see how that damn Kellerman can find anything wrong with me."

I didn't dare reply one way or the other. In the examining room the doctor had just finished checking him over when the nurse came for blood samples.

"Okay, Doc," George told him as the blood was drawn, "no exchanging my test tubes for someone else's so you can get me to stay here. I realize how lonely you are, but I've got better things to do than stick around to entertain you."

"Do you think I would intentionally inflict you on those poor nurses?" the doctor retorted with a grin.

We had to wait about thirty minutes while the results of the blood tests were analyzed, and that half-hour was unbearably tense for both of us, although George would never let on. We would sit in the waiting room, pretending to read the months-old magazines, unable to speak to one another. This time Dr. Kellerman called us back into his office.

"George," he said, "the nurses and I are going to have to put up with you a little longer, I guess. Your white count and platelets are low. They probably haven't bounced back yet from the last chemo. But we want to keep an eye on you for a few days until it improves."

For once George couldn't think of anything funny to say. As we walked toward the admitting office he said, "I'm never going to leave this place, you know."

"Don't be silly. Of course you are." I nearly choked on the words.

When the blood counts didn't come back up, they put him through another intensive chemotherapy program, but all it did was make his newly grown hair fall out. The numbers on the blood tests varied only slightly from day to day, increasing just enough to raise our hopes, only to sink again. Then the infections began, invading a system too weak to withstand the onslaught. They became more and more serious as the days went by, and the massive doses of antibiotics failed to halt their progress. George was fading away, and there wasn't a damn thing I, or anyone else, could do about it.

He slept most of the time. In his waking state he was just barely aware of his shrunken universe. I had brought the giant poster of Garmisch-Partenkirchen to hang on the wall at the foot of his bed. He would seem to study the familiar angles of the Zugspitz that rose up behind the spire of the Bavarian church as it gave him a view into another world. He had been stationed in Germany early in our marriage, and we always went to Garmisch while on leave. Over the years we returned there several more times, our Shangri-La, a place where we could shed our most pressing problems. But Garmisch was far away now, farther than it had ever been.

A smiling aide entered the room carrying George's breakfast tray. "You want me to help with it?" She was new to the floor.

"No, I'll do it," I said. I always helped with the meals as well as the bedmaking, the baths, anything I could do to keep busy. I had made the decision to sleep in his room to avoid long daily commutes and those hours apart—I'd go crazy wondering what was happening. But twenty-four hours a day of tedium wore me down. I welcomed any small task out of desperation for meaningful activity.

I uncovered the breakfast tray to survey its contents before I woke George. There was a bowl of lumpy oatmeal, cold as usual; soggy, limp toast; and a congealed mass that was supposed to be a fried egg. Every meal that came to the room was cold. As if hospital food wasn't unpalatable enough, it was rendered completely inedible by the long delay in getting it to him.

I wanted to dump it on the floor, to make a terrible scene. But the nurses and aides were already overworked. They didn't need a hysterical woman complicating their lives, and I'm not the type for the grand gesture, even at that bleak moment. Control was the word. I had to stay in control of myself. I knew if I lost it a little, I'd lose it altogether.

I thought bitterly of all the times I had complained about the meals to the aides, to the nurses and doctors, to the dietitians. They all agreed that it was important for him to eat, but they seemed incapable of providing anything edible.

I shook George's shoulder gently to awaken him. The combination of infections and medications had left him barely on the edge of consciousness, and when he opened his eyes, it took him several minutes to become aware of his surroundings. I raised the top of his bed just enough so he wouldn't choke and speared a tiny piece of egg to feed him. But it made him gag, and he managed only to drink a little coffee and eat a quarter piece of toast.

And I knew he only ate that much for my sake. I took the nearly full tray out to the waiting cart in the hall, my hands shaking with rage. I was powerless to help George. I couldn't stop his illness, I couldn't assuage his pain, I couldn't even see that he got a goddamn meal worth eating.

I tried to read for a while but I couldn't stop thinking about the food. If the doctors and dietitians couldn't improve the situation, what could I do? My self assurance, as usual, had vanished the moment I walked in the hospital door where the doctors are gods, the nurses their messengers, and I am the obedient servant.

But by nine o'clock I had convinced myself that I had to make one last attempt to remedy the situation. After thirty-four years of marriage, it all boiled down to one question: could I or could I not get George a warm meal?

I took the elevator to the first floor where I had seen the hospital administrator's office. I entered the outer office and spoke to his secretary. "May I see Mr. Troxler, please? My husband is a patient here."

Surprisingly she didn't turn me away or claim he was too busy, but announced my presence over the intercom. Within a few moments, he came out to the reception area.

"Mrs. Gates," he said, "I'm due in a committee meeting in five minutes, but if you'll come into my office, I can speak with you briefly."

I entered his pristine office furnished in mauve and pale green expensive-looking period furniture. It seemed to have no relation at all to the stark hospital corridors just a few steps away.

"Please sit down," he said, gesturing toward a chair.

"Thanks, no," I said, too angry and nervous to sit. "It's the food. My husband has spent weeks in here and we've spent tens of thousands of dollars and he can't get a decent meal." I didn't give a damn about the money, but I thought it would get his attention. "The only thing he has to look forward to is his meals, and they are not only lousy, they are cold. I beg him to eat because it's so important, but to tell you the truth I wouldn't normally give the stuff to my dog."

I was really wound up, and Mr. Troxler sat silently while I went on and on. Finally I stopped, on the verge of tears but determined not to cry in front of him.

He looked at me thoughtfully. "I'm sorry to hear that, Mrs. Gates. Please let me see if I can do something about it for you. Now, if you'll excuse me, I must get to my committee meeting."

I walked slowly back to the room, totally drained. Mr. Troxler had seemed nice enough, but was he just saying he'd help to get me out of his office? I really didn't expect anything to come of it.

I was sitting in the green chair, reading a paperback, when an orderly came into the room at 11:30 carrying a covered meal tray.

"Is this Mr. Gates?" he asked. "This is his lunch."

It was a full hour earlier than lunch normally came. I got up and walked around the bed and took the tray from him, thanking him. I set it on the bedside table and lifted the cover. There was a piping hot plate with chicken, mashed potatoes, and green beans.

"His meals will be brought up directly from the kitchen every day," said the orderly. "Mr. Troxler's orders."

I could hardly believe it. I felt a surge of joy as I realized that at last I was able to make a tiny difference. A feeling of hope went through me as if this might be a sign that circumstances could change, the future wasn't carved in stone.

Before I could prepare to help George to eat, Dr. Kellerman strode into the room.

"How's it going?" he asked, his usual greeting, although he knew far better than I how things were going.

"Things are looking up," I said. "We actually got a hot meal today. I talked to Mr. Troxler, and he's having George's meals sent directly from the kitchen so they aren't stone cold when they get here. George might even be persuaded not to blow up the kitchen when he gets out of here." I always tried to provide a quip when he couldn't.

Instead of congratulating me on my accomplishment, Dr. Kellerman's face took on an expression of sadness. That was unusual for him. He always kept his emotions well hidden behind a mask of benign congeniality.

Finally he spoke. "I came to tell you that George is not getting enough nourishment, and we're going to have to feed him intravenously. The nurse will be down here shortly to start it." He looked down at George, who lay there with his eyes closed, evidently unaware of either of us or our conversation, and then he looked up at me again.

"I'm truly sorry," he said, and then he left.

I stood there a few minutes, my hand still on the lunch tray. Finally I took off the cover again, picked up a chicken drumstick and began to eat it. I looked out the window and could see two construction workers sitting on the edge of the concrete floor five stories up, a big tub of fried chicken between them. They, too, were eating drumsticks.

Somehow I knew then that I would be all right. Maybe I couldn't change the course of George's illness, but I'd learn to cope. Somehow, you muddle through, even when you're most certain that you can't.

THE ANNIVERSARY WALTZ

Nancy Wambach

The wife sensed movement behind her, a stirring from the body occupying a twin hollow in the well-used mattress. Her eyes snapped open and she squinted at the clock: 6:00 A.M. Familiar dry-ice fingers gripped her heart. Turning heavily, she gazed at the skeletal body twitching beneath the sheet, at the cracked, peeling lips murmuring in a language he seemed to have invented lately.

"—with the existing isomorphism between Boolean equations and digital children, experiments in a mortgage can be performed without manipulating hardware hurt—"

Something had to be done about his chapped mouth. Plucking a tube of Vaseline from the nightstand that lately functioned as a pharmacy, she uncapped it and gently applied balm to the parched, but still familiar, landscape. With her thumb, she rubbed away the saliva that had collected all night in the corners of his mouth. Absently she wiped it off onto the hip of her cotton nightgown.

"The proton half-life should be ten to the thirty-second power years before descending into leptons or photons."

"Well, good morning, Sunshine." She kissed the dry forehead and salved mouth, then rubbed her own cracked lips together. "Happy anniversary." David's vacant eyes almost seemed to return her gaze, focusing on a spot just above her right ear.

"The larger number of slow neutrons greatly increases the probability that a neutron released by a fissioning dog will cause another nucleus mother to fuse."

Again she wondered if this could be some mysterious tongue spoken by those about to "cross over." David had been a physicist specializing in space propulsion. During their twenty-year marriage, he rarely spoke about the technical side of his work, but in these last days, he jabbered more and more in a disconcerting bastardization of what their children called geek-speak.

It was a family joke, that cliché, "Well, he's smart, but he's not a rocket scientist."

She, Judith Anne Nelson, exactly twenty years ago, had married an honest-to-God rocket scientist. This was supposed to turn out differently.

She glanced again at the photograph on their bedroom wall:

A young bride, eyes closed, leaned up to kiss her groom. Dressed in a white crepe gown festooned with seed pearls, she carried white roses, orange blossoms, and stephanotis. Having just removed the delicate veil from her face, David's left hand, newly ringed, brushed her creamy pink cheek while his right arm pulled her to him.

"C'mon, honey, let's get you to the potty." She'd devised a new language, too, apparently—one hardly resembling the baby-talk they'd sometimes enjoyed during sex play.

She walked around to the other side of the bed and gently pulled back the covers. Under hips now no bigger than knuckles, she saw a dark yellow stain. Her shoulders sagged. Oh, shit. Why hadn't she set the alarm to rouse him in the middle of the night? Why hadn't she noticed the ripe ammonia odor before now?

But then, why would she? Lately the room always smelled of seasoned urine, medication, vomit, disease, despair. Sporadically, when she remembered, she filled the house with cut flowers from the grocery store, but they never covered the stench. Within a few days, the stems rotting in the vase contributed to the room's sickening bouquet.

"You know, hon, when the nurse comes today, maybe she can show us how to use those special pads she was talking about."

"Special pads"—a euphemism for diapers, another vocabulary word to add to her new language. Gently she tucked her right arm under his knees and felt the hatchet bones press into her flesh.

It was a muggy October afternoon. Kneeling with David before the altar, she gazed at the ten-foot Christ looming agonized on the cross above her. As a child, in this very church, she'd always noted His bent legs and wondered if that hollow spot behind each knee was sweaty. This thought had always nauseated her until she comforted herself with the firm reminder that, even if Mary Magdalene didn't think about wiping the backs of the Savior's knees, surely Martha would be carrying a towel.

Dampness was collecting in the backs of her own knees. Could she be a "good" wife? Would she be ready, clean towel handy, for better or worse?

David winked and squeezed her hand. He'd always found her fleshy palms and the backs of her knees irresistibly succulent, had pressed his lips into them, run his tongue from the bottom of her buttock to her ankle and then back again, always pausing to savor the knee.

She managed to lift his lower body and remove the pajama bottoms, finally pulling them off over his feet. Carefully, she set him back down on a dry area on her side of the bed. She tucked her arm under his shoulder blades and helped him swing his knees and drop his feet to the floor.

"Honey, can you put your arm around my shoulder?"

"This gives vertical displacement and a pier height—"

"C'mon, David, help me here."

She grasped the cold hand at the end of the leaden arm and lifted him off the bed to a standing position. Wrapping her arm around his bloated middle, she braced her shoulder to carry his weight. Judy took a small step, then waited as David shuffled to keep up. She used his arm around her shoulders as ballast, keeping him from toppling over and pulling her down with him. Step, shuffle, step, shuffle. They made their way together.

The band had just finished the first selection of their standard wedding repertoire and were tuning up for "Anniversary Waltz." Soft tinkles echoed as waiters glided between tables, pouring coffee, clearing silverware. Guests smiled as their spoons made languid circles in china cups. An elderly aunt touched the rosebuds on a centerpiece while her husband of fifty years gently nodded off for a moment, chin resting lightly on his chest.

Hanging crystal fixtures created glowing crosses of light against a dark cathedral ceiling. Geometric patches of reds, greens, blues, and yellows glowed on the ravaged buffet table, giving odd iridescent hues to the potato salad and Swedish meatballs, tinting green the plundered turkey carcass that sat abandoned like the wreckage of a sunken ship.

David, tall and robust, cut in on Judy's perfunctory, at-arm's-length waltz with her father. He took her into his arms and pulled her close. Although neither of them had ever been a particularly graceful or enthusiastic dancer, their bodies, from the beginning, had fit like two praying hands.

Family and friends watched as Judy, her eyes fixed on David's, picked up a corner of her long white skirt. She smiled—just a bit smugly—at her prize, then laid her head on his shoulder.

Thank God the years of waiting were over. Now she'd be safe, secure, cherished forever. This dancing partner was nothing like her father, with his explosive and unpredictable temper, with his pattern of abandoning her just when she needed him most.

As their joined bodies glided in circles on the dark polished floor, the singer began: "Oh, how we danced on the night we were wed."

They reached the bathroom entrance and she gasped at their twin reflections in the mirror. A short, overweight, middle-aged woman returned her startled gaze. She wore a stained and faded pink nightgown; greasy tufts of uncombed hair drooped onto her forehead. Feet planted firmly, she grasped the arm and middle of an eighty-eight-pound hairless man naked from the waist down. Both parties were gray of complexion, one with red, puffy eyelids, the other with sunken, hollow sockets from which no light shone. The eyes of the man were downward. The woman stared directly ahead.

Then she felt a warm trickle hit her leg.

"No, hon! Wait'll I get you to—"

She turned and guided him to the toilet. Dropping to her knees, she steadied his torso with one arm and directed the last drops of urine into the bowl. Lately, his penis had become misshapen, like an obscenely fat, overboiled frank. Wiping splashes from the floor, Judy kneeled submissively, a vanquished hostage before a deranged foreign dictator.

His was the first male organ she'd ever actually looked at, stared at. All right, yes, there'd been previous gropings with an occasional college boyfriend, of course—but always in the dark and only because he'd placed her hand there. Growing up an only child—and with parents who, it seemed, had been born wearing pajamas and bathrobes—she longed to see a complete man, pored over art books and pictures of nude sculptures.

At nineteen, on a trip to Florence, she actually saw the testicles of a street artist fall out of his shorts, then stared as he furtively tucked them back inside. That same day, her exasperated girlfriend dragged her away from the statue of David, muttering, "For God's sake, Judy, you need to get laid!" And she did. Get laid, that is. Often. And well, for almost twenty years. With her own David.

When the dripping into the toilet bowl ceased, she dried and lifted him. They resumed their shuffling to the bed.

She grabbed the can of baby powder and liberally sprinkled the grotesque organ and flaccid balls. Rummaging in a chaotic bureau drawer, she found his last clean pair of pajama bottoms and struggled to slide them over his legs and under his wrinkled buttocks.

She was exhausted, wrung out, and he hadn't had his breakfast or medicine yet, and it was only 7 A.M. and this was her twentieth anniversary. She needed to lie down, just for a second, but the only remaining space on the bed was wet, so she collapsed on the floor beside him.

"Just let me rest for a second, hon."

David moaned. The pain, their familiar enemy, was returning to peek from the shadows, threatening to pounce if Judy relaxed her vigil.

"I'll get your morphine now."

"That would be the inverse cosine function."

"Yes, David. Whatever you say. That's what it is."

Grunting, she hauled her body up off the floor and headed for the kitchen. This sacristy housed the glass chalice in which reposed the precious morphine, currently the only god they could count on to give them solace, rest, relief. She retrieved it from the tabernacle, a top shelf, attempting vainly to keep five other items from flying down and pelting her head.

Judy noticed a half-empty bag of potato chips lying opened on the counter and she poked her hand into it. She crammed a load of broken ones into her mouth and chewed absently, wiping the crumbs from the front of her nightgown. A few fell down the bodice, resting between her breasts.

The salt burned her lips and she reached for a glass on the counter. It smelled like week-old milk. She vowed to wash a load of dishes later.

Yesterday a hospice nurse had helped her bathe David, had wiped the excrement from his anus and turned him to prevent bed sores. Politely, she turned her eyes from Judy's tears when David winced at her ministrations. This woman was one more witness to the stinking, fetid underbelly of the family's fear and desperation. When she'd asked for some water, Judy hastily rinsed out a glass from a pile on the counter, running her finger over a white stain at the lip. "I'm sorry. I haven't gotten to the dishes yet."

And not today, either.

She filled the glass with tap water, drank several gulps, grabbed more chips, and washed them down again. Within three minutes, she'd finished off the bag.

Now it was time to serve David his anniversary breakfast. Using an eyedropper, Judy measured out the twelve drops of morphine into a clean shot glass. She carefully rinsed a coffee cup and filled it with a cloying, sweet concoction designed to provide nutrients to the dying. Counting out the multi-hued pills and capsules, she pondered the irony of force-feeding David the vitamins and minerals, the blood thinners—and especially the little orange tablet (one-half, three times a day) that regulated his heartbeat.

She placed all the items on a tray, added the nitroglycerine patch last, willed her arms to steady themselves, and carried the provisions back to the bed. She sat beside David and raised his body to rest against her chest.

"C'mon, baby. This is good stuff. Let's get it down."

"A routine of the interstices."

"Right. Open up."

First a pill, then a sip of the drink. Massage his throat till he swallows. Another pill. Three drops of morphine. More drink. Another pill. Another three drops. Again and again. Slow and easy. Make sure he's swallowing.

She'd learned from yesterday's fiasco, knew better than to rush him. Just as she congratulated herself on the record time with which they'd completed the medicine procedure, David looked directly into her eyes, assumed an expression of clarity, and spat the entire pill/drink mixture in her face.

She had sat for a second, staring. When she blinked, a tiny tablet sticking to her eyelid dropped onto the bridge of her nose. Her fists clenched and for a second—it was only a second—she felt the urge to smack him as hard as she could, to erase the sight of this monster who'd invaded her home and kidnapped her husband.

Instead, she wiped her face with a corner of the bed sheet.

"David, can you tell me why you did that?"

"The blood! Can't you see the blood?"

As the photographer crouched before them, they wielded the silver knife above the cake. Devil's food it was: How daring and defiant of convention they thought they were to refuse the traditional white whose dryness they found loathsome and inappropriate. This day demanded a sweet, rich moistness.

Instead of the traditional plastic bride and groom topper, they had chosen fresh flowers: yellow and white daisies, mums, tightly curled rose buds. Judy loved the name of the roses: Honor.

They executed the cuts where Mr. Andre, the wedding consultant, directed. They extracted a dark, pungent slice and fed each other. David picked a small crumb from the corner of Judy's mouth, placed it on his tongue, swallowed, and replaced it with a kiss.

When the last pill was safely down, she needed to tidy him. Removing the stained pajama top, she reached for a clean replacement. Of course, the drawer was empty. Her aspirations to give him clean sheets were also too ambitious since, without help, she couldn't lift him to arrange clean sheets—even if she had clean sheets, which she did not.

She sat on the floor beside the bed, leaned against his bony arm, and wept for a few seconds.

It was only 9:00 A.M. And it was their anniversary.

"This procedure is valid . . . for radices . . . larger than ten."

On schedule, the morphine was kicking in.

"Okay, honey, time for a nap. Let's make you comfortable."

She arranged the pillow under his neck, the way he liked it. She opened the drapes. In the light she glanced down: He lay writhing, a giant, bloated, hairless albino spider, a concentration camp refugee, a poster boy for famine relief efforts. Quickly she covered him with the top sheet and blanket.

A wave of dizziness and nausea engulfed her. She needed to lie down again, somewhere softer than the floor. She sniffed a towel from the pile in the corner. Not too bad. Dry, too. She spread it over the urine stain still ripening on David's side.

The Hyatt Regency Honeymoon Suite: Piles of barely worn clothing decorated the floor. The lovers rolled, giggled, whispered, perspired on satin sheets that absorbed a nightful of sex-stains. Judy sniffed David's musky semen, rooted her nose into his belly and chest, licked his collarbones, ran her fingers through his thick, curly blond hair. His chest was her own furry mattress; the locks on his head, a luxurious personal toy for her fingers.

Later, she lay on her back, gripping his shoulders. Silently she thanked whatever power might be responsible for this comfortable weight above her, this delicious thrusting between her legs. She turned her head and moaned as David nibbled her neck and shoulders.

Still later, he held her face in his hands and whispered, "My God, you're beautiful. I can't believe you're mine."

She'd waited so long, panicking often that she might never find him. Her eyes filled. As tears streaked down her cheekbones and into her ears, he kissed them.

"David, don't ever leave me."

"Never. Didn't I already promise you that today?"

"Well, my love, shall I sing you to sleep?"

She collapsed beside him on the bed and took his hand, so bony now that he wore his wedding ring on the middle finger. He'd become silent—already dozing, she guessed. She lay beside him, her uncombed hair brushing his bald head. She kissed his temple.

It was salty-wet.

"Oh, how we danced on the night we were wed."

Her voice cracked, the bruised notes stumbling and limping—but every word rang clear.

THE NET

Dale Matlock

I just looked into my own despair
Deep gorge
Raw, Bottomless, Dark, Silent.

Ballet slippers poised
the cheering crowd beckons
Time to cross the tightrope.
Tense, excitement in the anxious crowd
or is it me?

Hushed now, comes the world's cavernous ache.
At once the wind, the wavering, engulfing cold surrounds.
Midway through the crossing the laughing abyss resounds.
The tightrope shudders.
Descent, a plunging fear entwines
And then as suddenly I become the net
that saves the fall.

—Nancy Matlock (1947–1994)

"They found some suspicious cells in my abdominal fluid today. I'll have to go in for exploratory," my wife Nancy told me in January 1993. Her words hit me with a horrifying impact. It was the "C" word again. I thought of the poem she'd written after a bout with breast cancer in 1974. That time her fall was in check.

But now, where was the net?

Nancy had lived in a health nightmare for years, so it seemed like ancient history since that first lump was found in her breast nineteen years ago. Now all those memories of hospital waiting rooms, antiseptic smells, and pontifical medical pronouncements returned, endlessly looping through my senses.

That first time, "Ace," her surgeon, attempted to explain the procedure to me, but I couldn't quite grasp the ramifications. It was surreal, and I clung to the thought: "It is going to be okay because it has to be okay." But we were both badly shaken. Nancy had lost a beloved grandmother to breast cancer some years before her own was discovered. This genetic fact had a tangible presence, igniting a flash of fear that was diminished only when no metastasis was found. But as we were to discover, no physical symptom is minor after cancer.

Two open heart surgeries for tumors followed over the next six years. These surgeries called forth a fearfulness that beseeched: "Enough, please, enough!"—but courage, bolstered by angry defiance, carried us through. "I have to raise my kids!" was her mantra. I wanted terribly for us to resume our family life. Nancy had suffered unfairly, more than enough for one person it seemed. Wasn't it someone else's turn to walk the tightrope?

It had to be okay.

And, for over twelve years, it was. However, the intervening years brought numerous incidental hospitalizations and consultations with the medical clinic regarding mysteries-made-manifest. Seemingly minor discomforts to outright painful episodes haunted our days as her body went through its plunge to self-destruction. During this time together, we saw our son graduate from college and follow in Nancy's footsteps as a teacher, and our daughter take her first college courses.

Then, in 1993, it came again—cancer—tentatively identified as ovarian, and leaving us in limbo for days as they debated strategies and procedures. In the interim, I felt impatience; time was slipping away. Nancy, on the other hand, seemed at ease as she welcomed the steady stream of visitors to her hospital room, talking about the future as if there was one. But as the surgery day approached, I saw that Nancy's idea of tomorrow was not mine. Fear ripped a jagged edge of doubt onto my waning confidence when she called in an attorney-friend to write her last will and testament.

Where is the net? It's going to be okay—it has to be.

Maybe not this time. Our family doctor was grim-faced, misty-eyed as he pushed open the heavy door, exiting from that exploratory room of revelation. "It doesn't look good," he said from within his own pain, a pain that would soon overtake us all. Overwhelmingly. Irrevocably.

Her release from the hospital in late February was unlike those other homecomings. The ovarian cancer was like an entity with its own existence. Why weren't we allowed to know of its presence long before it crept to such an advantage? If only I had insisted she see her doctor when some early indicators started appearing, instead of joining her in dismissal, attributing symptoms to stress at the end of a hectic school year. So many whys and what-ifs clanged in my thoughts. I believed it was now, once again, time to gather our defenses to keep this cancer at bay, to put it behind us and move on with our lives. Hadn't we managed to overcome those previous calamitous scenarios?

Where is the net?

Our immediate concern was to stop the physical suffering—pain, she announced, as the most horrible ever. Nancy broke down that first day at home. "I'm going to die," she cried. Unlike those earlier times, she now appeared tired and weak. On the brink of defeat. As I wiped away her tears and tried to comfort her, the fear and anguish were palpable. I gently held her, wanting very much to shield Nancy from this demonic imposition, reassuring her that we could soundly defeat this malignancy. I wished to be strong for both of us, but I wondered if my heartfelt reassurances had a hollow, insignificant ring. It was then, hoping against hope, that I knew it would take more than the two of us to become the net that breaks the fall.

Seven months; seven sessions of revolting, gut-wrenching chemotherapy followed. Early on we had a glimmer of hope when the cancer markers in her blood disappeared. And this hope remained beyond chemo. Nancy's enthusiastic assertion, "I kicked cancer's butt!" brought a cautious optimism to a scene overshadowed by her self-described "hairstyling-by-Dow-Chemical."

The decision to change the "soup mixture" on treatment number seven, by introducing a new drug into the recipe, brought on a myriad of allergic reactions and a nausea that reached to her very soul. She decided that it would be her last treatment, that it was time to stop the chemical assault. She wanted to return to the classroom in the fall; for the first time in months, our old comfortable routines began edging into our lives once more. With some hesitancy, I started to relax as I viewed the future.

And I told myself again: *It is going to be okay because it has to be okay.*

I hoped that all would be well, but if not, perhaps she could be persuaded to resume her treatments. She was at relative peace with her Destinies, having come to a hard-won reconciliation soon after the chemotherapy started. It began with a dream/vision of a Native American. As Nancy explained it, his chanting and healing dance imparted to her the profound effect of being healed, not cured, in mind and spirit. He gave no verbal communication despite her entreaties for clarification. This dream/vision occurred just once, but over her last year exerted a powerful influence over our family, and others within our circle of friends. We all felt Nancy's peacefulness descend upon us. It helped us accept the possibility of losing her.

Two days after this vision, Nancy was given a hoop drum as a gift. There was no obvious connection between her, the gifter, or the vision.

In the coming weeks the shared drumming of others became a vehicle for reflection, meditation, and journeying into the realms of the subconscious. We began a long introspection, listening to the voices of our inner selves, taking small steps, and crossing our own tightropes in an effort to embrace mortality and gain a spiritual strength unthinkable a few months earlier.

About six weeks after that fateful number seven chemotherapy, her strength rebounded. She returned to teaching, throwing herself with a vengeance into education, the classroom, and into a bitter political campaign to defeat a state ballot proposition affecting education. My joy at seeing her zeal, her satisfaction, her absolute contentment in attaining her bliss was tempered by my concern, for as time passed it seemed that she had shouldered an excessive burden in her crusade to make up for time lost. Or time not to be.

But after only six weeks, in late October, signals from within her body raised the flag heralding danger. Early November brought a ballot victory in the state election, but no personal victory. The news from her oncologist was again grim—markers were found. The cancer had returned with ferociousness. The net was quickly fraying beyond repair.

The doctor's plea that she resume the chemotherapy fell futilely against steel-clad determination that she would let Fate run its course. She asked us for our support and complicity in her decision, as if she needed permission from us to end the suffering.

It was unreal, yet I heard myself say, "Yes, yes, I'll carry as much of this load as I must." But my heart pounded, *not okay, not okay!*

We talked about her approaching death in a straightforward manner with family and friends. This honesty gave us a period to process thoughts, adjust to feelings, and formulate some basis of acceptance. Nancy's courage in acknowledging her approaching death turned her despair into acceptance and began for me an attempt to resolve my impending loss. Cultural pressures discourage the inner journey, the search for a center, but Nancy's spiritual experience invited us to explore the connection between life, illness, and death. Tearfully, we agreed not to view her cancer as a full tragedy, for tragedy has no redeeming quality. With finality, I saw that I too would have to surrender the need to control, to surrender in order to heal myself, to endure and gain peace of mind.

Attempting to cope with this void in my existence has directed me to trust life and view the universe as an interconnected, orderly whole. With calmness, I can now read Nancy's last comments regarding her poem:

If I were to rewrite my poem about the tightrope walker, she certainly would never fall. She would pause, steady herself, regain her balance, tune in to the vibration of the life-cord and move forward. And she would be smiling with her peaceful, rhythmic stride.

The end came in less than four months, awash with the smell of spring blossoms, a sea of green grasses, and the fading sound of drumbeats telling the new world, "Okay . . . because . . . it is."

ANGEL WING

S. K. Duff

At Christmastime you once gave me pieces
of a broken angel too fragile to hang
from the tree; like a beautiful bird with a broken
wing. I nurtured this cherub's breaks and bandaged
its terra cotta fractures, grew close to its patchworked
seams. Its place in the season now an honored tradition.

Today, I peer into the sky and am embarrassed
by its blueness; and the minuteness of my selfish catastrophe
unraveling like an elbow hole in a woolen sweater
birthday-given with love, too dear to ever throw away.

Exhausted after a bath, water hangs from your chest
like beautiful beads. I bury my face there
contributing liquid crystals to the strands as we
embrace, your arms hang heavy around my neck
offering jewels of a reciprocal beauty.
My hold will no longer ground you.

In the butterfly chair you recline. An inverted
cocoon of sorts, thinner and frailer than days passed.
Your three-day beard circles your velvet mouth . . .
Bones stack like a card house. Today's
undetermined illness is the spade that crushes
all hope, collapses ambition from your voice . . . .

This morning may my words penetrate
and comfort a heart that lives in fear.
I wish for you to break free through
all barriers, as a young monarch instinctively
taking flight into the light of day.

ACCEPTED ALTERNATIVE

Joelle Steefel

My hands smooth the soft fabric, feeling for some vestige of my husband; some energy or residual warmth. I fold and pack Steve's suits and jackets methodically, his favorite sweaters and worn jeans. I set aside a navy blazer for his nephew, the belt with the monogrammed buckle for his father. Pajama tops are for me. The good watch and cuff-links will go to the safety-deposit box for our children. My nightmares, the ugly pictures of his last days I plan to lock away as well. I have two kids to finish raising.

"You're young, you should get on with your life," say family and friends. For once I listen. California feels right. I find work, new friends, learn to carve, drive freeways, and make investments. Illness and death were another life, until yesterday. Headlines in the morning paper screamed "Hospital Investigation." Last night death and doctors became dinner party conversation.

"—who's been suspended."

"Who?"

"The doctor."

"The one who gave the morphine overdose?"

"The child had leukemia. She was suffering," responds a physician friend. "She was dying. We use morphine that way." He bangs a spoon on the table. "It's an accepted alternative."

Accepted alternative! The words reverberate against a vault of memories I've tried to keep buried. Memories of IV dispensers and squeaking gurneys, spinal taps, and radiation. Tapes of more clinical conversations begin to play in my head. The kids and I standing in the doorway of a pea-green hospital room chatting with doctors.

"How's he doing?" I ask, expecting their usual cheerful response.

"You know we're trying," says the head oncologist. "If he were seventy-five with grown kids, we'd have let him go days ago."

"Let?" I look at my husband, horrified. The doctor assures me that Steven is beyond hearing our conversation.

"But he's so young—you, all of you, it keeps us trying new things."

His resident sidekick focuses on the two teenagers flanking me. "Tumors give off calcium. It affects thinking, muscles, even his heart."

"It has the same affect on me," I respond. "Shouldn't we give the new drug more time?"

"His kidneys are still holding calcium."

"You said the level was down."

"It's a long way from normal, and it's affecting the brain." The brain—I inhale. This is news to me.

"But the new drug?"

"It can't reverse the damage. There's no reversing it." He looks at his clipboard and mumbles, "If this regimen doesn't work, there's really nothing. Maybe one alternative."

I have to touch my husband. The emaciated figure with transparent skin, protruding cheek bones, and bald head bears little resemblance to my Steven. Even his eyebrows have thinned. Awake or asleep, his stick-thin arms claw the air in slow motion. A macabre conductor orchestrating the click and gurgle of dispensers and tubes. His moments of consciousness are few. I thought it was pain killers. He greeted me this morning with a kiss, alert, but within minutes he was holding the *Journal* upside down.

He's battled lymphoma for two years with me and the kids as cheerleaders. We've seen bad times. This phase will pass like the others; it has to. "The new drug will work," I repeat. "It just needs time."

I hear the agitation in my son's voice. "What do you mean there's an alternative? You just said there's nothing more to be done. You're not making sense!"

"We're trying to tell you—morphine controls pain." The doctor drops his voice. "It can also suppress breathing. It's the quantity." The oncologist peers from Anne, to Ryan, to me.

"How long do you want him to go on like this—in so much pain? His heart is strong, it can pump for weeks!" The hiss and click of equipment fills the room. White arms claw the air. My heartbeat in my ears. Ryan and Ann look at me—to me.

An alternative. The idea is beyond grasping. The last few months career through my head: fishing in Montana, the family in Sun Valley, business in Memphis, treatments sandwiched in and around all of it. We were living with cancer, managing it. Now it was managing us.

Steve's voice comes back to me. "Let's have coffee by the stream, watch the sun come up. Who knows how many more . . ." That was the day before I brought him to the hospital. I thrust shaking hands into my pockets.

"This is not a decision I can make alone," I announce, looking at my children. Their faces carry Steve's genetic stamp: the long-lashed, dark eyes, the curve of his lips.

It's August, the school semester has started early. The kids join me daily, after class, their books and backpacks tossed on either side of

Steve's bed. A homework assignment offers Ryan an escape. He must write an essay. But the mounting pile of crushed yellow paper in his corner proves that escape is impossible.

Ann's teachers are more understanding, but she has no way out. She paces and ministers; a cold compress for Steve, a cup of coffee for grandpa, a sandwich for me.

The doctors suggest we summon the rest of the family to the hospital. Within the hour, father, stepmother, sister, and lawyer gather with us in an antiseptic doctor's lounge. We sit facing one another from sticky vinyl chairs, across a linoleum abyss. A bright summer day pours in through the wall of windows: a cloudless cerulean sky, remnants of snow reflecting from mountain crevices—the kind of day that ordinarily lifts my spirits. At that moment, it signals how out of step I am with the world.

"Why couldn't it be me?" My father-in-law begins his daily mantra. The doctors appear on schedule.

"We have the results of the lumbar puncture." I feel like I'm in a classroom. "The cancer has spread into the spinal fluid. The problems aren't just calcium—they look irreversible."

"Irreversible," flashes off the wall in neon. I am the woman in Munch's "Scream," and just as silent. My mother-in-law begins to wail. My sister-in-law weeps quietly. The children and I clutch one another.

"We can radiate the head, add chemo to the spinal fluid, and see. At best, you could get two months, then face this again."

"They would be painful months," he assures us. He removes his glasses and wipes his hand across his forehead. "There is one alternative."

In that instant forever becomes finite. My head fills with questions mundane and cosmic: *How do I raise the kids? How much should I ask for the boat? Have we said our last good-byes?* It occurs to me fleetingly, that what he's suggesting is illegal. He could lose his job. But I'm much more focused on the two months. Should I keep him alive for two more months? Am I totally selfish?

"Selfish!" I answer myself. What's worse than inexpressible pain? I'd be keeping him alive for me.

Together we review the alternative: allow calcium to build up, coma to deepen, then up the morphine. Sobs turn to unrestrained tears as one by one, I poll the family. One by one they say, "Stop the pain. Use the morphine."

Within the hour a standing order is issued: no therapeutic medication, no tests, no meals. We watch as Steve's swallowing becomes more difficult, his breathing labored. He doesn't respond to our words.

The children's wretchedness is beyond my help, my own beyond sensing. We take turns wiping his lips with lemon swabs. At the end of the day, his parents and sister kiss him good night and leave in search of respite. Friends take the kids to dinner. I take a short breath and return to find the doctors with a night nurse I've never seen before. The door is closed.

As they have each night for two weeks, they stand on either side of the IV machine, making small adjustments. It takes a moment for me to realize what I'm seeing. Clear, tear-shaped drops of morphine fall faster and faster. I watch in horror. "I'm not ready," I want to yell, but I will never be ready. Within minutes his arms float down to the covers. A stethoscope confirms the finality. For the first time in a two-year, all-out siege, Steven is finally pain-free.

In those years, in another place, there was not an accepted alternative, only the alternative of sensitive doctors, and their willingness to risk careers for what they believed was humane.

I rejoin the dinner party with difficulty and comment only on the chocolate mousse.

THE LAST SIGH

Carl Stancil

Your struggle for breath is unbearable. I am at your bedside. The time between your shallow gasps increases. Before the long pauses a little saliva drips from your precious lips. Two minutes. Three minutes . . . You just give a sigh. Then nothing. Michael is at my side and places his hand on my shoulder as I move closer to you, but there is no holding on. I turn toward the clock. It's 8:45 P.M., Sunday, the 20th of December, 1992. Time has stopped. You have stopped breathing. I must let you go. You have completed your work here.

Perhaps you are in the friendlier place that you sought. You look so peaceful. We wash and oil your body and dress you in a rose nightgown, with your favorite sachet pillow beneath your head and your electric blue scarf around your neck. Your cape with its fearsome dragon encircles your shoulders with a rose on your breast. The wooden Akido knife which Glenn carved for you lies at your side atop a scabbard adorned with Swiss alpine blooms. Your nearly hairless head is topped with the Nepali hat which we brought from Kathmandu. You had begun to wear it each day. Your eyes are slightly open as if you are awakening. Your lips look as if you are about to speak. The progressive cold of death is creeping through your body. Your smooth cheeks are becoming colder with each touch. You are slipping away.

Friends and acquaintances file through; some sadly at ease with you; others, seeing their own death, contort in pain and fear. Thank God they leave. A peaceful solitude sets in. I ring the meditation bell to welcome the night as we have so many nights before. I turn from the window and see your face lighted by the soft glow of candle light. I feel your spirit present. I spread my arms as a priest preparing for benediction. "Great Spirit, take Rosmarie and find for her a friendlier place. Rosmarie, your work here is complete. It is up to us to carry on."

I have no sense of what has just taken place. Tears fall freely. I cry for myself; she doesn't need my tears.

MENTOR

S. K. Duff

You never went anywhere without returning to me
with duty-free pleasures: Belgian chocolates and bottles of Lagerfeld.
Favorites, potent enough to linger in your absence. You always
liked to fly, even after a blue raven was discovered soaring across
your chest. Out of the clear blue black crows of Cancer
crossed your path, marking your heart with butterfly wings

one spring, followed by a winter of chemo. X's marked
the spot where my treasure was buried. Months later
I fished in holes of ice for suitable words, unfrigid.
Shooting off at the mouth with stabs at pleasuring you;
while your hair fell like virally stalked husks around
your feet. Your mourning pillow looked as if a survivor

of Hiroshima had lain there. In patches of Emmett Kelly
silence, you clowned words so firmly believed. After
a particularly bad bout of vomiting you quoted Euripides:
"Nothing is hopeless, we must hope for everything."
Such phrases coupled with fear and liquids of the body
composed the lethal concoctions we ingested then . . . .

Now when I am lost, my compass points to your example.
Your hands wet with breath . . . Your tears taking brave leaps
from the arcs of lashes . . . Forty days between radiation treatments.
You created vast bodies from a constellation of two black stars—
those small drops on the tiles were oceans of hope. Your constant
orgasms of optimism blinded your moments of rage.

Even as your eyes became riddled with CMV you still
had the faith to envision a cure. You believed your autumn
would ultimately bring spring. I hold this true—myself
a fallen man, holding on by frayed ropes; my palms blistering
and burning as I pull myself up to your example. My own death,
beneath me, my feet dangling above its gatorish gnash.

I REMEMBER YOU

Sheenagh M. O'Rourke

A flat line,
As I bent to kiss you
I breathed in your last breath.
Somewhere a radio was playing
You are the wind beneath my wings.

Inside an implosion,
My head, heart and soul
Caught in a cloud of purple rain,
Gazing blankly into a sea of jumping stars,
Echoing, echoing, you must maintain standards.

Head held high,
Inside silent screaming,
Tag on toe, blue body bag zipped.
That toe I once kissed, that body I loved.
That warm soft skin, now hard and cold as ice.

My love gone,
Night, day, meaningless.
The hand that touched my face
The head that gently rested on my breast,
His touch, his feel, his kiss, no more, no more.

Silk skin nights,
Now harsh as cotton,
Cold feet, cold heart, cold bed,
Long nights of longing roll into long days
Long weeks, silent barren years. I still remember.

ON THE SHORE

Penelope Dugan

My lover, Ingie LaFleur, died six days after her fifty-second birthday, one week after our twelfth anniversary. Among the survivors listed in her obituary, I have the designation of "domestic partner." And I was the domestic one, staying at home while Ingie traveled throughout Eastern Europe, recording and interpreting the shifts and tremors of that part of the world she knew so well.

I am not the historian of political movements that Ingie was. Instead, I record the personal—Ingie's and my life together—recreate her voice and face against further loss.

Our life together changed on March 13, 1992. I became the keeper of the appointment calendar, the note taker at meetings with doctors, the researcher of Ingie's inoperable brain tumor—an anaplastic astrocytoma, grade three. My own adrenaline sped me up while the phenobarbital Ingie took to prevent seizures slowed her down. She avoided my growing file of articles, computer printouts, and pamphlets. I thought she was in denial.

To Ingie, my library searches, calls to the National Cancer Institute, and attempts to follow up all leads must have seemed frantic. I knew I couldn't do anything about her diagnosis, but I thought if I found the best doctors, I could buy her more time. I realize now my presumption. What medium of exchange did I have? If I used every minute, I thought we would be given more as reward. We weren't. Ingie lived fifteen months after her diagnosis instead of the two and a half years predicted by the neurosurgeon.

While I mailed sets of Ingie's MRI's to radiologists throughout the Northeast, she sent faxes to members of Congress demanding an end to the Bosnian arms embargo. I accused Ingie of being more interested in Bosnia than in her own brain. She said that her brain was her favorite organ, but she knew more about Bosnia.

My internal clock remains set on Ingie's medication and meal schedule. I wake at midnight, then at four, and again at six. She needed a bagel upon waking to keep her nausea at bay. Now I fix one for myself. I am not in a race with time anymore. Tasks take longer. I forget what I'm doing or what I need to do.

Today I went to the grocery store to buy cooking oil and bought instead a wandering Jew, a Boston fern, and a spider plant. I hang the plants in my new apartment, put the break-offs from the wandering Jew in a glass of water on the window sill, and remember the cooking oil. I go back to the store to buy the oil, as well as broccoli, mushrooms, onions, and garlic—Ingie's "perfume of the Balkans."

Maybe I'll cook a real meal again. The smell can't bother Ingie anymore. But I don't cook. I live on bagels, cheese, beer, pretzels, and herring from a jar unless I'm invited to dinner by friends. They comment on how well I'm doing. I force myself to be positive and upbeat. I come home exhausted and have a beer to ease the tightness in my body from holding myself together. I share pretzels and cheese with the dogs. They don't like herring.

I walk the dogs by the ocean a half block from my apartment. At daybreak, we have the beach and boardwalk to ourselves. I think how the boardwalk and its ramps would have been ideal for Ingie's wheelchair. I ache to be pushing it along. Here it would be transformed from the symbol of her failing body into a seaside stroller.

A long-distance swimmer, Ingie delighted in the ocean, where, she said, she was weightless at last. Afraid of water and unable to float, I stood on the shore, holding Ingie's glasses and towel. I fell in love again each time she emerged from a swim, hair streaming water, sleek as a seal. With near-sighted confidence, she strode into my toweled embrace. Now I stand empty-handed.

Ingie and I could never discuss her death. She called death, "the great unmentionable." When we were told the tumor might spread to her brain stem, I asked Ingie if she wanted to be hospitalized at the end. "Do what's easiest," she said. Everything doctors told us might happen to Ingie over a period of months—the inability to move her arms and legs or turn her head, the loss of vision, and, finally, speech—happened in a period of days. Ease never entered into my decision. Technology couldn't save Ingie, so she spent her last days at the camp, the place she loved, cared for by friends she loved.

Early on her birthday morning, Ingie opened her eyes. Lil, her secretary and friend, wished her a happy birthday. Ingie responded slowly, "I'm so hap . . . hap . . ." and closed her eyes again. Lil talked to Ingie about her birthday and all the friends who were in the house. Ingie kept her eyes closed, but smiled. I kissed her on her forehead. Lil said, "Foreheads can't kiss you back. Kiss Ingie on the lips." Ingie's lips kissed back.

She responded to my kisses until her last day.

We talked and read to Ingie throughout the days, hoping for the times she would open her eyes and be with us. We played tapes of her favorite Bach and Mahler and Schubert lieder. Once, I walked into our bedroom to the sounds of one of our rock and roll tapes. Ingie opened her eyes and said, in her raspy whisper, "This music is shit." Then she asked me for cheese. I said that I couldn't give it to her, that I was afraid she would choke on it. "Sooo?!" she responded. I suggested plain yogurt instead.

"If I'd known the menu, I wouldn't have come," she said, and closed her eyes.

In the middle of Saturday night, two days before her death, Ingie's eyes opened again, "Tomorrow, I'm going on my journey."

Too tired to think straight, I asked, "Where are you going?"

Her eyes closed. "I don't know."

Later in the morning, Ingie was agitated and said that she wanted to go for a walk. I held her hand and watched her face relax as I talked us through a walk of our shared memories. I described the silver birches, the flowers on the path, and the sunlight on the lake. When Ingie squeezed my hand, I made the description more detailed to include the wetness of the grass on our bare ankles, the mayflies circling us, the size of the stick our dog, Seamus, carried in his mouth.

Ingie died at seven o'clock the next evening, June 7, 1993. She took two quick breaths as if she were going to dive and was gone. Twenty minutes later Seamus broke the stillness of the room by bounding to the bedroom door off the terrace. He danced on his hind legs, scratching at the door and barking until I opened it. The dog raced around the lawn in wider and wider circles and ran down to the lake shore where he plunged into the water, lapping it as he swam. Watching him, I felt hungrier than I had in weeks. I needed to eat before we bathed and dressed my love's body.

I wanted to put off the final acts for Ingie for as long as I could. I wanted her to stay in the house. I wanted to do ordinary things again, to eat, to drink, to pretend she was resting. I wanted to be alone with her, and I wanted to be away from her. I wanted to tell everyone to go away, and I wanted them to stay. I wanted to throw myself down and beat the floor with my fists. Instead, I went into the kitchen to drink wine and eat goulash while the other women who had taken care of Ingie went into our bedroom one at a time to be with her.

When I returned to the bedroom, Ingie's face had lost the gray pallor and become translucent. We bathed her body and dressed her in her favorite red and blue dress with a yellow sunburst on the bodice. My sister tied a purple scarf around her head. I worried that she would be warm enough. I took off the sandals we had put on her feet and replaced them with wool slippers. I wanted to wrap her in a sweater but my sister took the sweater and put it around my shoulders. My teeth chattered in a cold only I seemed to feel.

Four days after her death, Ingie's ashes were given to me. She used to joke how she wanted me to scatter them in Dubrovnik, Paris, and Leningrad, so finally we would travel together to the cities she loved. She laughed with friends about a happy wanderer like her getting together with a nester like me. I couldn't scatter Ingie's remains. I needed to know where they were. We dug a circular rose bed on the hillside outside our bedroom window, overlooking Lake Champlain.

Friends returned for the service and to share memories. Liz recounted the signs and wonders of Ingie's last week—the disabled crow that appeared by the back door on the first day of Ingie's dying. The colorful air balloons that we could see over the lake from Ingie's window. The hummingbirds that hovered outside the window for the days of Ingie's dying and then vanished with her death. The silver sky with its horizon of gold that dawned on the day Ingie died. The cry of the loon on the night of Ingie's death and the third loon that appeared in our cove the day after to join the resident couple there.

Ingie would have laughed at this talk. She would have said that a crow is crow, a hummingbird is a hummingbird, and a loon is a loon. They aren't signs of anything beyond themselves. The wonder is that fifteen women and two men dropped what they were doing to drive hundreds of miles to take turns nursing a dying friend. Celebrate human actions of solidarity, she would say.

I continue to find Ingie's notes to me tucked in books or among my papers. One reads, "Be of good cheer, my plucky Penel. Win or lose, we have each other. Our love has been strengthened by struggle. All my love, Flower." She must have thought of me in the future finding these notes and taking comfort from them. They show me, instead, who and what I lost.

I can't forget. I can only remember. I think about the floating rock my sister picked up off the shore. To a non-swimmer, the floating rock offers the possibility of one day doing what now seems impossible. One day, my body may relax enough to float. One day, I may not have to be conscious of the grammar of grief, the need to substitute "I" for "we" when speaking in the present tense. One day, I may leave the shore and swim.

NOW

Diane Quintrall Lewis

They say I'll feel worse, I tell her.
What's worse? my friend asks.
Worse appears before me:
my silent ride in the ambulance at 3 A.M.;
those aggravated days of his
lying almost naked in intensive care
with tubes and machines,
the shunt in his skull draining
a mixture of blood and fluid;
the nurses, gentle and subdued
marking charts, shifting pillows;
the last day when his arm
turns blue, then his body—
so blue I can't stay and run
from his room saying
that is not my husband.
Waiting is worse until the phone
rings and the voice says, *expired.*
Better is when I lift
the soup spoon to my lips
and feel peace and wonder why
am I eating now
and wish I could keep eating
so the peace won't leave.

END OF THE WORLD

Layle Silbert

The city on Fifth Avenue outside the hospital lay in an otherworldly aura of deep night; a few inhabitants not asleep were still abroad on lonely errands. Take a taxi. Don't tell Ben. Poor Ben hadn't shaken the influence of his childhood. His father, who'd never found the golden land he emigrated to, worked as a house painter, a baker, a cobbler. For Ben, until grown and out of college, taxis were exclusively for going to the hospital, which indeed he'd done four days before. *He'll never know,* she said to herself, and stepped off the curb to hail a taxi.

Sitting back in luxury, windows open on the unnaturally warm January night, in her head, she played the evening in Ben's hospital room over and over. It had ended when the nurse said, "Go home. It's after midnight." But how could she leave him among these busy strangers? A formidable crowd surrounding him, doctors, nurses, a technician, were in her way. How urgently she needed to lean over, kiss him on the forehead, say what she could for comfort. No way even to catch his attention. Between white-coated shoulders she caught sight of his face, bewildered, eyes open, staring at nothing. She left her telephone number written large on the window sill, where for a moment she saw Central Park, dark, speckled, across the street and turned to go.

Giddy with fatigue, she left, carrying her camera around her neck. Through that long day there'd not been a chance to use it. Bring it back tomorrow. She'd already photographed him throughout the years; in his bed, but more often out of it in dozens of settings, some stranger than a hospital.

Good-bye, good-bye, she said a little sad song to herself as she passed other rooms along the corridor, some with doors open, some not.

So many good-byes, the first long ago at the train station, seeing him off to the West Coast and then to China. He'd lingered too long and had to leap onto the last car as the train slowly began to move. She waved and waved until it turned off in the distance. After that there'd been other trips and more good-byes until she began to go with him.

The taxi ride ended. Leaving the tranquil night, she opened their apartment door, looked around as though she'd been away for weeks instead of only since morning. She touched the back of a chair to connect with belongings familiar and strange at the same time, set the camera down where she'd see it and remember to take it in the morning.

Suddenly she was ravenous even though she'd done away with Ben's dinner. "You eat it," he'd said waving off the tray. "I can't." She didn't argue with her hunger now. With the morning newspaper to read before tomorrow's plopped outside the door, she sat down with cold chicken.

The telephone rang. Half-past one. She wiped her hand on a napkin, picked up the receiver. The ring had already told her; before the doctor spoke, she knew. Old news. He made a little speech explaining the need for an autopsy. "Of course," she said, giving permission.

"Come down in the morning. Now get some sleep," he closed the conversation.

Everyone wanted her to sleep. Before she left, the nurse said, "Get some rest." To go to bed now to sleep peacefully would be an outrage. She didn't try. Sleep was of no interest.

Abandoning the chicken, also of no interest, she stayed at the telephone. Wake them up, wake up everybody, wake up the world. Ben is dead, his abundant brain extinguished. The death she'd feared endlessly, hoped for with shame, spat at, despised, doubted, had no connection. It felt as though she'd opened a door and been shot.

With no sleep, as early as she dared, she set out in new alertness, camera in her bag. As she sat in another taxi, the remembering began. On a Christmas day ten, maybe fifteen years ago, as he sometimes did on holidays, Ben decided to go to his office to work and take advantage of solitude and quiet. In the afternoon she went to the public library on Forty-Second Street open on the holiday, spent the afternoon reading, basking in the hush of the near empty reading room. Later, they had their Christmas dinner in a restaurant also open on the holiday, almost empty.

At the hospital, in the room she'd left so few hours ago, Ben's bed was made, sheets tight, as though nothing at all had happened here. In the other bed the drunk with cirrhosis lay in the same stupor, unattended.

Another doctor, a young woman in a white coat, took her in hand. First, belongings. Overcoat, hat, scarf, paraphernalia from Ben's pockets, book, billfold, papers from the night table drawer, all stuffed into a shopping bag and then the Sunday paper he'd been saving to read.

"Can I see him?" she said as she put the billfold in her bag.

Leaving everything behind, they descended to a room in the sub-basement lined with oversized cabinets up to the ceiling holding people-sized containers that slid in and out. Nobody paid attention to the smell—foul, unmistakable. The drawer containing Ben was slid out halfway, too high for her to see him well. Gingerly she touched his naked arm, chilled, splotched, his beard pointing up at an unnatural angle. The doctor stood to one side with another doctor, also in a white coat, who appeared to inhabit this room. They watched. *How does a person behave in a place like this?* she asked herself.

She took out her camera, checked light and exposure, focused, took pictures from as close as she could, raised her camera to the height of the drawer, took more in the heavy silence. "Enough already," Ben had said many times. "No more." But he stayed where he was and let her photograph him over and over. This was her way to keep him alive.

Slapping the cover on the lens, she turned, confronted the impatience of the two doctors.

Back upstairs, as she put Ben's overcoat over her arm, picked up other belongings, the woman doctor said, "If you'll excuse me, I have patients to look after." Beginning to move away. "I'm sorry," she added.

"I know," she said. "You said that already."

With nobody to displease and still numb, she took yet another taxi. The street where their apartment building stood was the same, the morning sunshine the same. How could that be? Mary, the basement tenant, also the same, puttered in the small garden in front. "Oh," Mary said. "How is your husband?"

"He's all right," she said. Didn't Mary see his overcoat over her arm? Leave Mary out of it.

She'd already spread the news to as many people as she could through the night, awakening them each without mercy, friends, Ben's boss, his sister in another city, her own, in yet another city.

She closed the door behind her. The apartment was all hers now. Dutifully she hung the coat in the closet. When sometimes Ben simply flung his coat down, it was she who'd hung it up in the closet with a flare of irritation. No more irritation. It had slipped off as a loose garment falls off one's shoulders. Now she could sit where she wanted, do as she pleased, eat as she needed, spread herself into all the corners, she thought with a stab of shame.

Not yet, not yet, she wasn't ready for freedom. But she knew it would come. Slipping the camera from her neck where she'd left it, she slapped the lens, as was her habit, thought, here was where she had the last of Ben.

Still morning, the sun blazed merrily on the garden below the back bay window and danced on the furniture. She sat down to face the end of the world with Ben.

WAVES OF ABANDON

S. K. Duff

Green hands flutter from limbs in a silver
maple patch; their white palms softly wave to
some unseen good-bye. Stuttering crickets

are silenced by a familiar cry. There, an old Lab
is mysteriously tethered. His tail wiper waves,
an auburn fan in slow motion. Stroking the rust

of his scruffy coat, stick-bone-struts are felt beneath
the tent of his flank. These bones, frail as twigs
underfoot . . . He laps my face as if reading Braille,

drinking me in like an elixir. Eyes cataracted
and foggy ignite lamps of recognition.
I back into our past . . . *you* tethered to machines

and IV's—your brown puddles full of emotion,
in a body emptying of breath. A nurse's bark
breaking the blackest night: *"Let him go."*

CROSSING POINTS

Rondi Lightmark

My mother, who has always been the best person to sit on the other side of the kitchen table, shares a different look with me these days. When we gaze across the table at (and through) one another now, the old roles crumple and we turn to philosophy. We can do this because I am catching up to her. Our bodies contain similar spaces created by loving and hard places left by pain. We are both widows. So we can talk about the crossing points.

She, who was born at home on a Minnesota farm in the 1920s, raised her four daughters with detailed stories of how each of us came into the world. We all arrived between 1945 and 1956, a time when birthing a child was a colorless and cloistered piece of scientific precision. My own birth story reflects this era. My mother describes how after I was born, I was whisked off for evaluation and cleaning and then ceremoniously brought to her arms several hours later. She took the carefully wrapped bundle that was me and began unwrapping it to count my fingers and toes. "Don't touch her!" admonished the nurse. "She's sterile!"

The nature of my beginnings had no counterpart to balance its strange message about the taboos that exist at the thresholds of life until several years ago, when our family history matured to include the telling of the stroke and swift death of our father. Despite the fact that he was in a coma, there was no doubt in any of our minds (so our story goes), that he waited until the last child flew in from California to make the circle complete. Then he let go with a great heave; it was almost as though he burst out of his chest, took a mighty leap upward, and was gone. Some moments later, we were ushered out of the hospital room in a state of collective awe at his magnificent leave-taking. My next-youngest sister turned back for one more look. "Don't touch him!" admonished the nurse. "He's toxic!"

I don't want to imagine what happened to his body once the door was closed and the hospital moved into its familiar rubber-gloved routine of dealing with that strange euphemism called "the remains." It's not what any of us wanted, that wrenching of the shell that had housed his spirit from the sacred hollow of the family. It was wrong: the loss of the possibility of touching him in farewell, of knowing all he gave us to know about death. This could have enriched the telling, nourished and taught our traveling, because we had felt through our skins into our bones some aspect of earth in winter, the differences at the heart of seeds and stones.

Then last summer, my husband Jim had a seizure and we found that his cancer had spread to his brain. Jim hated doctors and hospitals, but a combination of ignorance and fear led us initially through the familiar round of tests and radiation. And, when the pain began, there were the black holes and ravings produced by morphine and all the attendant drugs that countered its side effects.

But Jim stayed home, eventually giving up all drugs, preferring to allow his body, in its wisdom, to let him go. A home health nursing agency became our biweekly support system, along with a sympathetic and courageous woman doctor who mostly from afar coached me in the old ways: the poultices and compresses, the massages and herbal remedies, the simple knowledge and work of women who for centuries have known the loving management of birthing and dying.

Because the state of Vermont permits "taking care of your own" from the moment of death to burial in your own backyard if you have room, I was able to promise Jim that no stranger's hand would ever touch him.

I'm of the generation raised in abstractions. My grandmothers, and my mother too, knew the metallic smell of passages, the steamy odor of lye and ashes, the feel of diminishing warmth inside a fresh-killed chicken or the way to watch for a fever to turn. They knew about doing things because you had to, or because you had promised. I didn't want that look of grim endurance I have seen in some dark, curling photographs. I wanted the look in the eyes that came from knowing how to keep moving.

Jim stayed for four months. His fierce-hearted and sorrowing mother and I took round-the clock shifts to keep watch with him. Outside, fall burned red in the air, then grayed into November. Loving friends left food on the doorstep, raised money to pay the bills, and planted scores of daffodils in the lawn. "Don't you want to take a break?" they asked, concerned and wondering. I didn't. It was like being pregnant, I told them. The whole house was pregnant with life and I couldn't step outside it until it was time. Was I afraid? Yes. I prayed for some ancestral wisdom to pulse through my veins. I'd never been a midwife before.

No, that's not exactly true. A neighbor around the corner had invited us twice to share in the home birth of her sons. Although I had carried no responsibility those times, I knew well the sound of pain and effort, the dance of fear and exultation, and the presence of light in the room after.

When Jim left, I was alone with him. Early morning, dark, and then a rush of rain. He left so decisively, without struggle, that I touched his chest and shook him gently, querying in disbelief. Then I called to his mother, his sister and my mother, who had joined us in the last days, all still asleep in the heaviness before dawn. Then I cried: relief, triumph, loss.

What is something that is neither toxic or sterile? Perhaps it's the road where beauty walks. We washed and tended Jim's body, his mother and I, just as we had every other darkening autumn day. And even though his body had been nothing but fragile bones and huge hands and slender feet before, it was full of him. Now it was empty. But the light was there.

I have a fantasy about those of us who have held family, lovers, or friends until it was over. Some people are waiting for me to look familiar again. I will not go back because my hands have taught me something ancient and wise.

My fantasy is about a time and a shared state of mind that honors death for its secrets: the transition from fear to knowledge that comes with holding your lover's body when it becomes cool and hollow. The quest for a description of the light—it's like the glaze on long grass in October afternoons. It touches everything. And there's the sense of the open space behind your breastbone when you wake. You know you've been somewhere, but it won't write itself down.

How would things be different, if we weren't afraid of the crossing points? In my lighter moments, I imagine it this way: you come into a room of people who knew you before your life took on a strange shape. Instead of turning away or looking awkward, they burst into howls of grief and celebration when they see you: howls, because you know something of a great mystery, something you can give away (when I told this fantasy to someone recently, demonstrating right there in a parking lot, crash! a nearby tree fell over with my first howl).

Or you find yourself in conversation with a complete stranger on a bus. You swear to yourself that you are not going to say anything and sooner or later your story comes out. This story is important, why apologize? It hides some kind of magical key to everything. The stranger asks for one of your tears as a blessing, because of where you have been.

ARMS

Greggory Moore

I opened my arms up
And she laughed
A joke between lovers
I could never explain
      (nor would ever want to try)
Her eyes went sad just then
For we both knew that now
The smiles were numbered
But what we never saw before
was that
They always had been

It all ends
Everything

Chapter Two
Interrupted Conversations

What are the words of letting go? If we could manage one more talk, it would be a loving conversation of echoes, called out through the universe:
   Goodbye,

         goodbye.

   I forgive you,

         forgive you.

   I'll miss you,

         never forget you.

   I love you,

         love you, too. . . .

         —Molly Fumia, *Safe Passage*

We never imagine in the activity of our daily lives that a simple conversation, a joke, a debate, an anticipated tenderness, an argument such as mates will have—all those ongoing moments of a couple's daily life—will be our last. Unless we are like the wise old grandfather who marked each parting by holding his loved one's hands to offer a small prayer of blessing, we generally leave threads of unfinished conversations with our many daily good-byes. We think our time together is endless.

But the unimaginable happens, with a shock that hits like a thunderbolt. The line goes suddenly dead, mid-sentence, with no warning, leaving filament trails of *whys, if onlys, what ifs, I didn't get to, what did he/she mean? how did he/she feel? Did he/she hurt? Why wasn't I there?* Why, why, why . . . .

When the conversation with a lifemate is snapped with the terrible finality of a sudden death—murder, suicide, accident, or natural trauma—there is a bereftness, a shock, a numbing bewilderment and anguish different from any other loss.

There are many interweaving conversations in the circles of our lives: professional, familial, and the casual daily dialogues of friends and acquaintances. The most intimate of all, the conversations with our mate, provide the greatest closeness and full knowledge of another human being's core. This relationship encompasses the intellectual, the physical, and the emotional—every aspect of ourselves.

Our mates know us as no one else does and the words we share reflect this intimacy. They are an integral part of our daily lives: our sleeping and eating habits, our recreation, our relationships, and our economy. When that life is wrenched away, there is no preparation for singleness, no wrap up, no good-byes.

It's final.

It's over.

And it's now.

The stories in this chapter are the wolf's lonely howl to the moon for its lost mate. This howl comes out of the deepest recesses and darkest corners of our aching soul. These are voices of grief, of incomprehension and of longing. They are solitary cries that echo in the night. Some will reverberate through a lifetime; others will fade as new conversations begin and continue in the endless circle of life and death.

DEATH IN THE COOL EVENING

Ginny Stanford

I've always called it love at first sight, the compelling visceral attraction that overpowers competing instincts, any tendency to caution or reason. When Frank said hello, I fell in love with his voice. By the end of that day, I was sure I loved everything he had been, was then, would ever be. He was wildly enthusiastic about my painting—there's nothing like being understood. In the weeks that followed I read from his manuscripts and made drawings based on the poems. He bought me notebooks and different kinds of pens to try out.

"Paint an old man sitting by a coffin waving at the moon; a fat lady shelling peas and a centaur behind her; a blind Gypsy holding a conch shell. Paint a white horse breaking away from a funeral hearse; a scarecrow wearing a kimono. Paint smoke rings," he said.

Back then I was sure of many things. I believed Frank and I would always be together, and that time would only bring us more of what we wanted, as if the course of our lives had been set to trace an unwavering line upward toward happiness and achievement.

I have never regretted leaving the Midwest, although sometimes I miss the farm—our rambling house with the front porch that wrapped around two sides, the elaborate garden we had, all the land. Sometimes I miss the prairie and its views of each day's beginning and end. I loved watching that sky. Things are different in Northern California. Coastal hills, ghosts of old mountain ranges barricade the eastern horizon. I don't see the copper edge of the moon rising out of the earth like I used to, but nothing the Midwest has to offer can compare with the sight of that enormous red crescent sinking into the Pacific in the middle of the night.

Bodega Head is where I go to watch the moon set—November and December are the best months. I've never been scared to take the path on the crest of those high cliffs alone late at night. Perhaps I should be. A buck deer and I met once in the dark; I saw the white smoke coming out of his nostrils before I saw him.

Frank had been the one so at home around water. I never thought I'd end up feeling the same way. Now I can't imagine leaving here. Living on the western edge of this continent, so far away from where I began, is reassuring to me now—the whole country behind me; two mountain ranges, two time zones, and eighteen years now lay between me and the hot, oppressive summer of his death. I've had plenty of time to go over that Saturday, wonder why I didn't see it coming, parse every sentence I uttered—every word—comb through everything I did but wish I hadn't, and everything I wanted to say but didn't. As if my taking out one part could have changed the outcome.

He died before I had time to finish his portrait.

In May he said, "Copy this Gauguin and paint me standing in front of it. Call it 'Spirit of the Dead Watching.'" A Tahitian girl is clutching her pillow in fear, her bed a sumptuous pattern of blue, rose, yellow, and bright orange. A spray of phosphorescent flowers decorates the wall behind her. At the foot of the bed is another woman, hooded, dressed in black. She sits, staring impassively ahead. She is *manao tupa-pao*, the spirit of the dead watching. I thought it was a great idea. I thought he had the best ideas.

"Why don't you pose in your kimono?" I said.

We buried him barefoot in that kimono. At first, the funeral home refused. They insisted he wear a suit and shoes; claimed it was a state law. Sometime in the weeks after his death I rolled up the canvas and placed it in a corner of my parent's attic where it remains.

"I love you," was the last thing he said to me. He said I love you, and I said, "Don't give me that crap."

Saturday evening. June third. He had betrayed me by having an affair and I had found out. I was hurt and humiliated and angry enough to put him through a wall. *I love you.* It was the first time I didn't automatically answer back, *I love you, too.* I barely tolerated the hug he tried to give me, my arms stiff at my sides. He tried to kiss me, and I turned my head so that his lips only grazed my hair. Then he left. Forever. He left me in a room and shut the door behind him as he left. He took three steps across a hall into another room and shut another door and shot himself.

In the span of the longest five or six seconds I have ever lived through, Frank fired three shots into his chest. Three pops, three cries. All I had was sound. I couldn't see him; I could only imagine what he was doing in another part of the house. With the sound of the first shot time stopped, changed course and went backward through the second and third shots, then reconstructed itself into an endless, directionless loop. Before Saturday, June third, time was a straight line. After Saturday, a loop.

I heard a sharp crack, a hard slap, an angry teacher breaking his ruler against a desk. I heard the crack and just as sharp I heard Frank hollering, "Oh"—surprised. I heard him step on a copperhead, get stung by a yellow jacket, smash his thumb with a hammer. I watched him jump into Spider Creek, heard him hit the cold water and yelp from the shock. *Pop, Oh! Pop, Oh! Pop, Oh!*

After the third cry I knew he was dead. Imagine the wall is telling you a bedtime story. Go to sleep now, it might say. That is how the news was delivered. A quiet voice from somewhere inside me said flatly, *It's all over; he's killed himself.* I didn't want to move. But the same silent voice was ordering me out. *Get out, get out,* it kept repeating. *Call the police.*

I didn't want to look. *He's blown his brains out,* the voice said. *Don't go in there. Save the memory.*

Death had changed his eyes from hazel to pale porcelain green. I climbed onto the bed where he lay and sat astride his crooked body, amazed at the sight of three small red holes ringing his heart. I put my hands on his chest. While I waited for the police I tried to memorize every detail of his face before I never saw it again. He looked through me toward a distant place and I tried wishing myself there. *This is real,* I repeated, working hard to convince myself; *this is real, this is real.*

I spent the night in a Holiday Inn. I was afraid to close my eyes, afraid to dream, afraid to let sleep seal the day and lock it into history. *Tomorrow,* I thought, *he will be irretrievable.* Finally, against my will, I slept, and not fitfully as I had expected, but deeply. During that long deep sleep—more like a coma—I didn't dream about Frank. I didn't dream at all. He sent no messages, instructions, or last requests and I felt no trace of our connection.

His funeral was like every funeral—inadequate. Stand up. Sit down. Kneel. Pray. Get used to it. I remember the missal in my lap. It was a deep, lush, luminous red. The soles of my black shoes clacked on marble tiles, each step echoing through cavernous silence as I made my way to a pew. What I remember most clearly is Frank's casket—so small and far away—bathed by a pool of dim light. It glowed in the darkness of the church like Sleeping Beauty's glass coffin. I see thick white candles burning in giant brass candlesticks at his head and feet. I think of a clearing in the forest, and all the animals in a circle waiting for Sleeping Beauty to open her eyes.

I don't know if the first year was the worst, but it was the most singular. Then death was new—every day unique, the first of its kind to be lived without him—and the point was simply to survive. The first year, I couldn't imagine there would be a second one. I anchored myself to painting and stayed busy. It was hard to concentrate on art because I kept expecting someone to burst through the door of the studio and shoot me. I scoured Frank's poems for ideas and ways to stay close to him.

All that year I looked for windows, mirrors, thin fingers of light, something to slip through, some way to find Frank through faith or will, on the other side of pain. I dreamed of secret passageways, walls that were really doors opening into life, and Frank vibrant, splendidly alive on the other side of those walls. My nights were full of second chances.

What I saw before me was a desert of time, a white monotony of absence and regret that I could never cross. I imagined him waiting at the end of that long first year with fresh water and a laurel wreath, waving from the finish line to spur me on. "You made it," he might say, "and I'm your reward."

For years I saw him—a gesture, a wave, a blur. His promises were everywhere. *Set me as a seal upon thine heart, as a seal upon thine arm; for love is strong as death.* I thought it was him. I worked hard at forgetting but he stayed with me, beside me, behind me. I felt him waiting, like the fog waits to come in on summer evenings. *Just roll in over the hills while I sleep,* I told him. *You can disappear with the sunrise.*

Once I thought I saw him, but it was the light hitting my windshield. I thought I saw him, but it was a blue jay in a bay tree. I thought I saw him, but it was a curtain blowing through a window. I saw a man waiting for the bus and thought it was him. I saw a shadow dancing across a wall and thought it was him. I was expecting him. I had the red carpet out. A black cat jumped down out of a tree and I thought it was him. I heard something like his voice, but it belonged to an owl. I thought I saw him, but it was smoke from a brush pile. I thought it was him, but it was my longing, my regret. Sometimes when the phone rang I imagined he might be calling. I said, "I love you, too." I said it often in case he might be listening.

I studied the photographs I'd taken, looking for clues, and found the other woman in his face. At the point where she entered our lives I saw lies cross-hatching, shadowing his cheeks, filling in below his eyes with darkness. The smile began fading in and out; it grew less frequent. Finally his jaw became a clenched fist, clamped down tight on honesty, choking it back; his face seemed fossilized. He looked driven, wild, worn out in the last pictures. I decided she had killed him.

The fifth summer I opened one of his books and read a poem on the last page and I remembered our life purposefully. To console myself I painted a meadow like the meadow at the farm—prairie hay turning copper in October light, intersecting an eastern sky infiltrated by the beginnings of darkness. I painted my longing as a red silk kimono with its pattern of tiny pink and white gourds, floating above the tall grass. The seventh summer I took off my wedding ring and put it in a pine trunk. The eighth summer I gave all his records to the library. I couldn't bear to listen to the music of our life. The tenth summer I wore his Saint Francis medal.

I painted his portrait during the thirteenth summer and we became friends again. I began to celebrate his birthday once more.

On the fourteenth anniversary of his suicide I fired a twenty-two revolver at a paper target. It felt a little like murder. *Did you feel the pain? How were you able to keep pulling the trigger? Why didn't you drop the gun? Why did you leave?* I hit the bull's eye twice.

Three months later, on August first, I celebrated his birthday for the first time in a long while. Instead of a cake, I bought a package of twelve-inch red tapers. I collected all the candlesticks in the house and arranged them in a circle on the dining room table and put my bouquet in the center. It had all his favorite flowers: bachelor buttons, mixed with yellow coreopsis and white cosmos, tied with a red ribbon. I'd picked them from the flower bed by the front door. The fog was beginning to roll in and soften the long shadows that fell across my deck. I lit the candles at dusk—fifteen in all—and stepped back to take in the sight. *He would get a kick out of this,* I thought.

June third comes and goes. I grow older and Frank remains forever twenty-nine. Time has taught me, among other things, that death is persistent and enduring beyond my capacity to imagine it. People still ask me, *Why?* I used to have an answer. Now I say, *I don't know.*

The day we met, Frank read me one of his own poems. It remains my favorite simply because it was part of such a remarkable encounter. The irony has not been lost on me.

DEATH IN THE COOL EVENING

I move
Like the deer in the forest
I see you before you see me
We are like the moist rose
Which opens alone
When I'm dreaming
I linger by the pool of many seasons
Suddenly it is night
Time passes like the shadows
That were not
There when you lifted your head
Dreams leave their hind tracks
Something red and warm to go by
So it is the hunters of this world
Close in.

ATOMIC BOMB

Christopher Koch

The light switch illuminated your bloodless skin
The blinding flash seemed surreal, disorienting
Touching your cold stiffness releases my scream
The roar was distant, not part of light or space
The shock wave hit my chest and knees
I felt deaf and prayed for blindness
There were no birds, laughter ceased, safety evaporated
In denial my fingers trembled through lifeless hair,
  flicked across rigor
I stumbled through the questions and hours,
  relying on training and armor
The fallout lasted longer than I expected
The radiation sickness came close to killing me
Feeling the blast of your decision shifted my foundation
720 days and I still survey wreckage and rubble
The crews follow procedure and are hopeful
The explosion of light altered the spin of my world

I tilt my view above the ruin

LETTER TO A MURDERED MATE:
WE NEVER GOT TO SAY GOOD-BYE

J. E. Tibbals

Honey,

We never said good-bye. How can a life end this way? How can two worlds be shattered so fast and irreversibly? We read about murder in the newspapers, see it on TV and the movies, but it can't really happen to us. Can it?

It was 4:30 P.M., December 16, 1993. The phone rang as I stood at the stove cooking dinner for your return from Boise that evening. The cold, calm words of your uncle sliced through my heart, cleanly, quietly, and thoroughly, catapulting my whole being into a world of shock and numbness. The tears would come later . . . in torrents.

Details emerged that evening on national news, more in the police and coroner reports that followed.

Items Found:

(1) Victim and brother of perpetrator: shot 8 times, 7 exit wounds in the back; 4 shots right abdominal area, 2 shots upper chest area and contact shot in right ear;

(2) Business partner of first victim: 7 bullet wounds;

(3) Perpetrator: one contact wound to right temple area;

(4) One 45 caliber, semi-automatic handgun with three magazines; two empty clips, one clip with three live rounds;

(5) Note: "These people bought their bullets."

These are the facts; cold, hard, stark. How can they relate to who you are . . . were, a living, breathing, loving, spiritual entity reduced to items on a police blotter? A man who couldn't stand the sight of blood; who boycotted violence in entertainment and in life.

They say you died around 9:30 that morning. The S.W.A.T. team didn't even enter the scene of the massacre until 11:00. On TV, they always arrive within minutes. Aren't they supposed to take risks? What if you had been only wounded and lay bleeding to death before they arrived? There was no help for you that day. And I wasn't there. Why not? Why didn't I go? You didn't want me to. Did you somehow know the danger? Why didn't you tell me? Weren't we always there for each other in the big moments of life? We had been together for over ten years and now we hadn't even said a last good-bye. They told me not to come to say good-bye because of that last bullet. Why did I listen? Could it have been any worse than the haunting visions in my own head?

The day before, December fifteenth, we still had thirty years together ahead of us. The hard part was over. After the agony of both our fathers' deaths that year, we had some money to start our married life together in a beautiful home in the Santa Cruz Mountains. The next day, December sixteenth, that world is gone. It took a few seconds; that's all. I sent you off to Idaho with a light kiss—a portent of a warm and happy Christmas together. All that came back was your wallet, keys, and raincoat (where was the blood? Did they clean it? Did you leave it in the car? There must have been blood).

Three weeks later, UPS delivered your ashes into my hands as I mindlessly trudged the hills of our home, uprooting thistles, berry bushes, dandelions, frantically seeking a physical pain and exhaustion to match the psychic. The bargaining had begun. Maybe if I got the yard beautiful enough you would come home. Just one last touch, one last word, one last look. One last something. Please . . . .

We didn't even say good-bye. Who closed your eyes that final day as they stared sightlessly at the ceiling; your body shoved into a black body bag by strange hands; hands just going through the motions of another day's work? Newspaper photos showed you (or another victim of the massacre?) being carried out of the carnage in that body bag. This image will never leave my mind.

What was death like for you? Eight bullets entered your body; the last one in your head. Did you know what was happening? Did you have time to think? Did you know that this was the end . . . for you, for us? Were your last thoughts of me, of pain, of what you were leaving behind? Did you look into your brother's murderous eyes at that last moment? What did you see? Hatred? Anger? Insanity? Perhaps you experienced a moment of incredible fright and disbelief, but then you were gone.

I have haunted doctors with my questions. They assure me that at that close range with a Colt .45, you were dead within seconds. And during that time, you must have been in such shock that there was little pain or understanding; a disconnecting. I want to believe them, but I don't know; it's so hard to trust again. Will I always be this obsessed with the brutal details? Will I forever wonder what happened to your physical body during those last moments?

What I do know is that for me, you are murdered again and again. The video replays itself in my head. I awake at night almost feeling the impact of the bullets hitting your body. I relive the thud of emotions of that phone call that started the crumbling of my world.

Two years later, however, there are times of happy memories. You will always be my golden boy. I'll forever see you on the tennis court; the place of greatest fun and challenge for you, or hiking our beloved redwood trails. I will never have to witness the physical degeneration of a rugged, healthy man or the emotional degradation of a cancer-ridden disintegration, a debilitating stroke or heart attack. You will always be fifty-two and gorgeous.

But I mourn for all the things we now will never share. My passion for wolves has brought the joy of a wolf-dog puppy into my life. My daughter's wedding you were so looking forward to. Your pride in her was as great as if she were your own. We never got to share our first spring in Bonny Doon, with hillsides of wildflowers—ginger, sweet peas, ceonothus, buttercups, and wild strawberry. The creek on our property burbled all summer long as I sat on our deck and listened to the quiet of the redwood forest and thought of the joy we had looked forward to and now will never have. And our dreams—what about our dreams? What do I do with them now? Where do I put them?

But always I will remember and love: I picture the scenes of our life that delineate who you were. You, standing by my father's bed as he lay dying of cancer. A special visit to assure him of our forthcoming marriage and of your commitment to loving and caring for me the rest of my life. Life's little ironies.

I remember, too, the phone call from your brother telling of your father's suicide. Throughout those days of picking up the final pieces of his life, you remained cool and calm. Weeks later you allowed the tears to come. Your head always processed information first; then your heart. The opposite of me. We balanced one another so well.

I remember our last day together—an unexceptional day of working in the yard of our new home, building a wood pile—you chainsawing, me carting and stacking. Our last shower together; the sweetness of our last light kiss as you got in your flashy red sports car for the Boise connection; me to the airport to pick up my daughter.

Where are you now? When all the radios, TVs, and myriad manmade distractions of the world cease, my heart aches to know and understand what happens after death. Was that all of you contained in that black sealed box from the Boise coroners? Or are you out there in the night and in the cloud formations as I look out to sea?

I feel closest to you when my body is immersed in the natural world, or in my dreams. Some part of you must be inside me; our lives were so connected. I try to grasp some tangible concept of your being, but find only fragments. Your ashes; dispersed since, in your beloved redwoods and over the mighty Victoria Falls in Africa, a place we longed to visit together. Your tennis racket; your office filled with thirty years of business papers and notes. And the less tangible: the ache in my heart and the cloudiness of my vision as I try to refocus on what and who I am without you.

And so, my dear, this unraveling of our lives begins. Am I afraid? Not for my physical self; not for things or people or happenings. My fears are of nothing concrete. Sometimes I fear an emptiness of what's left in my life; of an inability to form another connection, even if it's just with myself. I fear no one will ever excite me again; arouse that awe-filled lurch of my heart when I first laid eyes on you. Who will suffer my pets as they sleep surrounding my vulnerability since that long ago day in December? Our common passion for animals was one of our strongest bonds, and I loved you so for it.

Good-bye, my Donald. We never got to say good-bye. If only I had told you all these things in your life, or at least whispered them to you as your life bled away on that cold floor in an Idaho office. If only I could have cradled your head in my arms one last time; to tell you of my love again; to put into words the great difference you made in my life. How proud I was to have touched and experienced your nobility; an old-fashioned concept, yes, but true. My heart, which you held in your hands for our ten years together, I knew was in safekeeping. I have not known a greater trust.

Last, and most of all, I thank you for the gift of your love; a love that gave me the strength to survive your loss.

SHATTERED

Karen Calcaterra

The only place I could even close my eyes was in his room, otherwise sleep was out of the question. The quiet beeping, pumping sounds seemed to calm my racing thoughts. I gently held his hand, kissed his chilled, clammy skin, and prayed for his recovery with all my soul, as if somehow the intensity of my prayers could keep him alive. This man was my life, my beloved husband of twenty-five years; soulmates; best friends; partners in all endeavors. We raised two children, weathered financial difficulties together; we were teammates in all of life's activities. This was all some horrible nightmare, some horror flick in which Carl and I held the starring roles. It just couldn't be happening. Not to Carl! Not to me!

This morning the clicking, whirring sounds of the assorted machines hooked up to him lulled me into a sense of false security. The monitor showed reasonable numbers for his intercranial and blood pressures, the enemies in the battle he had waged so courageously these two days past. Actually, the monitor showed better numbers than he'd had in the whole time he'd been here. Yesterday the doctors called him the "miracle man" because despite odds of one in a thousand he'd made it through that second day. God had answered my prayers—he was alive. An EEG and brain flow test were scheduled for early today and my hopes were high. He looked healthier, somehow more restful. An hour later my life, as I had known it, ended. Carl was declared brain dead.

As I recall those three days spent in the intensive care unit they seem a horribly blurred mini-drama played out in shadow characters. The memories come back as a mass of decisions, prayers, and horrors. It all started on that Friday morning, my last day of school before the long-awaited summer vacation.

"Honey, will you set the alarm for 7:30? I'm not going to aerobics this morning. I'm breaking into my lazy summer routine." I gently teased him about my free time each summer. This was to be no exception—or so I thought.

He held my hand as he sat on the edge of our bed and reset the alarm for me. "A kept woman again? You going to laze around for three months while I have to put my nose to the old grindstone and support us, huh?" he said in a teasing voice as he kissed my forehead lightly.

"Love ya, hon. Don't forget we're meeting the Fogartys tonight for drinks, so don't work over, okay?"

"Okay, I won't. Well, I'd better go. Someone in this house has to work." He leaned over and gave me a final kiss before leaving for his job as a heavy diesel mechanic. He loved working on those giant haul trucks in Butte's open pit copper mine. He used to say he could fix them in his sleep.

My morning progressed without incident. The last day of school for teachers in our district is very laid back—lots of joking and chatting—the relaxed pace of closure. The call came to school at about 11:40 A.M.; I almost didn't take it. Figured it was a joke; get me to walk to the office for a dial tone.

"Mrs. Calcaterra, Carl's been hurt in a fall at work. He's gone to the emergency room at the hospital. We'll meet you there," his supervisor calmly told me.

One of my fellow teachers insisted on driving me to the hospital. My body was in full panic. I couldn't rid myself of the fear that this wasn't just a broken bone. My breath was labored; I was strangling in fear. He just had to be okay. He couldn't be hurt seriously. God, please help him. I prayed and sobbed on the ride to the hospital.

Once there, I was ushered to the "family room" facility off the emergency room. My fears increased when the nurse told me that perhaps I should start phoning family members to come as soon as possible. Each physician and nurse I met provided a variation of "he's had a serious blow to the head."

I recall being so incoherent that I couldn't remember my sister's last name or the phone number I called every day. Representatives from Carl's company came to sit with me. I felt revulsion for his supervisor. I remember thinking irrationally that somehow this was his fault. Wasn't he responsible for ensuring that his employees were safe?

When the neurosurgeon arrived, he tried to explain what was wrong. He showed me X-rays of three distinct cracks to Carl's skull. His condition was rapidly progressing downward and surgery was imminent. I was to remember, "This was very serious . . . very serious . . . very serious. There are no guarantees."

Just before surgery I was finally allowed to see my husband. It is the most difficult of hospital memories. My wonderfully handsome, forty-five-year-old husband's face was ashy white. Blood poured out of both ears and from the back of his head. His eyes were half open and staring sightlessly. He was hooked up to a breathing bag. His work shirt had been cut off. He was unresponsive and in a deep coma.

"Honey! Honey, can you hear me? Carl, sweetie, you have to wake up." I pleaded with him, believing that somehow when he heard my voice, he would rouse or stir—anything. But nothing happened. He just lay there sightless, oblivious to everything and everyone.

They said he'd never regained consciousness after slipping from a truck tire fourteen feet in the air, striking his head on the cement floor of the garage. I persisted. I held his hand, crying and talking to him. "Honey, can you hear me? Honey, you're going to be all right. They're taking you to surgery now. I'll be right here when you get out. Carl, can you hear me?" Still no answer.

As they wheeled him past, my knees buckled and I sank to the floor sobbing. This couldn't be happening! Just three hours before he'd been normal, healthy. My chest hurt; that same chest tightening until the day he died. My body reacted, constricting with fear and pain, my mind numb. I couldn't remember what people said to me. I sat almost in an out-of-body trance, praying the same prayer over and over—"God, please let him live. Let him be okay. God, I can't live without him."

As I look back, I arranged the three days of his hospitalization into three categories. Day One—surgery and prayer. Day Two—lack of blood pressure and high fever, more prayer. Day Three—return of normal blood pressure and cranial swelling.

Day One brought little medical hope. The most encouraging statement made by his surgeon: "We'll just wait and see." An internist gave him less than fifty percent chance of living through the night. Neither of these opinions were acceptable.

"He'll do just fine with those odds. He'll make it, just wait and see," I defiantly told the doctor, daring him to contradict me.

Day Two, memories of a blood pressure so low that his perfectly healthy kidneys were affected; he would need dialysis later on. They were unsure his body, so traumatized, could withstand dialysis. An intense fever raged from pressure on his brain stem. All through the night they stripped him naked, draping an electric cooling blanket across him, cooling the room itself by means of the open window that allowed the cold mountain air inside. His room was so cold I had to wear a coat and put on a blanket just to be with him.

After the fever and that night's fight for a normal blood pressure, the next morning Carl looked so pink and healthy. I felt a sense of semi-calm, the first since his accident. He had breathed on his own for four minutes; I cried with joy. He had a cough reflex, the first discernible action since being admitted, another cause for celebration and hope.

But along with this improved blood pressure came another night of hell. His intercranial pressure rose to 66—previously a reading of 20 sent nurses scurrying to charts to make adjustments in medications. I became a roaming lunatic. I couldn't bear to watch the monitors, their numbers showing a dangerously swelling brain, yet I couldn't stand not knowing what they said. I paced from his room to the waiting area and back. At about 4:00 A.M. his intercranial pressure seemed to stabilize, even starting to decline. He had made it through another night! Things were going to be all right.

But at nine the next morning, the brain flow test showed that Carl had no blood flow to the brain whatsoever. They told me that clinically he was dead.

"Do you want to consider organ donation?" the nurse gently asked.

Numbly, I sat with my two boys and listened to the organ donation representative explain how the process was done. I signed forms and released his body for transplant surgery. I remember asking that they replace the bandage on his head so people wouldn't see him with his head shaven, wouldn't see him without his exquisite thick, black wavy hair. People came into the room, said their tearful good-byes and filed out. The boys and I cried over him a long while, holding each others' hands and his. I bathed his kind, gentle, peaceful face with the flow of my tears. I kissed him everywhere. He was so warm, he didn't seem any different than he had three days ago when they said he was only in a coma. How could he be dead now? I finally was able to let go of his hand and leave the hospital. That was the last time I saw him.

We had him cremated. He told me each time we attended the lengthy Italian wakes for family members, "Don't ever do that to me! I hate it when people sit in the room with a body and laugh and joke about things. Cremate me and spread my ashes over Fleecer," the mountain where he and the boys had often hunted. I remember being at the mortuary, going through the motions of funeral preparation in a surreal mode, not really there; almost viewing myself doing these activities from outside my body. I lost a whole week of my life. I know I attended the funeral, I remember hearing consoling words from hundreds of people, but my mind told me that I was still in some crazy nightmare. I remember lying in bed at night praying for the nightmare to end, so I could wake up and hold Carl—have him tell me everything was going to be all right. My mind couldn't even begin to fathom a life without him.

Immediately following his death, life was like an animal coming out of hibernation—disoriented, sensing the world as familiar, yet strangely different from what it had known before.

In some ways my life since has been a blur. I go through the motions. But nothing seems the same. When I'm alone, I sit in my chair, the one across the room from his, staring at it, willing his return.

Voraciously I read any book on loss and death, but they create more questions than answers.

"Where is Carl? Can he see me? Does he hear me when I talk to him?"

My niece related to me a dream she had in which Carl, standing at the foot of our bed, watched me sleep, then turned to her, saying, "Tell Aunt Karen that I'm all right. She's worrying about me and I'm okay. Tell her that."

"But why didn't he try to contact me? Why couldn't I feel his presence?"

At first, I just felt empty and alone. Surely if he made an effort I would be able to feel his presence. But I knew that dreams were not a medium available to Carl for contacting me; I had been dreamless since his death. Unlike many people who have experienced the death of a loved one, I drop into bed and sleep like I myself am dead. In the morning I awake feeling tired, but amazed that I was able to sleep. So if contact through dreams were out, would he contact me at all?

About three weeks ago, I was talking to him—as I continue to do—and I felt a tingly pulse through my body, raising goose bumps on my skin. I wondered, was this sensation a response from him? I repeated the question and felt the same tingly reply. I now know that Carl is able to contact me when he chooses. He doesn't speak to me in words; he just lets me know that he is present and with me. I can't describe the comfort and peace I feel when he is present.

Through my husband's dying, and the time since his death, I have realized many things about myself. I am a survivor. I loved Carl as much as is possible for me to love another human being. No two people were ever closer than we were. But even after his death, knowing that I will face life without him, I still love it, and will create the best possible world for myself and my two adult children. Without him somehow each day is a new experience. I feel fear for my ability to face these new experiences alone, yet I am still able to feel joy, laughter, and a sense of peace with life in general. Life now is different; yet it still holds the possibilities of joy and fullness.

Carl still lives on. He will see the progress of his sons and view his yet unborn grandchildren because I am not alone; he is within me. I will face my life with hope and the knowledge that I can indeed go on without his physical being. Love never dies.

MOURNING SAUL

Nancy Kassell

Sunday, August 11, 1991, four days before the first anniversary of our living together, Saul was killed in a bicycle accident. I'd known him for three and a half years. He was my best friend and the love of my life. Although I had grieved other losses—my mother's death from cancer, the disintegration of my marriage, the end of my academic career— nothing prepared me for Saul's sudden death. We didn't say good-bye. Well, I did, but I don't know if he heard me.

Saul awakened me early that morning. I knew that he had planned to go for a quick ride. It was to be a "working" Sunday for both of us. As a respected dealer in antique scientific instruments, he was in the midst of restoring an antique telescope, and I planned to edit a chapter of a book I was writing and do some reading.

I heard Saul downstairs in the kitchen and the slam of the basement door, but drifted back to sleep. Later, I would recall being roused from semi-consciousness by the sound of distant sirens.

Getting up at my leisure, I went downstairs and found his simple five-word note: "The cats have been fed." I never imagined it would be the last words I would ever receive from him. I went about my tasks, but by noon I felt very uneasy. Saul was a considerate man; I trusted him completely. What was I to think? Had he run into a biking friend and gone for a longer ride? He would have called. I cleaned the kitchen, read the newspaper, and began to set deadlines. If I don't hear from him by one o'clock, I'm calling the police. Don't be silly, I told myself; he's a grown man and he's only been gone a few hours. Time passed. I tried to read. More time passed.

Five o'clock was the final deadline. I called. There had been an accident that morning. The unidentified victim was in a coma. Hadn't I heard the bulletin on radio and TV? I hadn't. I was told very little and questioned at length. What was he wearing? What kind of bicycle did he have? What time did he leave the house? The description seemed to fit. A policewoman would drive me to the hospital. I found Saul's wallet on the bedside table and located his address book in case I had to call his family. The victim had two broken legs, I was told. I worried how we would manage Saul's convalescence in his eighteenth-century house with its narrow passageways and many stairs. He was a very active man, not likely to endure a period of disability with much patience.

The news at the hospital was far worse than broken legs. There were head injuries so severe that there was no chance of recovery. Saul usually wore a helmet, but he hadn't that day. It was too hot.

"We looked at the CAT scan and there was nothing to fix," said the gentle resident in ICU. When I saw him, it was hard to believe that the bruised body, the head swollen to twice its normal size, was Saul. I stroked his arm, but he didn't respond. I spoke to him, but he didn't answer. What I heard and saw was beyond comprehension. Shock is another state of consciousness; ordinary ways of perceiving and feeling are suspended.

I made phone calls. While his family traveled from points across the country, I sat by the bedside and talked to Saul. I wanted him to know he wasn't alone. His facial muscles twitched when I told him I would always love him; that it was all right for him to go if he had to, although in my heart I didn't mean it. The neurologist had told me that his injuries were "incompatible with life," so I wanted to let Saul know I was with him no matter what. I felt that some part of his spirit was still with me until noon, the day after the accident when I first acknowledged the flat line on the brain scan, the complete absence of reflexes.

Finding a life companion when you're in your fifties is an unexpected miracle. As an only child, as the wife in a difficult marriage, as a divorced woman and single parent, I had become overly self-reliant. I had too much of a good thing and I knew it, but I kept hoping that I would find an ally and life partner. In Saul I found more than I ever imagined—a loving, spiritual, but intellectually challenging companion, whose passions matched my own.

When someone you love deeply dies, life and death are confounded. Part of me died with Saul. Existence became a kind of living death. Mourning became an acknowledgment that I didn't die too, although sometimes I wished I had. I was finding my way back and the trip was exhausting.

The first year after Saul died I took care of his house (his son, who no longer lived at home, kindly told me to stay as long as I needed to) and helped to liquidate his business. Most days I could manage to do only what was necessary; the rest of the time, I stared at television. Writing would have provided a respite from grieving, if I had been able to concentrate. About all I could read was the newspaper. The hardest time of the day was in the late afternoon, when Saul and I would have met in the living room for a drink. I found myself watching "Where in the World is Carmen Sandiego?" on PBS, wondering: *Where was I?*

A year after Saul died, I moved back into my condominium with the cats—his, mine, and ours. I felt ready to leave his house, since it no longer held his presence. Though I was back in my own space, I never felt completely present without Saul. I had lived alone for many years before I met him, knew the value of solitude, and had never been a woman who took her identity from a man. But all that didn't seem to matter. Shock had provided a kind of emotional insulation for many months, but eventually I had to face the reality of starting over. I shuddered at this task of moving on. What if you just don't want to do it any more? What's the point?

In my old/new home, I began the process of reconstructing my life. For the past three years, life equaled work. Some days I'd be all right; other days I would pretend; still others I couldn't even pretend. I tried not to ask cosmic questions: *Why him? Why me?* At first, I'd set myself little tasks; one foot in front of the other. I spent a lot of energy trying to maintain a minimum level of comfort. Sometimes I would have to let everything go, to allow myself to feel the sadness, the rage, the injustice.

My daughters and friends have taken good care of me, but it is hard to comfort a person when she is inconsolable. And by now, I'm supposed to be reintegrated into life.

Mourning is about powerlessness: however fiercely I loved, despite all my efforts, this is how things turned out. "We looked at the CAT scan and there was nothing to fix."

I don't know what it means to "get over" Saul's death. I'm still trying to grasp life without him. I experienced the kind of love which I had only imagined for so long. At least I know now that such love can exist. But for now, years after Saul's death, I also struggle with the awareness that one does not live on memory alone.

And "alone" is the operative word.

MOURNING THOUGHTS

Gloria Rovder Healy

It was a gorgeous March day
      or was it April?
Months aren't important,
      it's the day
      I must forget

"I'm too tired," he said,
      "for flower shows."
      "Okay," I smiled,
"I'll drive Michael to his friend's."
      He grinned.
      "I'll be waiting."

Gone forever when I returned
      I cried angrily.
How dare he leave without
      saying good-bye?
      Later, I accepted, but
never, never understood.

      Outside my darkened window
    stately maples sigh sorrowfully
as I toss fretfully in my barren bed.
    Reaching out for him, I shiver
      remembering I'm alone

    Looking at our children
I mourn lovely times we shared,
    lonely times we didn't.
    Looking at our children
I feel an angel's tear fall
      upon my heart,
      I'm comforted.

THE WINTER OF MY WIDOWHOOD

Jeanne Quinn

The phone rang. It was 3:00 A.M. I knew without knowing, my husband was dead. By some weird freak of premonition I had dreamed of this very moment. Dreaded those nightmares when I'd wake up in a cold sweat, sit bolt upright in bed and he would turn slowly and ask what was wrong. Nestled in the crux of his arm once again, I was safe. He wasn't dead. He was here, to put his arms around me. Where was he now? Why didn't he roll over and take this nightmare away from me? The incessant ringing of the phone. Make it stop.

But this time it wasn't a nightmare. This time it was a call from the hospital. The jangling phone seared through the black night and I knew this time was for real.

I lay silently under the warm pink quilt, a feeling of lightness permeating my body as though, I, too, had become an ethereal being. I floated about in my mind, letting the words of the nurse penetrate the wall of refusal. Instantly, although I heard her words, denial encompassed my being. She said to come to the hospital; she hadn't actually said he was dead. I lay there, under the warmth of the quilt, taking my time. There seemed to be no hurry. Death had already come.

Slowly I crawled out of bed. The cold night air hit my naked body. I went into the bathroom and turned on a hot shower. I stepped into the steaming tub, the water cascading down upon my head, over my shoulders, covering me like a shroud. I turned my face upward and let the water hit me full force. Lathering my hair, I let the soapsuds drizzle softly down my skin. A mantle of foam collected at my feet and then rushed down the drain. With it went the feeling of that which I feared the most has happened.

Although I felt no outward sense of panic, I don't remember driving to the hospital. I remember the rain-swept streets. There were no other cars on the road but mine. Had it really rained? Arriving at the hospital, my hair still wet, streaming down my shoulders, a man saw me running toward a red sign that flicked "Emergency." "Slow down," he called, "they'll wait."

I smiled, waved, but couldn't stop my running feet. A nurse met me at the door and gently took my arm, steering me into a small office. She offered me a cup of coffee. I sipped the hot black liquid. It slipped slowly down my parched throat. A doctor asked my name, where I lived, how long I'd been married. But no one spoke the words. No one said he was dead. Finally I asked, "Is he dead?"

"Would you like to see him?" the nurse answered, nodding.

Like a child being led into the dentist's office, I was propelled into a small room at the end of the corridor. I choked back a lump that rose in my throat as the nurse pulled back a sheet. He was sleeping. I'd seen him like that every night for twenty years. Why was tonight different? All I had to do was touch him on the cheek and he would roll over and take me into his arms. But something repulsive crept into my heart. Something made me back away. A wall, a barrier I could not see, had come between us. I wanted to pound on it, break it down. But where was it? It was like he had been swallowed up in a whirlpool and something deep inside of me told me to stay back, not to get caught up in this whirlpool or I, too, would be sucked under. I wanted to run, but to where? I wanted to reach for someone, but whom? There was no one to say "April Fool!" or "only kidding." The nurse pulled the sheet over his face and walked me gently out of the room.

"Can we call someone for you?" she asked.

My mind raced as I remembered the five sleeping children I'd left at home. There was my mother or my brother, but they were far away. "No," I shook my head. "I'll be all right." Suddenly I wanted to be alone with my thoughts, with the last vestiges of quiet that would be mine for the next several days. I wanted to remember us, our alone times and the problems and privileges that only come between two married people that no one else can understand.

I drove home in the stillness of the night, the morning light not yet beginning to break. I made myself a pot of coffee and sat out the endless hours until the first stirrings of the children brought me back to the realities of the day. They would have to be told. Of course. My first thought was to let them go to school as though nothing had happened. "How could I think that?" I questioned my own logic. I called my mother.

The phone was silent when I broke the news. She uttered a deep sigh and said she would leave now, at dawn, and be there as soon as possible. "And yes," she took on a soft motherly, but insistent tone, "you must tell the children. Now," she emphasized.

My eighteen-year-old daughter, Tara, was the first to wake up and the first to be told. With the swiftness of wildfire, one by one, the children tumbled down the stairs, stirred by the unsettled atmosphere, the anguish of Tara's cry. "Dad is dead," I uttered not once, not twice, but so often I wanted to scream it from the rooftops. Let the world know the pain of anguish that lay in my heart, that rose in my throat, that throbbed in my head. They cried, they lay on the sofa, across the kitchen table, they went back to their rooms. Suddenly it wasn't five children anymore. It was ten arms, ten legs, five hearts, five heads, five voices crying out in anguish, each needing to express itself.

Suddenly the house wasn't big enough to contain all our energy. The phone. The phone would be our release, the conveyor of our energy across states, into other lives, to share the news, to let others help us carry our grief.

He had been such a healthy person, so vital and alive. This heart attack, which had claimed him in the middle of the night after working late at the office, was not possible. He had no heart problems. A freak accident, the doctor had said. What kind of a freak accident? Weren't doctors supposed to prevent freak accidents? Wasn't the medical profession supposed to save people? What happened? What went wrong? A deep stirring in the pit of my stomach, a feeling of resignation, of relief, of awe that our lives were not our lives, but from the God who gives life. He also takes it away and in His own time.

The ritual of being the dutiful wife, of receiving business associates, of making funeral arrangements, all this I performed like a trained monkey, like a person who had rehearsed this event all her married life. I did it; I felt nothing. I smiled, I hugged, I accepted condolences and shared memories until the last handful of dirt was thrown onto the grave; until the last bouquet of flowers was laid on top.

After the funeral, people came back to the house where neighbors had generously brought food that lay decorously upon the dining room table. I looked around at the faces; they were a blur. Their heads nodded as they spoke, like posies in pots nodding in the breeze, but I could not recognize any familiarity with family or friends. A buzzing sound of many voices filled the air like humming bees around honeysuckle. I could hear the mumbling of words, but not what the words were or decipher any meaning. They were eating, talking, laughing, sitting in my living room, taking up space that I needed to release the energy of my anguish. What did they want? They were like gossipmongers pecking away at truth. Did they want to see me fall apart? Did they want to feed on my carcass of woe?

I wanted to be alone. I needed to be alone, to fling my arms about, to fill my lungs with air and let out animal cries of pain. They had no idea. Everyone was so civilized. I was not feeling civilized. I was falling into the depths of sorrow. I came unstuck from the glue of duty that held me together during the formalities of the funeral. I didn't want to be nice anymore. I didn't want to be polite. I didn't want to be a together person. I wanted to be me, to feel deep inside, to wrench out my sorrow and these people were blocking me. They were here, still polite, still dutiful.

"Go away," I suddenly screamed. "Go home. Leave me alone."

Silence fell across the room. I saw no faces; I saw only the blur of tears that washed across my eyes and flooded down my cheeks. My mother came from somewhere.

"Come," she said, for long ago she had buried my father and she, too, knew my pain. "Let's go lie down." She took me gently by the arm.

A NIGHT NO DIFFERENT

J. F. West

On an April evening slashed by rain
you stop on impulse in your bedroom door
to watch her primp. How many heartbeats
have you watched her movements making right
the face that you have known so many years?
Caught in a study of her mirrored self,
she ignores you, piqued by a fine face
no longer young.
You ache to talk,
but what is left to say
on this night like a thousand wasted nights?
"Be careful, Sweet," you murmur.
"It's raining cats and dogs."
Her hazel eyes respond but do not focus.
She looks beyond and says, "I know.
I'll drive slow. Don't worry about me."
You return to your chair beside your child,
eyes on a world of color on TV.
You hear her heels mince past
and cross the floor. You do not turn.
She calls, "I'll see you later." You reply,
"Bye." The door slams. The end.
A leave-taking like a thousand leaves
of late. A night no different
from a thousand lonely nights.

And when you see her next, supine
on a wet cot, her skin blue-splotched,
hair wet, an anger at the ages on her face,
wrecked, drowned, destroyed, wiped out,
daybreak looms outside in gray squares
on a dead screen. Inside, the happening stops
briefly. The protagonist, you, stares
at the audience—two cops, a sleepy nurse.
The props are simple and austere, except
there is no switch to cut this happening off.

NIGHT-BLOOMING JASMINE AND SUMMER SHEETS

Mary Schultz

A boot heel clicked against the concrete of the front walk. I knew it was a policeman's boot, though I couldn't see through the solid front door. I knew what he was going to tell me. On this summer Saturday evening when the scent of night-blooming jasmine permeated the house, Hal wouldn't be coming home.

The two police officers each took a step back when they looked at me. The older of the two asked if the lady of the house was at home. I assured them that would be me.

"It's just that you look so young," the officer said.

"Is that Daddy?" asked three-year-old Tim, the youngest of our three children. He must have climbed out of his crib. There he stood, barefoot in his crinkle-cotton pajamas. I didn't answer him.

The younger of the officers asked Tim, "Want to wear my hat?" Then he turned to his partner and with a nod of his head he said, "I'll take the little guy with me."

Seven-year-old Wendy and four-year-old Jana slept while the more senior officer unfolded the news to me. Killed on impact. The motorcycle destroyed. Lost control. A street light standard. About a mile and a half away.

"Are you sure it's him?" I asked.

"Yes. Plenty of identification on him. Do you have family nearby?" the uniformed man was asking. I don't remember screaming or becoming hysterical. I suspect I didn't. I don't remember crying. I expect I did.

My family. My family. All I could think of was, please, don't call my parents. I begged him not to call.

"What about your husband's family?" he asked.

"His mother's in the hospital. Heart attack. God, I can't tell her over the phone."

"His father?"

"His health is almost as bad as hers."

"Neighbors?"

"Nancy. Next door."

I believe one of the men stayed with me while the other went to the neighboring house. Moments later, I think it was moments, Nancy came over and put her arms around me, saying, "Mary, oh Mary." This gesture, from a woman who'd never touched me before, forced me to comprehend what was in progress in my house.

"Does she have a doctor?" the officer now spoke to Nancy as though she were in charge of me.

"Yes," she answered.

"She's going to need something to sleep," one of them said.

In seeming seconds, Nancy's husband, Bob, was on his way to the all-night pharmacy.

I don't know when the police left, or when Tim went to bed, or how. Nancy tried to reach my pastor and discovered his number was unlisted. Somehow, she wrested the number out of someone.

Then she took me by the hand, led me to the sofa, sat me down and said, "Mary, I have to call your parents."

"No!"

"The thing is, they're going to find out at some point."

I must have lowered my head and acknowledged that she was right.

The pastor came. The drugs came. Neither proved to be much consolation.

My mother and father arrived with my older sister, who'd returned home to live with them. They brought a gallon jug of wine to share.

If Hal were home, I found myself thinking, *they wouldn't dream of barging into our house equipped with wine.* Nancy couldn't know what leaving me with them would mean. Anyway, she had her own three-year-old daughter and husband to tend to next door, along with all the ramifications of the fact that Hal was killed on the motorcycle he borrowed from them.

Mom, Dad, and Kathleen were already drunk when they arrived. My sense was that they were drunk long before Nancy phoned them. The extra wine was to keep the alcohol anesthesia from wearing thin.

They lamented the tragedy. Dad, who'd never had a civil, let alone kind, word for Hal, waxed sorrowful. Of course, before Hal and I were married, Dad judged Hal a hoodlum, and he wasn't entirely wrong.

Mom, who could barely stomach the fact that I, pregnant at seventeen, had dropped out of high school to marry my wild-streak misfit husband, bemoaned the loss. Experience told me that with enough wine, she'd recall every ugly memory and soon give them all voice.

Kathleen, connoisseur of wholly unsuitable men, probably understood my love for Hal as well as anyone in my family could, but she couldn't face the best day, let alone a cataclysmic day, without alcohol. And alcohol always transformed her into someone else.

I checked on the kids, then stood in the kitchen doorway, staring at the portion of my family that had arrived to help me through the night. I turned and went to our . . . my room.

I lay there for the longest time, breathing Hal's scent in the sheets, jumbled thoughts racing around inside my head like a continuous audio tape.

I wanted to call Hal back, demand, insist he come home instantly and finish our last conversation.

I then thought of the single moment earlier in the day when I could have taken an action that might have changed the course of our lives. I was putting laundry away when I heard voices from the patio next door. Hal was asking Bob if he could borrow Bob's motorcycle.

Right there in front of me in the closet sat Hal's helmet. The stuffing was coming out of it in two places, from a previous accident on his own bike, the one he totaled a year before. My impulse was to carry the red helmet to Bob and Nancy's backyard, where all the neighborhood men were sitting around drinking a beer. Then I thought the idea through.

I'm his wife, not his mother, I told myself. *I can't save him, rescue him, make him do or be anything.* I heard keys hit the concrete. Then I knew. He was going to ride. No protective gear.

That was hours ago. Now, I wanted to kill him for getting himself killed. I also felt so strangely betrayed by him for dying in the street, as though it was a breech of our intimacy. Not all thoughts are rational, I suppose, when one has lost a mate.

Then I felt how empty the bed was, hollow in his absence. For all the sturm and drang of our life together, we'd never slept a night apart, save the occasions of the births of our children. I wondered if I'd ever be able to sleep again without his body next to mine.

His body. Hal had one eyetooth that grew in at a funny angle, startling gray-green eyes, a huge chest, and arms proportionally too long for his torso. He'd always fought excess weight, and had a large man's physical strength. I pictured him holding a big and pregnant me on his lap the day my grandmother died, his huge arms around me, comforting me. In eight years of marriage, we'd made love a million times and fought just as many. He'd once bounced out of the shower wearing a towel like a feather boa and minced around like a chorus boy, making me laugh so hard I forgot what we'd been fighting about.

I could see him and hear him as he'd been just a few nights before. Jana had awakened crying in the middle of the night. Hal wrapped a robe around himself and barefoot, he set out to go comfort the child. As he made his way down the hall in the dark, I heard yelps of, "Aah! Uh! Ow!"

"What is it?" I asked.

"Jacks," he said, and then he laughed.

I couldn't imagine waking without him.

Yet, oddly, I sensed relief. His temper was often so out of control, he'd slam a door hard enough to break window glass. He loved speed and courted danger. He loved the children. And me. Yet he stormed around with an unfocused sense of unrest. Together, he and I were on our way to forging a next-generation dysfunctional family to rival those from which we'd come. Now, I'd have to complete the task alone. Alone.

I allowed myself to think about Hal, for his fate entailed a visual image from which I'd been trying to shield myself since the police had first come. What had gone through his mind just before life left him? Was he terrified? In pain? God, no one should have to die alone, or suffer a body torn and broken. Yet that's exactly what had happened. I ached so for him, I wondered if I were dead, too. I felt dead. Numb.

Ours wasn't the most viable of marriages. We'd been at the brink of divorce more than once. The strains of too many responsibilities too soon and the complete absence of preparation for earning a living were taking their inevitable toll. I responded to his accusations that I was cool and rigid by blaming him and his wildly impulsive streak. We were perennially young, broke, barefoot, pregnant, and frustrated. Rage was a frequent visitor to our home. And yet, we had a genuine home.

The love was real, the marriage was real, the man, severed in the street at age twenty-eight, was real.

I lay there and wept, breathing his scent in the sheets.

EXCEPT AT NIGHT

Cassandra Smith

The family doctor said he was sure it was Rickey's body. He had made a positive ID. It had taken the Marines more than a month to get the body bags from that far back in the bush. I heard that it no longer looked like him, the skin was dark brown from the sun and the hair buzzed close to the scalp. The dog tags were mangled, but wrapped around it was the necklace with my name on it. The doctor said that helped with the positive ID. There was no doubt.

Mother told me what the doctor said. The necklace made it a fact. Mother said it was time to accept facts. "It's not like my brother in Korea," she said. "In those days the Army didn't find all the bodies." Mother was telling me this so that I would feel more secure. She thought I'd stop talking about prisoners of war and miraculous escapes. She thought I'd accept the facts.

Around midnight, Mother came into the bedroom to tell me to stop crying.

"That's enough," she said. Her voice was thick with anger. "I think you've cried enough for today. There's no reason to make yourself sick."

She slammed the door, turned on the hall light, and walked down to the toilet. I heard the broken gurgle of water and the cry of a squeaky faucet. Across the room my sister whispered from her bed.

"He died thinking of you," she said. "I bet your name was the last thing on his lips."

"Shut up, you stupid fool," I said. "You've been watching too many John Wayne movies." I kicked the sheets. Across my feet lay the five-dollar black dress I bought at Woolworth's, the only dress I owned.

At the funeral, Rickey's mother sent his sister over to ask if I was pregnant. The ten-year-old whispered in my ear and I looked across at the mother's face. The minister finished his few words and called for the pallbearers. Her face was lighted and hopeful. Her fat fingers pink and rubbery. I was ashamed. The minister said "I wish I'd known the boy," he said. "The family should be proud." The Marine honor guard lifted the casket easily. Brilliant blue pillars. All around sat Rickey's brothers and his long-haired sisters. His mother looked away and stared out the window and then back to my face with a pleading look. I should have been. I would have been.

That last night he laughed at me. On a cheap hotel bed, squeaking under his body. His heat. His desperation. I ran out into the street and back to the dorm. My roommate, waiting up late, asked, "Did you? It happens that last night. Just before they ship off." She'd been watching too many old movies.

The day after the funeral Mother found me crying in the attic. She walked up the stairs, gently and softly, and stood in front of me.

"You're making yourself sick," she said. "He was a Marine. He wouldn't like this. This weakness of yours," she said. "He'd be ashamed."

I sniffed. The dust and the thick attic air clogged my nose and throat. My father's Army Reserve uniform hung from the rafters. Scattered around me were his flight bag, his hard polished shoes, his dull green fatigues. Paraphernalia for a weekend of war.

"You're like me," Mother said. "Once you start crying you won't be able to stop."

She took me to the kitchen, made a cup of tea, then led me to the front porch. She set out a lawn chair. The neighborhood kids rode their bikes back and forth. Mr. Calloway walked home from his job at the post office. Joe Prather crossed his path, heading to the corner store for his nightly can of beer. Nothing had changed. The traffic purred from Puritan Avenue, punctuated by a backfire or a bus transmission grinding in the distance.

That last night I ran from his body. His steam. His insistence. Reluctance. Persistence. When I jumped from the bed and buttoned my blouse, he was relieved. He smiled and reached out his hand in a sign of peace. Of forgiveness. I stood by the door shaking and tried to breathe. *There are other girls for this,* I repeated in my head over and over. Girls with bright lips and loud voices. Girls who laugh with their mouths wide open. He sat up and balanced on the edge of the bed, his head cocked to the side like a German Shepherd. Still speechless. Still smiling. His forehead wet with perspiration. I ran out of the room and down the burgundy hallway. I ran from him. Across campus, through the library and into the dorm. Away from myself. Into my room and my roommate's face, round and pock-marked. Her face placid and anxious. "Did you?" she repeated. "Did you? It so often happens."

The next morning back at his hotel room I knocked hard on the door, prepared to do what needed to be done. He leaned out of the door; a towel wrapped around his waist. His body—the perfectly carved killing machine they'd created—shone beneath a glaze of water. His hair was dense and wet and suddenly I wanted him again. In the cold, bright, harshness of morning I wanted him. Not knowing what wanting meant. Not understanding what I should want. I reached out to touch his naked shoulder. He jumped, squealed, and began to laugh.

"Let me get dressed first," he said.

From behind the door he was still laughing. A thick guttural laugh from deep in his chest. The sound of a hollowed-out log beaten by sticks. The violent laugh of a wild man or the gentle laugh of a bear.

"I'm proud of you," he said opening the door. "You kept your head last night. I know now I can depend on you." His lips spread across his wide teeth. "Even if I'm far away. With all these college boys around, I know I can depend on you."

He bent down to tighten his shoelaces, then rolled back the cuffs on his sleeves.

"That drill sergeant was wrong," he said. "He tacked your picture up on the rifle range. He said you were a whore. 'Those dreamy-eyed ones,' he said. 'They pretend to be shy. But as soon as you're in 'Nam, bam, you find out she's a slut.'" He walked over and held me lightly by the shoulders.

"I'm proud of you," he said.

"I want to. I didn't mean to run away," I tried to apologize. "I don't want you to—" He bent over. His lips burned my ear and then my eyelids.

"I couldn't be any happier. I had to come up here and see you. I wanted to see what this college stuff was all about." He reached in his tee shirt and pulled out his dog tags. Standard issue. I'd seen my father's a thousand times hanging over the doorknob to his bedroom. Two metal tags covered with numbers and letters. In case of emergency, father explained. In case I can't talk for myself. Wrapped around Rickey's tags was the necklace I'd made for him. The beads were in psychedelic colors and my name was in tiny alphabet beads. He had looped it around his dog tags. He pulled it out. The whole Marine, hippie, high school girl-friend, twisted mess. Smiling, he dropped it back down his shirt.

"My lucky piece," he said.

This is what I believe. There was another kid in his unit. Same name, different spelling. It was easy to mix them up. They got each other's mail. I do not believe Rickey died in Vietnam. It was a practical joke. I believe he exchanged dog tags with the other guy. That's the kind of joke he'd play. I believe he was trapped and couldn't get a transport home. Maybe he has amnesia. That last mad scramble in Saigon. I need to wait.

I need to dream.

The fantasy continues: when he shows up on my doorstep he calls me by my childhood name. He recognizes me beneath the years and the pounds. He's younger, taller, the eyes are crystalline blue, though I remembered them as brown. Eighteen years old, maybe twenty. That wide alligator smile. His head is cocked to the side. Somehow the eyes aren't quite human. They are translucent and without depth, but the corners are twisted up in a friendly gaze.

"I'm Rickey's son," he says. Inside my house I see that the boy is a man. He reaches around his neck and pulls out a small canister dangling from a string. He twists off the lid and pulls out my high school photo, its edges frayed like soft cotton. The image is blurred except for two hard pinpoints of light where my eyes had been. I'm ashamed that he's found me like this. I smooth back my hair to readjust the ribbons of gray. He begins to laugh in that same wild, unrestrained way. He lifts me, effortlessly, high into the air.

"I knew you'd wait," he said. "I knew you'd be a virgin." Like Odysseus he reaches out an arm and tells me of twenty years of wandering. Of capture and hardship. Of moving from village to village. Crisscrossing continents. He's the man I escaped on that humid, sweaty, November night, and sitting before me, his legs outstretched, he tells tall tales.

Since he's twenty, I become twenty. His chest is solid and unmoving. I rest my head in the crook of his cool marble arms. I sleep. I dream.

In the daylight, when the gray birds scream without stop and the children play games of skill and speed, the lines are clear and precise. But at night, alone, when the evening birds sing and the moon burns orange, then white, I lie in the arms of my killing machine, pregnant with his son.

Chapter Three
Broken Mirrors

How queer everything is today! And yesterday things went on just as usual. I wonder if I've been changed in the night? Let me think: was I the same when I got up this morning? I almost think I can remember feeling a little different. But if I'm not the same, the next question is, Who in the world am I?
—Lewis Carroll, *Alice in Wonderland*

Thousands of shards of broken glass lie around us. Carefully we pick up the largest, and peer into it; a giant staring into a tiny, jagged mirror.

A relationship has died. This broken pile is what is left of our life. We cannot see a whole self any more; only ragged little pieces: a saddened eye; a defeated mouth; one lone tear moving slowly down a cheek; a shattered heart. We search each fragment for a clue to our identity, but they are just fractions of what once was; disconnected, unfamiliar, distorted; like a kaleidoscope. We ask the broken mirror to give us a name.

Broken mirror on the floor, who are we now if we are no more?

But the shattered looking glass is silent.

Once, in a life that seems so long ago, we remember looking into a perfectly shaped, undamaged mirror. We took the reflection for granted; it was who we were. We were partner, husband, wife, lover. In its reflection we saw ourselves, our daily life . . . and another image— our mate. The mirror reflected our shared life, our history, our intimacy. We were understood. Loved. Reflected.

Then in one instant, it is gone—there is no image, no sense of place, only pieces of a life. Fractured memories.

Broken mirror on the floor, who are we now if they are no more?

Again, the mirror is silent. We become confused; disoriented. We should be the same person we were before the death. Outside it looks the same. But inside, it is so very different. Nothing feels the same. We are no longer The Mate. The Life Partner. The Best Friend. *Who in the world am I?* we ask ourselves again and again.

We must find the answer. We touch a shard, but its smooth former borders now cut deeply, its sharp ridges reminding us of our loss. Or we stare too long and hard into one small sliver and are blinded by the bright light of normal, familiar daily life as it bounces off the sharp edges. We search for the identity we have lost; a name we recognize. Darling. Sweetheart. Honey. My Love.

In time we begin to feel a little different. We become dissatisfied with the silence of the broken mirror and begin to seek another, whole reflection. We may try to glue the broken pieces together again, but too many are missing to make it complete. We begin to understand that we can use the broken mirror as a foundation for rebuilding ourselves.

The stories in this chapter are about being lost and being found, of building something different from the pile of broken glass that once mirrored our life. These stories describe the most frightening identity crisis of all—the loss of a mate and the relationship. Some find another mirror, another identity; another reflection to smile back at them. Other stories tell of people who choose to go on alone, accepting that the only image in the mirror will be their own.

These stories tell us that it is not easy to climb out of the deep, dark rabbit hole of grief and loss. It is not easy to find a new reflection, another way to see ourselves and to be seen. But we must remember Alice's question, *Who in the world am I?* and know that somewhere there is a reflection that fits; an answer to the question. It's just not found in the shattered remnants of a broken mirror.

AFTERWARDS NOW

Ida Fasel

I rustle left-over leaves into round.
A long-legged spider tangles in the rake
and I think of the way of its web, trap and sting.
A whack across my eyes from a protruding branch.
A stab of thorn through gloves.
Who devised the torment?—the question old
when Eliot asked. And answered Love.

A black pool from watering broods over
the primroses you divided and replanted.
Little cells of beauty multiplying fast,
so different from those spreading in blood
across the sheet, my hand lightly
on yours not to add to pain.

I'd lift you from the rack where you lay stretched.
You helped. I held you: the thinner you became,
the thinner I did. I sat you tall at the window,
and you accustomed yourself to brightness,
grass blending its green with common
red and white clover. We saw the immediate thing
up close, a leaf always a leaf, a flower a flower,
a life not forever lost.

Morning moves in its course as plastic bag
after plastic bag fills, pressed to hold more,
dragged to the curb. I have quieted the street.
You helped. You help. One world is not enough
for either of us now. This gardening has no end.

ATTENDING TO DETAILS
(Excerpted from *Grieving: A Love Story*)

Ruth Coughlin

I am new to this thing called widowhood.

No one can tell you about grief, about its limitless boundaries, its unfathomable depths. No one can tell you about the crater that is created in the center of your body, the one that nothing can fill. No matter how many times you hear the word *final,* it means nothing until final is actually final.

It has been just over four months since the day Bill died, and still I am paralyzed. I am a woman without a country, an alien who has dropped to earth from some other planet. I am in a capsule on the moon, bouncing from side to side, floating in space, but I cannot imagine emerging from the capsule to offer one small step for mankind. I keep thinking I will see a 224-point headline that reads DERANGED WIDOW FOUND SUSPENDED IN OUTER SPACE, and then realize that the headline refers to me.

I rarely read newspapers, and when I do, I give them only a cursory glance. Newspapers, after all, were a bond Bill and I shared, what with his reading four of them a day, and with our morning discussions about what was good in the world and what was bad in the world frequently blossoming into full-blown, morning-coffee arguments.

I have turned on the television set once—to tune in to the proceedings of the Democratic National Convention, mostly to commemorate Bill, a lifelong Democrat and a politician to his very core. At thirty-one, he had been the youngest person ever to be president of the Young Democrats, the kid who welcomed Jack Kennedy in 1960 to the state of Michigan, the same year that he himself ran for lieutenant governor. Bill would not have missed the convention for the world.

As it turned out, he did.

I am incapable of looking at baseball, the sport we both loved and watched together endlessly. I cannot remember who played in the World Series last year, and I am not inclined to find out, even though I know for a fact that we both saw every minute of it, as did we the Super Bowl.

Mail-order catalogs flood into the house, and I, a former fool and catalog maniac, throw them out immediately, not glancing at a single page. There is no piece of clothing, no trinket, no gadget I want or need. Magazines arrive in the mail and go untouched. Because it was one of Bill's weekly rituals to do the *New York Times* crossword puzzle, I can barely pull the magazine out of the mailbox, let alone read it. Books, our passionate and shared interest, are tossed onto stacks in every room of the house, their spines uncracked. I will get to them someday, I know, but I cannot figure out when that day will be.

I do not play the music Bill was drawn to, from Mozart and Mahler and Puccini to Jimmy Buffett and the Beach Boys and Nat "King" Cole. I do not turn on the radio, because I cannot decide which is worse; the thundering sound of silence that envelops me night and day or the reminder that it was Bill's habit to play the radio at all times, while he was shaving or showering or writing or reading.

There is not a second in the day that I do not long to hear his voice, listen to his advice, yearn to hear the laugh that made everyone around him smile. It is not possible for me to envision a life without him, and I know with a frightening surety that I will not be able to get along now.

I am using his toothbrush and comb. I am wearing his shirts, their largeness a small comfort in a universe in which comfort has been swept away. I am wearing his wedding ring, inscribed with the initials RLW, RUTH LOVES WILLIAM, on the middle finger of my left hand, next to my own wedding ring, which I cannot contemplate ever removing.

I have taken as my own the Mont Blanc pen he so treasured, one of the last gifts I was able to give him. My old key ring has been replaced these days by the first gift I ever gave him, a gold-and-silver St. Christopher's medal suspended from a silver circle.

I have not moved his eyeglasses from the table next to our bed, and the seven dollar bills I have found in the pockets of seven of his jackets remain unspent. They never will be. I have had one of his jackets altered to fit me, sort of, in anticipation of a dark and cold winter's night when I know I will prefer to wear Bill's coat rather than turn up the heat.

The Greek sailor's cap he preferred to wear once he lost his hair sits atop a pile of books in our living room. I caress it and hold it to my lips more often than I would like to admit.

In his office at home, I sit surrounded by thirty-five years of a man's life. Papers, books, letters, partial manuscripts, manuscripts that never got published, notes to himself written in his squirrelly hand—reminders of those things he hoped to accomplish on any given day. Cabinets, bursting with the accouterments of the life that once was his, await my opening them.

In a drawer I have been able to go through for no more than a few minutes, I find his passport, one of the lottery tickets he bought every week, each bearing our special numbers—my birthday, his birthday, the date we were married—two Kennedy half-dollars, and, unaccountably, my college diploma.

If I need something from his desk, something as mundane as a paper clip, an elastic band, or one of his black felt-tip pens, I am overwhelmed by panic, opening the middle drawer so quickly and closing it so fast I know I am in danger of banging it on my fingers.

"You have to realize this is final," says Bill's doctor, with whom I have kept in touch. He is a compassionate and remarkable man, this Dr. Craig J. Gordon, this oncologist whose zeal and dedication lead him to believe that he can save the world from the corruption of cancer.

I think I know about final because I, who have never before seen a death certificate, now have a dozen copies of Bill's. It is a gruesome thing, this piece of bureaucracy, this plain document stamped with its official seal, this lifeless record that has the power to destroy your sanity.

Decedent's Name: William J. Coughlin. Informant: Mrs. William Coughlin. Marital Status: Married. Surviving Spouse (If wife, give name before first married): Ruth Pollack. Immediate Cause (Final disease or condition resulting in death): Carcinoma of Unknown Primary Origin. Cause of Death: Abdominal carcinomatosis, Hepatic Failure related to metastatic carcinoma. Disposition: Cremation.

I look at this piece of paper and my vision blurs. I am underwater, I am twenty leagues beneath the sea, the air is being sucked out of my lungs, I cannot see the sky.

I have had to furnish copies of this document to too many places, too many people: The American Bar Association, the Michigan Bar Association, the lawyers for the estate, our insurance carrier, the banks behind Bill's personal credit cards, the utilities companies, the mortgage company. There are, it seems to me, far too many people who need proof that my husband is dead, and that is exactly what I have. Proof. Certification. That he is dead.

What I am forgetting as I mail out copy after copy of this certificate is something that I didn't know and am just beginning to understand.

What no one ever really tells you about is the one thing that should be the most obvious: that you will never see him again. The decedent. William J. Coughlin, deceased. He was alive one dismal, rainy Saturday afternoon in April, and then he was dead. Never to be seen again.

I know that Dr. Gordon is concerned about my welfare. I know he means to help me by discussing finality. He has, after all, seen patients die before and has been there to comfort their survivors.

"This is it," he continues. "There's no going back. You have to begin to accept it."

The idea makes the hole in the middle of my body triple in size. My heart beats faster than I can ever remember it beating before, my hands start to shake, and I begin to notice that I have forgotten how to breathe.

In these few short months since Bill's death it is difficult to know what I know or what I have learned or what lies before me. I know that I believe that life is too short. I realize it is essential to say it now, do it now, and that I must acknowledge what another Bill has told me: the secret to life is that it ends. I know it is important to cherish those things that go beyond value before you lose them, and that, as F. Scott Fitzgerald said, there are no second acts in American lives. I now agree with my mother: in life, there is no such thing as a dress rehearsal.

As far as I can tell there is only one certainty, a certainty that is as solid as the realization that he is dead, and it is the sure knowledge that I have now learned, am continuing to learn, another language, the language of loss. Like the language of music and love, it is universal. You don't need a dictionary, you don't need a translator, you don't need a thesaurus.

All you need do is go through it once, just once, to get it. Bereavement. Grief. Sorrow. Mourning. Devastation. Loss. Despair. The books or newspaper articles you read or the advice you are given will or will not help you. What I have come to know is that you do what you have to do to go on. Some people will call it surviving, but you will know that it is a matter of just going on. You do what you are capable of, you do what you think will cause the least amount of pain. To yourself and others.

There is no right or wrong to widowhood, or to loss of any kind. Nobody's written the rules, nobody can tell you how to play the game, and if they do so, the rules may or may not apply to you. You make them up as you go along.

"You must be one tough lady," a woman says, when, not too long after Bill's death, I telephone Federal Express to change, for the sake of ongoing business, the account name from his name to mine. Federal Express does not require a copy of the death certificate, but this is the first time, except for having had to call the authorities, that I actually have to talk to a stranger and say that my husband is dead. I almost choke on the word, and I am embarrassed to hear the catch in my voice.

"At a time like this," the woman goes on, in a not-unkindly way, "it can't be easy. What I mean is, attending to these kinds of details, and all."

"Details and time are what I have a lot of," I respond. "The details are hard enough, what's harder is the living."

UNSTITCHING

B. B. Adams

This is worse than watching Humpty Dumpty fall—
he was only himself.

We weren't born like this,
joined at the heart
and the hip—
self-made twins.

We did it to ourselves,
sewing our bodies and souls together,
our memories and future—
a stitch at a time.

We felt the needle's prick only once,
pulling nylon thread through our hearts—
leaving a deep, sweet ache
that never goes away.

Stitching our hips together was a snap—
the drops of blood, the mingled juices
and the babies—
proof of our oneness.

Stitching our heads together took longer—
14,965 stitches,
each one a bead on a rosary
telling a familiar tale.

Then I caught you, one night,
pulling them out one by one—
disconnecting us like a hopelessly tangled
switchboard.

Frantically, I tried to tie them back
but couldn't make your end stick.
Then I got mixed up, and found more and more
threads you'd snapped.

One night, nearing our 15,000th stitch,
I dreamt that I was helping you,
breaking thread after thread
when the needle broke—

And then you were gone—
leaving me with a broken needle
sewing stitches
to thin air.

MY SONG, MY MUSE

Eva Kolosvary

SILENCE
My legs—crooked and bloody, arrived first, but in my heart there was a
song—my parents called it a cry—

I knew it was an ancient melody—thousands of years old—the
ballad of my ancestors. I carried it with me through adolescence and
when I was seventeen and met you, I knew that you'd understand it. My
song echoed back and forth—it grew into several voices—into a full
orchestral suite, a chorus of friends sang and danced around us . . . I
thought it would last forever, that it would grow with every passing year,
but suddenly my life fell apart—I heard the requiem of eleven oncolo-
gists singing the death sentence.

The song in my heart is silenced; there is a hollow emptiness in
the nights. Lying alone in the king-size bed, I reach over again to touch
your heart with my song.

WHERE IS MY MUSE?
My Muse lives within me—deep, deep inside. I have always felt its presence. The companionship. As a young child I talked and played with
her. I dreamed with her. She completes me into wholesomeness. We create together—collaboration is so natural—so easy. Sometimes she teases
me—she hides from me and I have to find her. It can take a long time—
a long search—a desperate search, but what a reward when finally I get
a sight of her and we embrace . . . .

My life is broken now—and my muse has left. Maybe she wasn't
mine. Maybe she doesn't like my sadness, my tears, and my loud cries
into the nights.

I am so desperate. My past was so good—how can I continue my
life without Paul and my muse? Maybe they are together—just hiding
from me like in my childhood. Maybe I should call out loud—call out
to her—and they will arrive together hand in hand, my soulmate and
my muse.

THE TWO WIVES

Nancy Kassell

There should be a myth about us,
The Two Wives who speak
across the rim of death,
but womantalk is seldom recorded.

I must tell you, dear Elizabeth,
that after you died,
he drifted all night,
your oxygen canisters
still under the bed
his only ballast.
Knowing celestial navigation
was useless.
"Grief" is not indexed
in any of his rare books.
A separate devotion, fierce and angry—
that's what you had with him.
I know men's impatience, their muteness,
I have taught other men how to talk.
Don't blame yourself. After I moved in,
I found your dressmaker's form
wearing a flowered shift still unhemmed,
yarn with the crochet hook
still in the loop,
in the sewing room, an accumulation
of patterns.
That's what marriage becomes:
patterns, easy to make,
hard to fit, hard to finish.

I sheltered him, steadied him.
"Talk is our compass," I said.
Your spirit became the star
shining over the daylilies
asleep in the garden.
None of us foresaw what would happen.

I buried him next to you.

WHAT THEY WANT TO HEAR

Paula Porter

People say I'm handling it well,
      coping,
      adjusting . . .
But they don't know I go to sleep every night
      hugging a pillow
      pretending it's you
      and praying not to wake up
      another morning alone.
People want to know how I'm doing
      making a new life . . .
      going on . . .
I give a sad smile and say,
      "It's rough."
      "Thanks for asking."
      "I'm managing."
Words they want to hear.
People comment how strong and brave I've been
      through it all . . .
      your cancer,
      your fight for life,
      your death.
But they can't understand that
      my strength
      and bravery
      and hopes
      were buried
          with you . . .

REQUIEM FOR THE SAD TIMES

Marsh Cassady

Tom and I have just moved from the house to the apartment. The last of the kids—Sally's and mine—had moved out into a harsher world than I ever knew. Rapes and muggings, drive-by shootings, corner drug deals.

You know how it is when you move. You must deal with the cardboard boxes you drag with you for years, rarely ever opening. But the two-bedroom apartment is a far cry from a five-bedroom house.

For Tom it was easier. He'd been married too, but Penny was still alive. The memories were stored mostly at her house. I was forced to carry mine with me, distilled over the years, consolidated.

I knew what was in those boxes. Another me, a different lifetime, a distant world where dreams were supposed to come true.

Some of it was easy; I split it among the kids—some going to Iowa, some to Oklahoma, some to Katie right here in Fountain Valley.

Then I found this note. It must have gotten damp somewhere along the way, no doubt in the fruit cellar where it was stored when Sally and I lived in Kokomo.

Brown, crumbly, words here and there lost forever.

"Tonight is one of the sad times," I'd written. I mentioned something I still remember, "the night after a formal, standing on your porch, the light pale behind you, the bittersweet smile of love on your face."

The note, written two years after our marriage, was a lament, an apology. I loved her deeply, but we got off to a bad start, both enrolling in graduate school, getting into debt, trying to cope with our new relationship. I couldn't tell Sally what bothered me most. Jesus, I grew up in a tiny town of 1500 people. Fifteen hundred people. I didn't understand being queer. At first I thought everyone felt like me; that it was just part of life.

I learned at college that wasn't so. Two freshmen boys were caught in bed together. They were shunned by the rest of us. Dear God, that was a different sort of time.

There's openness now. Or maybe it's because I'm no longer a small-town boy.

Sally . . . Dear Sally . . . .

She died. Fifteen years after I wrote that piece. Fourteen years ago now. I went on, raised the kids as best I could. I'm not cut out to be a father . . . .

The kids all know what Sally didn't. I think they've forgiven me.

I'm sitting in the middle of the living room surrounded by memories. I spy the Roy Rogers coin purse that belonged to Sally. He was her first love, she said. Why is the purse still here? When Sally knew she was dying, she gave all her things away, dividing them among the kids. I felt bad about that, so I split up my stuff, too. The little wooden box Dad had made, my special stones, my Tom Mix badge, and my secret code ring.

Maybe Sally put the purse away at the last moment because she couldn't bear to part with it. Now here are all these other things I haven't been able to part with.

I've been sitting here for hours, sorting through boxes. Tom comes out of the second bedroom. "About finished?" he asks. "It's getting late."

"I don't know what to do with this stuff," I tell him.

He smiles, shrugs. He has only one box, a box he's carried with him for years. I never thought I was much of a saver. Sally was the saver. Yet I have every scrap of paper with her handwriting on it and every article of clothing she owned.

And suddenly I think: *if Sally were alive, I'd have discarded these worn out clothes; I'd have thrown away these miscellaneous grocery lists, these notes of appointments long since kept or canceled.*

My mother once remarked, "You know, Sally wasn't a saint."

"No, Mom," I answered, "she wasn't." But she's the closest to it we'll ever find.

I pick up the piece of paper and read it again. "The porch light, pale behind you, and the bittersweet smile of love on your face." She didn't want me to leave. But my friends were waiting in the car.

I hold the paper close. I'm surprised it no longer smells musty. "Oh, Sally . . . ."

I want to bring back those innocent times. But then again I like what I am right now, more than I liked any other me. *I wish I could share this with you, Sally,* I think. *But how could I? How could you understand?*

I've led two different lives since Sally died. The father rearing his kids, never being as open about himself as he'd like. And the second life—the year since Tom and I took the apartment after Katie moved out.

I sigh, hesitate, toss the appointment and grocery lists into the wastebasket in the kitchen. I gather the remaining items, the essence of all my lives, and place them into a single box like Tom's. I close the lid, carry the box to a shelf in the extra bedroom—Tom's study. He's staring at the computer screen, fingers clicking the keys.

What if Sally had been the gay one, and I straight? Would I have understood? I doubt it.

Who do I blame? Myself, my parents, God, society?

Just last week I talked to my daughter Rachel, getting a divorce after less than a year of marriage.

"We knew we had problems," she told me. "We thought marriage would solve them." How could she believe such a thing? How could Ronald believe such a thing?

But isn't that what I believed, too? That marriage would cure me—Sally loved me, right from the beginning, so I couldn't disappoint her. I couldn't walk off that porch forever.

Sally.

I pick up the note once more.

Tom loves me, accepts me when I'm impatient, frustrated, depressed, cranky, nasty. Sally loved me.

Tom is now. But Sally . . . will live in my heart forever. I fold the note again and again and again, then toss it into the waste basket.

"Tom," I call. "Tom!"

He sticks his head around the corner.

"Yes?" he says.

"I love you," I tell him.

"I know," he answers. And then he smiles.

WHAT IS LEFT

Carol Mahler

Because my husband is dead, this house
feels like a cavern at a cliff's base
Now the sea filling its chamber
is sorrow. On the rock-solid counter,
is a red plastic ring, egg shells, a feather,
his photograph in foggy glass, a stone-
ware plate, kelp tablets, a chipped bone
china cup—a ragged tideline.
Shipwrecked chairs and tables line
the sandy floor where the cat dashes
for crab spiders and silverfish.
Every moment I survive him, I am in
over my head. Clouds of children's
paintings drift above my head.
Tonight, I am stranded on our bed:
I taste salt on my skin—sweat, tears, or sea—
what is left is here with me.

PARTNERS

Ellen Ohrenstein

Widows receive a lot of advice. "Sell your house and go traveling."

"Don't sell your house and don't go traveling."

"Don't sell your house and do go traveling."

Anna found the third piece of advice was best for her.

She loved the cottage where she and Walter had lived so amicably. She loved the flower beds and the curious snails, the stone fireplace and the bookcases—though her loneliness was sore at times. She could afford to keep the house, she found, but she'd have to get a part-time job. Walter's friend, Harry, affirmed her financial decision; he liked to give good advice. This was before he made other advances.

She found a job as an aide at a branch library, and worked three afternoons a week. Evenings came lonely, but there were her cats and her television set and as many good books as she wanted to snuggle down with. And she liked to think about the portrait of Andrew Carnegie on the library wall, with his merry, wistful smile. The portrait reminded her of the one in the town library in her childhood, where she'd learned to love books—and here he was again. Sometimes Harry dropped over in the evening, and she gave him a cup of tea and some Toll House cookies. He'd done this every now and then when Walter was alive, and it felt like home by now. All this wasn't enough, of course, but it was something.

Anna began to see a certified grief therapist, a motherly lady named Marguerite who'd been a widow for seventeen years. Marguerite's card had been on the bulletin board at the library. They had a few private sessions together, and then Anna joined a Widows' Group. She felt this was an investment in herself. Anna loved these once-a-week meetings. She loved the way they all encouraged and supported each other. Bella, as she learned, knew how to change the oil in her car and replace the washers in her faucets. Marylou had talked to contractors about the new foundation she wanted to put under her house. Shelby had kept trying to do her own taxes but finally found a CPA she could talk to easily. Marlena began to realize a lifelong dream and took a ceramics class. And old Josephine, the dance teacher, shared the story of her own transition years ago, as she taught them dances to keep their muscles flexible.

They were proud of each other and of their new skills, and proud of Anna for working at the library after she'd been a home-person for so long. They took to dropping in at the library to see the book displays she'd arranged. They would nod at Andrew Carnegie as they browsed for mysteries or romances or good family stories, or looked for books on subjects of practical interest. Anna was pleased to help her friends this way.

Although she felt lucky she had a house and a garden and two cats and a job she liked, she agreed that realizing some lifelong dreams would be a marvelous thing to do. As she sorted out those dreams in front of the fire one night, she decided to try for something small and specific at first—something that she and Walter had long thought of doing together, but never quite had time for. It was to spend a weekend at an old inn on the coast; rest together; listen to the ocean; and be restored. Harry had hinted he'd like to travel with her, but she told him she needed to do this alone.

She remembered an old teacher she'd had years ago, a widowed lady named Elizabeth Lantern, who'd told her how important it is to do special things alone that bring joy.

"There's so much to tear us down these days," she used to say. "Let's discover ways to restore our spirits . . . ."

Elizabeth's way had been to take a journey to an old inn on the coast, where a person could rent a room at modest cost, walk on the beach, read and write letters, and reflect on the direction that her life would take. Anna decided to venture to the coast on her next three days off work and find Elizabeth's Inn.

Bella offered to take care of her cats, Marlena presented Anna with silver shell-shaped earrings for a getaway present, and Marguerite affirmed Anna in her choice. "It's good to start with a small dream first and learn success. A lot of small successes build up our spirits—then we can change our lives in bigger ways."

Anna wasn't sure how much she wanted to change her life, but she would think about that later. Her children kept urging her to move to the Bay Area to be closer to them, but she wasn't ready for that. Right now, she needed that small success.

What were the worst things that could happen to her on the journey? To get a flat tire, she decided, or to find that the inn was a disappointment, or that she'd spent too much money. Well, she could live with any of those setbacks—so she wouldn't worry about them. The best thing that could happen would be that she'd succeed. She smiled. She'd feel worthy then of the wisdom of old Elizabeth, who'd always shared with the class her own gentle optimism and belief in life. Anna had often thought of Elizabeth across the years. Even when Walter was alive, Anna had felt Elizabeth standing at turning-points in her spirit, encouraging her, trusting her judgment, challenging her to choose well. She hadn't heard from Elizabeth for a long time. Anna wondered if there was a chance that they'd meet at the old inn.

Anna packed a journal to write in, some letters to answer, and her walking shoes; then she added the novel that her almost-daughter-in-law had lent her. She would be happy—this she decided at the beginning. She wouldn't let the group down. Of course, she could be upset with Walter for dying and leaving her alone; of course, she could be irritated with her son for not marrying sweet Suzanna; of course, she could be irked with Harry for not being the man of her dreams. She smiled. She'd met the man of her dreams already, once. Wasn't that enough? He had left her a widow. Of course, she'd like to hear someone breathing beside her in the night, but she didn't think that Harry would do. She wanted to develop her own dreams so she wouldn't become vulnerable to Harry. Oh, Harry had his good points, but she needed her own centering. She'd begin this weekend to find the restoring solitude that Elizabeth had suggested long ago. Maybe another time she'd ask someone else to join her—her sister, maybe—but not yet.

Anna's car didn't get a flat tire. She stopped at little coffee shops along the way, soaking up the beauty of the ancient trees, admiring the girths made out of redwood, loving the texture of the redwood grain. When she reached the coast, she gasped at the great expanse of blue and white that seemed to stretch on forever. She loved the sea birds with their graceful sweep, and became exhilarated by the sound of the surf. She pulled off the road and poured over the AAA map. Yes, here was the coastal town where the inn waited, and here on the back was the street map, with the X she'd already marked at the corner of Fir and McKinley Streets where Elizabeth's Inn stood. It was as the guidebook had said: "Quiet; set back from the traffic . . . Old World charm."

The landlady received Anna in an apron and fuzzy house slippers. "It's my feet—my aching feet," she explained. "I'm growing old, but this ocean air makes me want to get out and about!"

She gave Anna keys to two vacant rooms. "It's a little climb either way, dear. Number six on the second floor has a queen bed, and it looks down on the garden. Number ten, on the third floor, is a single, but it looks out over the rooftops to the ocean. You can see the sunset there." Anna decided that stairs are good for the heart, so she accepted the keys pleasantly.

"This is a good walking town," the landlady continued. "And downtown you'll find the library and little shops that sell art and antiques, and a good yarn shop where women like to meet. You'll like poking around. Where did you hear about us?"

"I had a teacher, Elizabeth Lantern—a long time ago. She told us that she comes here sometimes for a personal retreat."

"Yes, Elizabeth . . . She was a comfortable woman, and easy about her hearing aid. Yes, of course, I knew Elizabeth! Beautiful spirit! A widowed person, too, but still had a family to take care of. This was her healing place, she used to tell me. She liked the room downstairs here, with the fireplace. I use it now for my sitting room—do my crochet here in the evenings. She passed on a couple of years ago—you didn't know? We miss her. Was a guest here off and on for twenty years."

Anna felt tears in her eyes, and her smile crumbled. "I should have kept in better touch with her, but I had so many others things to do. My husband died, too, a year ago."

"These things happen to every one of us," said the landlady. "Death comes hard in our lives. I was a widow when I inherited this inn from my old aunt. Tried to run it by myself for awhile. Elizabeth came to stay now and then. I always liked her—cheerful and kind lady, who'd been through a lot. She encouraged me to take a class at evening school—Creative Widowhood, it was called. That was one of the best things I ever did. Still didn't know how I'd maintain the inn, but I was more optimistic about it after that. Was in that good frame of mind when I met up with Fred. He needed a good woman to anchor him, and I needed a man I could count on to fix the locks and do the plumbing. He liked the idea of a business venture as much as he liked the idea of marrying me. We make good partners."

"You have a lovely inn, so I guess your partnership works."

"Do you think you'll marry again?"

"How do we women know that?" said Anna. "I'm still grieving for my husband. I'm trying to work things out alone."

"You're still wearing his ring, I see. Well, that's the way to discourage the fellas. Me—I wore my old ring till I knew it was time to make a change. It takes a while to get to know yourself. I met some mighty fine women in that class. Learned to admire every one of them, and the strengths that we all have. Some women think they're only good at building up a man's ego and taking care of a home—till they find they have to cope in other ways.

"When their role of wife is gone, they feel like a ship without an anchor. Sometimes they're prey to every knight of the road who comes along, unless they develop a good sense of their own separate worth."

The landlady laughed. "Elizabeth, she helped me to see that. I never did learn to pound nails at that widowhood class—but I learned to hire it done. Then, by the time I met Fred, I was strong enough to know what was right for me. And Fred was right."

Anna smiled. "I'm glad. I've heard stories of women who marry the wrong men because they're afraid of being alone. But I'm glad you found the right one—and he found you."

"It was mutual," laughed the landlady. "Well, look around, dear, and let me know which room you like best."

Climbing the stairs, Anna felt the peacefulness of this old inn. She understood why Elizabeth had kept returning here. The sun shone restfully, and through the open windows she heard the sound of the surf. She glanced at the second floor room with the queen bed, overlooking the garden. Walter would have loved this. She turned away: there were too many shadows in the garden now. She climbed to the third floor. A picture of a solitary gull was on the wall at the landing. The gull stood on a piling, waiting in the pink-and-blue mist. She could come and go whenever she wanted, thought Anna. Then, the room—it opened to the west, with the sun pouring through the windows. A little vase with a golden rose stood on the cross-stitched dresser scarf. A breath of wind fluttered the white curtains as Anna looked over the rooftops to the sea. She was thankful for the journey, and for this journey's end. She decided on the upper room.

Unpacking a little later, she thought of the diamond that Harry had offered her. "I'm lonely without you," he'd said.

"You've been alone for five years," she reminded him.

"But I was used to it before you became widowed, too," he said. Anna wondered if grief and loneliness became deeper as time went on.

"Couldn't you love me?" he'd persisted.

"I see us as good friends, not marriage partners. But we could have lunch now and then—talk things over. You know, be friends," she'd responded.

"But we could be so much more! I don't snore. I pay my bills. I don't have a social disease . . . ."

"Oh, Harry! Don't try to charm me!" Anna had laughed. She knew then how good it was to laugh—and she wished she could learn to love Harry, and walk on the beaches with him, and go on his business trips with him. But it wouldn't be right for her now.

"A relationship goes somewhere," Harry had replied. "If we spend more time together, you might change your mind!"

"Maybe you'll find another woman who can be your partner for life," Anna had said.

Marguerite had smiled when Anna had shared this. "That's a decision we face if we're lucky! All these lovely men who want to be our partners. And they're good for us. They start us searching our hearts to discover what we really want in our new life."

Anna thought of this now in her attic room, with the town spread out below her like a scene from an old storybook. What did she want, more than being partners with Harry?

It was good to be alone in this place. She would read Suzanna's book, write her a letter. She'd find the town library—browse among the books on cats and gardening, and the women's journals. She'd poke around the shops for birthday presents for her children and mementos for her friends. She'd walk on the beach, find shells to take home. Maybe she'd get some little magnets to glue on the backs to make decorations for the refrigerator. She'd have this restful healing-time, then tell her children she didn't want to move—that she had a home already. When she went back home, she'd find more work to do. Her heart was still vulnerable, and that wasn't good for Harry or for herself.

"We widows are working with a dozen changes all at once," Marguerite had said. "No wonder we feel a bit unsure of ourselves at times. Our finances. Our homes. Our time. How we feel about being alone when so many of our friends are couples, and we're not included. But most of all it's dealing with that interior change—from being a man's partner to living our own life. So many women have difficulty with this, and they keep their grief too close to their hearts to discover their own potential. Of course we grieve—and sometimes how we long for another partner! But all in good time. First we learn to build a way of life for ourselves . . . ."

"Does it have to be either-or? Can't it be both-and?" one widow had asked wistfully.

"Of course, my dear," Marguerite had said. "We're still double, even though we're single. That's the paradox of widowhood, and it's the challenge. But why should we avoid this challenge by marrying again right away?"

Marguerite was right, thought Anna. She loved her home—she loved all the reminders of her old life with Walter. But she also loved her new women-friends, and the challenges of her new life. She was glad she had the courage to venture forth to find Elizabeth's Inn at last—this quiet place with the view of this other town, with its rooftops and its boats in the harbor. It all reminded her of the storylike worlds she hadn't explored as a young woman before she'd married, old-new worlds that could open even yet if she kept venturing into other ways of life.

The blue cross-stitched dresser scarf—how beautiful it was! She thought of the landlady sitting in front of the fire with her crocheting, in the room that Elizabeth had loved. Whether married or alone, women seemed to need to create patterns in handiwork during their solitary times. And this little room with its thoughtful woman-touches, this could be a home away from home—a partner of a kind—another world to put her in touch with herself when she needed it.

One day Harry would bless her for saying no to him. He'd find a good woman he could give his diamond to, a woman who would love Anna for her wisdom. Someday. She thought of all the widowed women she'd ever known. Elizabeth, years ago, who knew women's need for restorative journeys. Marguerite, who nurtured and encouraged the group of younger women. And old Georgette, the dance teacher, who taught them how to keep their muscles flexible. They all knew how good it was to have work of their own—how good it was to build a life of their own that they could count on.

Anna smiled. She looked at her image in the mirror. She liked the lines on her face, liked the steady look in her eyes. She put blue eye shadow on. "Blue—that's the color of wisdom," Marguerite had said one day, standing beside her in the mirror, smiling.

Anna slipped on the silver shell earrings Marlena had given her. "Partners," she smiled at the image in the mirror. "Partners," the woman in the mirror smiled back. They were lifetime companions, best friends. They'd never desert each other: they'd never let each other down.

Tomorrow she'd go to that yarn shop where women met, and find some blue thread—many, many shades of blue. She'd find new patterns and new materials to make some fine works of needlecraft during her winter evenings with her cats by the fire.

There'd be no warm hands to cuddle her breasts, no warm body to breathe beside hers in the night, no lean, hard strength to plumb the depths of her loving. Tears smarted her eyes as she breathed, "Walter . . . ." She'd had it all, and it was still with her. The golden rose in the vase on the cross-stitched dresser scarf gathered her thoughts together. The tears in the eyes of the woman in the mirror shone like twin diamonds as she smiled.

A breath of the sea breeze ruffled the curtain at the window, and all the rooftops of the town glistened with gold as the evening sun twinkled them into mellow new beauty.

CONCEPT: DEATH

Mari Stitt

Gone   Over   Ended
Quiet   Untouchable
Sorrow   Shadows
Memories live   nourish
reassure   ennoble
clarify   enlighten

Theme: Death is immutable
but something remains that is never lost.

The problem has been: I am left here, a mile high
in a mountain forest,
the one who loves the learning milieu.
Which option to take?
—Go to the university in the city?
—Stay on the mountain and be my roles?
—Keep on being here, writing, studying as a poet?
The answer
is the same it always has been.
I would not leave my love's place
and I cannot cease being what I am.

Half of what our children are
came from him
and most of my life has been
devoted to him
perhaps very little has changed
for him or for me.
Perhaps
nothing important has died.

CONSEQUENCES

Fanny Elisabeth Garvey

For quite some time it was difficult for me to tell people I am a widow. It was easy enough to write it on forms because all I had to do was put a tick in a little box with a sharp pointed pencil. But I found it very hard to say the actual word or spell it on a piece of paper.

There was no place for me to be your widow. People looked oddly at me when I told them you had been dead for almost fifteen years. You look too young to be a widow, they'd remark. What they meant is I must have been very young when you died. They were right. I was. And what they sometimes meant was, it was hard to believe. How could a Black woman be a widow? Wasn't I just a single mother?

I was twenty-four when you died. At an age when most people are only contemplating marriage, we had been together for almost six years. We had been married and in love and loyal and faithful throughout the late 1970s. People found that odd also. No one understood how we could be radical Leftists and live a traditional married life.

The whole time we were together, there were always questions to be answered. What's it like to be married? the feminists would ask me. What's it like to be married to a White guy? the Blacks would ask me. What's it like to be married to an intellectual? the working people would ask me. What's it like to be married to an Irishman? the Americans would ask me. What's it like to be married to the same person for so long? the liberals would ask me.

Then, suddenly as it had started, the questions stopped. You were dead. No one asked, What's it like to be a widow? No one asked me anything anymore. People just decided this was one more odd thing about me that defied explanation.

No longer having to answer questions silenced me. I would long for an inquiry, pray someone would say, What's it like? But no one ever did. I was no longer interesting. I had done something that people didn't like to talk about. I had become a widow.

I remember doing my taxes one year and noticing there was a status called Qualifying Widow with Children. But when I tried to see if this status would apply to me, I found that the government also did not bother to ask any questions. They wanted no answers or explanations. All they wanted was the appropriate paperwork.

And I had no paperwork. I had nothing left of you except a wooden crucifix, your favorite books, and a tiny incense holder I had bought for you in Mexico. I had no death certificate. No coroner's report. No photographs. No insurance settlement. No last will and testament. I had nothing to explain your death to anyone.

I stopped talking about you because there was no one to listen to me. Even God would not hear my voice. I prayed to Him. I begged Him to bring you back. I pleaded with Him to take me to you. I implored Him to give me someone to take your place. I apologized to Him for my loneliness. I hoped He would forgive me for my tears. I feared He would never forgive me for my longing for you. I wished He would listen to me.

Then one day I stopped asking Him to help me. I decided I was on my own. I turned my back on anything and everything that had been a part of you. A part of us. Our politics. Our religion. Our church. Our fidelity. Our humility. Our grace. Our books. Our ideas. Our determination. Our devotion. Our love. Our faith.

That was what you had brought into my life. We had cultivated them together. They were the things that kept us alive and happy. And I didn't want them anymore. I didn't want to talk about them anymore. I didn't want you anymore. I was on my own. And on my own, I would find a voice. It would not be the voice of a widow, because no one wanted to hear what a widow has to say.

I lived twelve years this way. You never existed. People would tell me how beautiful our child was and I'd nod politely. I changed her name on the birth certificate. I would not let her be a part of you because you did not exist anymore. Sometimes I just wrote Deceased, never your name, on the forms she needed for school records and other documents. I went along, on my own. You simply did not exist.

There were kisses and caresses from other men. Some of them were quite nice, others weren't. There were dresses and perfumes I wore for them. And there were dresses and perfumes I wore for myself. I stopped writing. I stopped reading. I stopped going to Mass. I stopped working on political committees. I stopped reading newspapers and journals and reports. I stopped watching public television. I stopped doing all the things you and I had done together. You were dead. You were gone. And I stopped talking about it.

I left the city we had lived in together. I left the people we had known together. I left the beach where we had swum and walked and made love. I left the books and records and artwork and plays we enjoyed together. I left everything that had to do with us and went out on my own.

I was good on my own. I worked every day and supported my family and I did as well as any working class woman could hope for during the Reagan years. Once in a while, something would remind me of you. But I would shove it away, throw it out, crush it before it could grow. I emptied myself, drained myself, cleansed myself of anything that had to do with you.

You were dead, but yet, you followed me wherever I went. You caused me to form a frown on my forehead, kept a worry in my eyes. You teased me. You cried to me. You searched for me. You lingered in the back of my heart and kept a constant pain churning there.

I married another man, a very cruel, selfish man. A man the exact opposite of you. He took from me everything I had gotten on my own. My money. My car. My strength. My reputation. My beauty. My clothes. My furniture. My credit. My image.

He left me with nothing but a pain in my heart. A pain that clashed with the pain of you in my veins. This made me very ill. I went to doctors. They told me I was severely depressed. They told me I needed therapy and medication. They told me I needed to be observed for seventy-two hours. They told me I needed to get over all this.

The questions started again. I knew it was time for me to begin talking because I was being asked to explain things. They asked questions and I answered them all. They went as far back into my childhood as I could remember. They went as far back into my teenage years as I could remember. They went as far back into my childbearing years as I could remember. They went as far back into my middle-age years as I could remember. They asked me questions and I answered them all.

I took the pills they gave me and I paid thirty-five dollars a week for one-hour therapy sessions. They asked and I answered. They listened and I talked. They wrote and I signed forms. They decided and I agreed.

I explained you away. I told them you had been a quick affair. I had chosen to have a child with you because I was a liberated modern woman. I had not been married to you. I had not been a Catholic. I had not been a university student. I had not lived with you. I had not loved you. You simply did not exist.

After all the questions and all the answers, the decision was made. I would move to another new city. I would get a good job. I would start all over again. I would be more careful about the men I got involved with. I would rebuild my credit. I would save and buy a house. I would go on again on my own. And I would never mention you or your name again.

I began to sleep alone. I bought a beautiful set of bed linens, all white lace, and sheets with roses on them. I bought beautiful sleepwear and lingerie, satins, silks, lace, sheers. I bought a new wardrobe. I got a new hairstyle. I wore new make-up. I celebrated my thirty-sixth birth-day and admired how good I looked for my age.

Then, one night, I saw you. I had just turned out the light and was admiring the shapes of the pine trees in the early Georgia summer outside my window. I lay in my white lace bed in my white silk sleepwear and was listening to Van Morrison sing "Moondance." There was no moon in the sky and the only light came from the million stars I was trying to count. Then I saw you.

I didn't know it was you. I could not recognize you because you looked different somehow. You looked weary, tired, exhausted. Your hair was thin and limp. It hung around your haggard face in tangles. Your eyes were sunken and circled with shadows. Your face was lined with the creases of tears. Your mouth was drawn down at the corners and your lips trembled. Your hands shook as you held them out to me.

I called the police. I told them there was a strange man in the woods outside my apartment. They told me to lock the windows and doors and turn on the air conditioner. I did this. The noise of the ventilation system drowned out the silence of the night. I bought a night light and slept with it near my bed. I kept the curtains drawn tightly.

But I still saw you. Sometimes you would be on the seat in front of me on the subway. Sometimes you would be walking past me in the grocery store. Sometimes you would be sitting at the bar of the dance club I liked. Sometimes you would be a delivery boy on the job where I worked. Sometimes you would be the bus driver. Sometimes you would be Black, other times White, other times Mexican, other times Asian.

I slept with you every time I saw you. I took you into my white lace bed and let you remove my white silk sleepwear. I fed you. I smiled at you. I went places with you. I dressed up for you. I kissed you and caressed you and made love to you.

Still, the shadows remained around your eyes. No matter what I did, you looked more ill each time I saw you. One night, you began to cry. You made the wind howl and the trees bend in fear. You made the sky bright with lightning. You made the earth tremble with thunder. You made the ground gag on the thousands of buckets of rain you splashed down. You sent a heat wave through my apartment that blew all my electricity. My night light was shattered as you surged through it.

I woke up during the storm and saw you standing at the foot of my bed. You were a wisp of a form, thin and sickly looking. I could see the bones trying to pierce your thin fingers as you reached toward me. The lightning flashed and I saw you heave with sobs. Your body shook and I heard your heart moan in pain. I stared, enchanted, at you and you began to speak.

I stayed up all that night. I didn't take you into my bed. I simply stayed up and listened to you. I let you explain things to me. You told me you had been afraid. Like me, you had tried to run away. In that moment when death spoke your name, you had cried out, begged for mercy, pleaded for more time. Your eyes had searched in vain for me. For your mother. For your brother. Your ears had strained to hear our laughter, our voices, our breathing. Your hands had clutched at the formless shadows of us that tried to hold on to you. Your mouth had burned with the dryness of lost smiles and kisses. You had longed to live long enough to smell the new spring grass, the budding roses and the first summer rain.

But none of us had been any match for death. You had been taken so suddenly, so cruelly, so painfully. Your brother tried to catch up with you, in a rush of heroin and whiskey. Your mother let her heart stop beating. And I froze a weak smile onto my lips, shook my hair of the dust of you, and trod like a zombie through the darkness in my soul.

I fled from you, the thought of you, the meaning of you. And for all those years, you searched for me, calling in vain. Making me run faster and faster, away from you, into places and things that frightened you as you followed me.

You told me all these things and more. How sorry you were to have left me. How I would gain enough distance to leave you behind forever.

Until your hands were entwined in mine and your eyes filled with tears. Until you trembled and shook and sobbed against my shoulder. Until I knew once again the warmth of your breathing across my chest, the silkiness of your hair against my cheek, the velvet of your arms around my waist. Until you made me cry with you, from the ebony of midnight until the violet of dawn.

Then I played our favorite music for you. I made tea for you. I encouraged you to sit on the edge of the bed so I could comb the tangles from your hair. I rubbed your sore shoulders and back as you lay against me. I smiled at you. I felt what you felt. Smelled what you smelled. Tasted what you tasted. Saw what you saw. Heard what you heard.

The next day I bought a sketch book. I began drawing you every night when you came to me. I drew you. I painted you. I wrote down what you said. I listened to you some more. I made up songs and sang them to you every night. I filled the entire book and bought another one.

Since then, I write every day. Everything you tell me, I record it carefully. I write that I am your wife. I write that I am your friend. I write that I am your love. I write that you have grown beautiful in the two years since you found me. I write that you are not tired and weary and sickly looking anymore. I write that you are no longer ill.

Since then, I don't sleep alone anymore. I lie down and wait for you to come. I take the hand you offer to me. It is warm and healthy and full of your pulse. I take hold of it and go wherever you take me. I journey with you through the things that kept us alive and happy. Everything that had been a part of you. A part of us. Our politics. Our religion. Our church. Our fidelity. Our humility. Our grace. Our books. Our ideas. Our determination. Our devotion. Our love. Our faith.

No one asks me questions anymore. I answer no one anymore. There are no more questions. There are infinite answers. I am your widow. I write this over and over again until I begin to smile. The love we knew fills me once again. I have everything of you. Of me. Of us. Of God. I am your widow and I love you.

ALONE

Margaret Blaker

A box of your letters I cannot recall
to life or read again: what do I fear?
To be transported back into a year
I knew so little of you and loved all,
known and unknown; stretched to the tall
frame and brain of you, having no clear
vision of life or love, only the sheer
ardor of dreaming you my all in all.

Now here alone, I stretch to reach you still,
erasing your pain, restoring the old smile,
your wry, dry slant on things; your will
to keep on, to keep up, and all the while
taking the falls for me—falls I now take
no longer dreaming, sensibly awake.

ORPHEUS AND EURYDICE

Nancy Kassell

I redid the bathroom in white
tile with a Victorian border—
berries fix the progress of leaves
plump as feathers—
white, the union of all colors,
an argument
for the possibility of moving
from nothing to desire.

Your death was an accident,
like Eurydice's. Playing in a sunny meadow,
she was bitten by a snake. You careened
down a hill, shattered your skull
into mosaic. I have descended,

like Orpheus, into the resting place
of shadows. I have seen the palace of black Hades
electrified
by your smile and Persephone, as charmed
by you as I am, unmoved by my song.

I retrace my steps without you,
beguiling myself up to light,
and cannot stop myself
from looking back.

Chapter Four
Going Solo

The dream of flight is suddenly gone before the mundane reali-
ties of growing grass and swirling dust, the slow plodding of men
and the enduring patience of rooted trees. Freedom escapes you
again, and wings that were a moment ago no less than an eagle's,
and swifter, are metal and wood once more, inert and heavy.
—Beryl Markham, *West With the Night*

Forever we had flown the airstreams together. With our mates as co-pilots, we shared the aerodynamics of flight. With the wind behind us, gently lifting and pushing us along, it was easy to take our time together for granted; we believed we could overcome all turbulence, all the daily maintenance required to fly safely to our next destination. When take-offs were treacherous, we held the throttle together, soaring on wings built for two.

Then, in what seemed like a blink in time, we were flying alone, our co-pilots gone. We have flown only tandem, so we don't know how to navigate the night skies alone. We don't know what to do when we stall. We don't know how to land safely on the ground. Those were the co-pilot's jobs.

It will take time before we learn to fly alone. Sometimes we even crash. Then, we glide confidently; at times turning to the seat beside us, proud of our accomplishment. But the seat is empty. We are alone. We can only hope that we know where we are going. After the death of a mate, the only flight plan is a hopeful guess.

Everyday details baffle surviving mates as we steer through this turbulence called grief. Toilets overflow and cars won't start. Children get sick. Holidays and special anniversaries approach. A child graduates. Another marries. The grass needs mowing and the roof leaks. Bills must be paid, yet there is not enough money.

Going solo is learning to make decisions about a life that no longer feels like it belongs to us. We must decide what to do with our mate's possessions. Do we keep them or throw them out? Do we stay in the home we shared or move out? Should we paint the house or replace the furnace? Fix the car, or buy a new one? How do we buy a car? How do we get a Christmas tree? Who will care for us when we are old and sick? We shiver at the questions we must ask. We shrink away from the answers we receive; they are not the ones we want to hear.

We have survived the death of our mates—our co-pilots—and now we must learn how to survive alone. This chapter speaks of these most difficult challenges in a world where life goes on, with or without us, never slowing down to honor our grief.

Thrown into the wind, we must learn to keep our nose up, our eyes ahead, the throttle of daily routine steady, and our senses acute. We have no experience, no flight plan. It is not easy, but eventually we do take off. And then we land, realizing at once that we've done it. We are flying—solo.

THE WIDOW'S CLUB

Miriam Finkelstein

We recognize each other on the streets of the city
Even when we're not wearing black.
We have all paid our dues.
We have become members of a club
That none of us wanted to belong to.

Some of us throw lace mantillas over our heads
And scratch our faces with our long red fingernails.
Others take long walks and write poems,
Travel to Amsterdam, smile in elevators
Listening to the voices in our heads.

Nobody reaches out for us in the middle of the night.
Nobody wakes us up with his snoring and has to be pushed back
To his side of the bed.
Nobody touches our breasts
Except our doctors and ourselves.

The subject for this evening's meeting is lamentation.
Next week we will discuss grief.
How it grabs you when you least expect it.
In the bank, in the supermarket, in the bathtub.
As you pull the curtain in the voting booth.
Like a mischievous lover, sneaking up from behind
Just when you were beginning to feel safe.

BLESS THIS HOUSE

Grace Brumett

JUNE 24, 1995

Another good-bye stands before me. In a little over a week I will leave this house for a new one, the first to know my steps without Michael. I have not yet packed a single box. I don't even have boxes. All around me lies the disorder of a family's daily chaos—dirty dishes on the counter, piles of laundry needing to be folded, dust on the window ledge, stacks of unread books and magazines on the coffee table, my desk littered with papers I must deal with someday, unopened junk mail and bills that will need a response—"Michael Brumett is dead now. Please close the account."

No, I haven't begun to pack yet. I'm in a jumble of emotions I can't predict or sort. How can I be so passive even as I take big steps? What keeps me from packing? Is it fear that now I must begin the hard steps of creating a life that is "mine" and not "ours"?

Am I making wise choices? Would Michael approve? I always depended on his advice. We made decisions together. Will this move take me further away from the shreds of us and the life we had together into the unknown reality of my solitary present life? Another letting go I must face?

"Grace, you are so strong!" I've heard it said so many times that it has begun to sound like a curse. Yes, strong. I don't know if fear is a part of my vocabulary anymore; panic maybe, but fear was blasted out the door by too many years of watching what one fears the most happen slowly in front of me—Michael, my mate of twenty-five years, dying bit by bit.

Now that is done.

Death is not the enemy. There is nothing more to fear. Dead is easy. It's the little things, the everyday things that are hard. The living. Like paying the bills on time; paying attention to practical details when I really could care less. Getting my youngest son to school. Fixing the car. How do I get it across town, then to work and back later to retrieve it all by myself?

Losing keys. Where are they? Don't lock myself out. Keeping track of things when I'd rather not be bothered, but panic when I don't. Making all the small decisions and some big ones without my partner to run it by.

And then reminding myself that I must stay soft and compassionate. It would be so easy to slip into hardness, bitterness, cynicism. I hear people agonize over so many mundane silly things, or so it appears to me in my self-indulgent state of mind. "Stop fretting!" I want to scream. Of course, the world will keep turning whether or not little Billy makes the baseball team (and what can you do about it anyway?); whether or not Clinton gets elected or O.J. convicted (and who cares anyway?); whether or not you buy the car (it's only money after all); whether or not adolescent Sara is in a constant, unbearable mood these days (it will pass, I'm sure). It will all work out. It's not the end of the world.

Stay soft, sympathetic, I remind myself. This is important, this stuff of life, even though at this moment in my life it may seem a luxury to worry about small triumphs, tragedies, and conflicts. It would be so easy for me to feel resentful. If they only knew what they have. Everything. Their husband didn't just die.

A world didn't just end.

And then there's that question I have at moments asked myself when I have dared to think of a future: *Will I ever find joy in my gut again and the capacity to dream?* I am so numb now. Numb and yet, whack!—so wide awake.

Such are the rambles of fresh widow grief that keep me from the business of packing. I must move to a new house. I am propelled by necessity. I can no longer afford this big one. But I also recognize my sense of relief that I didn't have to make this healthy decision to move on. It was made for me, which makes it easier. I may not have had the courage to break my inertia. I like to think the Great Mystery has once again come to my rescue. I've come to trust it that way.

Leaving this house has great significance. It will be my first move alone.

I could just go through the motions and act "normal," but recently I have found the value in honoring my inner journey in my outer life. When something is significant, as all "firsts" tend to be for a new widow, a simple ritual in acknowledgment of steps taken is empowering. So in the midst of all the boxes I must surely pack in this next, last week, I will pause here to do my spiritual packing, to beat a drum, to mark the moment with a little serious silence and a few words of blessing to this house:

They say a house has its own soul, that houses come to us for a purpose. They take care of us, hold us, guard our secrets, contain our passions. When we leave them, we leave a part of ourselves within them.

Indeed, House, what stories you could tell. The first time I stepped inside your door I knew you were a substantial house with a heart big enough to embrace all that was ahead. I sat awhile, asked permission to be here, and you received us. Thank you, House.

Thank you for witnessing these last three magnificent years of passage for my family. I brought Michael to you, it would seem now, in order to die.

And dying takes time. It isn't easy. It's a big deal. I brought him directly from the bone marrow transplant ward at Stanford—that science-fiction battle zone where he spent six weeks in isolation. Even the air wasn't safe for his body. They gave him a lethal dose of chemotherapy so every cell began to die. Then they tried to trick his body and transplanted fresh clean marrow in the hopes that it would multiply and replenish his dying body. We prayed each day, each moment. Me beside him, meticulously masked, gowned and scrubbed down because nothing organic or alive could come near him. We prayed and watched the computer stats hooked to his body along with the morphine drips and sterile food fed into his jugular. We rejoiced at each tiny rise in platelet and white blood cell count they recorded, hardly daring to hope, while not doubting for a moment that all things are possible. Many weeks later he re-entered life for the final stage with his family here in this house. Hopeful. He felt welcome—at home.

Now, the very creak of your stairs, House, is impregnated with images of Michael stubbornly pulling himself up with his own unfailing strength, up to our bed and the intimacy of our room. His salty smell still lingers in my closet. I smile in spite of myself at all the drama you have silently born these last three years. All the midnight-whispered assurances we gave one another as I would watch Michael endlessly, touching his whiskered drawn face over and over in the night, needing to voice again and again one more time, "I love you, Michael."

"I know," he would smile.

All the celebrations with the stream of friends coming to say goodbye. But not really. They came to hold Michael here a little longer with their love.

So many visitors received through your door for merry meals and intimate talks. Reveling in the holiness we all experienced living so close to the fragile veil that separates worlds. Exhilaration and utter exhaustion. And yes, again, the tears and the tears and the tears. All the anxious exchanges you heard with doctors and the announcements received on the phone, "I'm sorry. It's back and there's nothing more we can do." Our rallying cry, as we've always done in affirmation of life: "Then we'll go to Mexico and play!" Excitement within your walls of packing up one more time.

Music, friends, family agonizing each in our own way in explosions of anger, fear, panic, outrage, frustration, and sad and sad and sad. Our tears stained your proud wooden floors.

Good-byes. You witnessed extravagantly wild and crazy gatherings of good-byes with candles lit, incense burning, conversation through the night, people dancing, singing through your rooms, dope and liquor as medicine to loosen our minds and numb our pain. Guitars strumming, fire burning for yet one more, one more celebration of our agony.

You heard rage, harsh words, morphine confusion. You witnessed Michael's Tibetan vajra mysteriously, spontaneously ignite and flame on your hearth as an omen of release. You were patient as we continually redrew the line of hope and laughed yet again in death's face.

You rocked us in the desperate passion of our tender lovemaking, heightened by the inevitable separation looming imminently before us. You were quiet while we held hands in a circle for the very last time physically intact as a family, two days before death's visitation. Extra long. You gave us time.

Oh, House, right here where I sit Michael drew his very last rasping breath and with that final look of merging love, took me with him to eternity.

This last long year you have secreted what we have lovingly referred to as Michael's room—the closet shrine with Michael's ashes where each one of us has crept at odd hours to commune with spirit and lick our wounds.

I've walked your rooms now a full turn of the seasons retracing every step, every memory. Your walls have been safe enough to hold even the darkness of my grief until now I feel I can let go of these protective walls that have cradled my agony, my sleepless aching nights and vacant lonely days. You have served me well. The images are forever embedded deep within my psyche. The time is right to move on. I know this with a blind faith I have come to accept like a sleepwalker in the dark who somehow doesn't fall. I can close your door gently, firmly now, with the resolve that it is only by shutting one door that another will open.

JUNE 30, 1995

The house is empty now. Not one physical vestige of our life here remains. I have picked every tack, marble, and paper clip from the carpets. I have emptied each closet and drawer. I have scoured every inch, wiped every wall and light fixture. I have painted over the wall in my son's room where it exploded through those last weeks as an organic and growing mural of words and images drawn to mirror the pain, anguish, and transformation of a father's dying.

Now I sit, quiet inside and out, hearing only the silent echoes of this passing moment in these empty rooms. I am very still. It is afternoon, 3:45, forever marked for me as the moment of Michael's passing almost to the day a year ago. The light falls on the carpet of my barren room just the way it did at his passing. The same birds are singing sweetly outside, the warm scents of summer plants and the quality of the air evoke an instant connection out of ordinary time and space. I am right there again. Right here.

I bring to this spot a dark red rose I pick from our garden and sit on the empty floor—this spot where Michael left his body. The sunlight on my back through the bedroom window ignites my body. As I feel the touch of hot sun on my spine, there is a great sense of peace that reaches far beyond sadness.

I hear once more Michael's words of blessing he left for his children, spoken one timeless day in his dying:

> All is energy.
> It doesn't die.
> It moves on
> But remains one.
> It is something
> Can't be spoken.
> Keep a spiritual side to you.
> Look for the good.
> I love you and approve.

And it is enough.

COIN OF THIS REALM

Maude Meehan

This is not despair,
not the retreat into the deep wound
but a conscious living of each day

This is the placing of one foot before the other,
not the free stride of the unencumbered
but the careful tread of the initiated foot

This is learning how to walk
without familiar landmarks, alone
even in the company of others,
not ready yet for new direction

This is the living of each day, aware
that what you cannot predict
may still loose sudden tears, yet
that laughter too is possible

This is when you struggle
as plants in arid soil
strive without conscious knowing
to stay alive until the rain

This is a time for faith
that this most naked agony of loss
will ease, and not corrode the spirit

This is the time to trust that day after
labored day you will move forward,
open to joy as well as pain;
two-sided coin, you proffer for remembrance

DAWN

Diana Lee Goldman

The salty sea breeze was warm and gentle as it caressed my slightly sun-burned skin. After a day in the gloriously blazing sun, it was now a joy to watch that same sun set majestically into the ocean. I wanted to stop time. Everything in my life seemed so perfect. I was living a dream. I looked up into the eyes of the man whom I had adored for as long as I could remember. Quietly standing on our balcony, he wrapped a cotton shawl around my shoulders as we gazed at our view. The sea had begun a quivering silver-gray dance. A dramatic burst of orange fire seemed to spill across the inlet from the setting sun, a mystical carpet of color that spread across the water as if to welcome home a traveling God. The tropical smell of hibiscus rose up from our garden and the sound of the gentle lapping waves overwhelmed my senses with contentment. No words had to be spoken. Everything was said in the silence.

The tap on my shoulder shook me back to reality. "Excuse me, Ma'am, are you okay?"

"Oh yes, I'm fine, really just fine."

"Would you like to place your order now?"

"I'm really very sorry," I stammered. "Just one more moment please, I was lost in thought."

Our waiter left quietly and I looked across the table at the kind face of the man I was with. Other than the fact that he owned an advertising agency and dressed conservatively, I knew very little about him. He looked gently at me and asked if I would prefer to leave.

"No," I answered as a chill swept over me. He saw me shiver and stood up to wrap my shawl around my shoulders. "I'll be fine," I managed to say. I tried wholeheartedly to smile, but didn't know where to look except beyond the terrace and into another time and another place.

My heart was frozen. I tried to focus on the small boats drifting slowly through that radiant burst of color splashing across the water. All I could envision were complete families on board. The boats quietly disappeared into the darkness. I realized I was biting my lip so hard that it had begun to bleed. Blinking away tears, I looked down at the tiny flower arrangement on the restaurant table, but the lone orange hibiscus in the clear glass vase only made me feel vulnerable and caused my tears to spill down my cheeks. Trying vainly once again to smile and brush away my tears, I turned my attention to the menu.

The man across from me, sensing my extreme discomfort, once again offered to take me home. I became determined not to give in to the undertow of the past and turned to safe small talk.

"How old are your children?" I asked blankly. Soon I was telling him all about mine. I was talking faster and faster, trying to get in as much chatter as I could to enable me to stay afloat and leave the past behind. The lapping of the waves outside this seaside restaurant became a roar of panic in my mind. The view in front of me was Long Island Sound and not my beloved island cove, and the man across from me was not my husband. Brian was gone forever. Everyone said it was time. Time for the young widow to start dating. They said I was ready.

I smiled at the man in front of me and slowly listened to his story. The gentle lapping of the waves began to soothe the dreaded undertow. I ordered my meal and watched the sun finally disappear from sight. I was once again determined to face the dawn.

GIVING HIS BOOKS AWAY

Miriam Finkelstein

My books everywhere
On desk tops on kitchen counters
On the wobbly piano bench
His books in the bookcase beside the table
Where he sat reading every morning at six
Leaving me slumbering
Dreaming about our wobbly marriage
While he plunged
Into the cloudy swirling seas
Of psychiatric controversy

I scrub the dusty shelves
Trying hard not to look at the void
Then I place poetry novels short stories
In the sacred space
Courage or hubris?
So far no retribution
I drink my morning tea sitting beside
My beloved books thinking
If I gave his away it must mean
That I really believe
He's not coming back
Perhaps the only crime
Is empty shelves

A GIFT OF MEMORIES

Joseph F. Sweet

I never realized a night could be so dark. It was not late; only a little after six, but the low clouds blotted out the stars and the rising moon. I pulled into my driveway in my quiet neighborhood and parked near the side door of the house. No light shone in any of the windows. The noise of the tires hitting the stone driveway woke Daniel. He was tired from an afternoon of Christmas shopping. I lifted him from his car seat and carried him into the house. He barely moved except to rest his head on my shoulder. I put him on the couch and turned on the lights.

"Shh, Dan, Mom's still sleeping."

"Can I play with my new Turtle guy?"

"Sure, but please play quietly. I'll have supper ready in a little bit."

I sat at the dining room table, slowly and sadly unpacking the Christmas gifts we had purchased. I decided not to wake Barbara until supper was ready. I sipped a cup of coffee, barely attentive to anything save my hazy reflection in the cold, dark window.

"Will you read a book to me?" I hadn't heard Dan enter the room.

"Maybe later, Dan. I'm going to cook supper now."

"Okay, Dad."

I watched Dan retreat into the living room. He had his mother's regal features, but with my lighter coloring. His lean, strong body, large, round, doleful eyes, and thick hair also resembled his mother, but his fair skin and blond hair came from me.

While the macaroni simmered, I made a salad in the manner Barbara liked. As the macaroni drained, I walked upstairs to wake her.

"Barbara, dinner's ready. And I got most of the Christmas presents we wanted," I said as I sat down on the bed next to her.

"Huh, oh yeah. Good." She blinked groggily and rubbed her eyes. "I'm still tired. I'm going to sleep some more. I'm not sure I can come down for dinner."

"Okay. Did you take your medication?" Her eyes were already closing.

"Yeah, g'night."

I returned downstairs. The living room seemed cold and bleak, as if no amount of light could brighten it. I turned up the heat. Daniel and I ate silently.

As I cleared the table, he asked, "Dad, can you read to me now?"

"Later, Dan. I have to clean up." As Barbara became more ill, I had less and less time and energy for Dan. His requests always provoked guilt.

"Can I watch TV?"

"Sure. I'll sit with you after I finish the dishes. Let's watch one of your Christmas tapes."

"How about 'Sesame Street Christmas'? I like it when Oscar eats the Christmas tree."

"Yeah that's funny. The only thing he doesn't eat are those sad, puny branches."

"Dad, will Mom come with us to Grandma's tomorrow?"

I hesitated. How do you tell a three year old that his mother is ill, very ill, and she may not be able to share his Christmas with him? A boy's third Christmas should shine in his eyes and create a magic that leads him to appreciate wonder. There should be colorful lights and the delightful singing of bells in winter songs. A boy's third Christmas should not be dismal. I wanted to tell him all of this. I wanted to tell him how sorry I was that his mother was ill. I wanted to tell him how bad I felt that his Christmas had no joy. But, I could only say, "I don't know, Dan. I don't know if she'll come."

We both fell asleep as Big Bird continued his search for the source of Santa Claus' enchanted entrance. The blank hum of the VCR finally woke me. I carried Daniel to bed.

"Dad," he said sleepily. "We forgot to turn on the Christmas lights tonight."

"I know buddy, I know. We'll get them tomorrow."

Work crept along slowly the next day. Not much was done during Christmas week. Most of the staff attended the party down the hall, but since celebrating seemed profane to me, I volunteered to cover the office and answer the phone.

Feeling lonely, I called to check on Barbara.

"How are you feeling, Hon?"

"Terrible, just terrible," she cried. "I'm so weak, and I'm ruining Dan's Christmas."

"No, you're not. Everyone understands. We just want you to get your rest."

"No, you don't understand." I could hear her crying. "I can't give Dan anything. I can't shop for him. I can't make a holiday dinner for him. I can't even help decorate the house. I love him so much, and I can't give him anything."

"It's not your fault. I know you'd give him the world if you could."

I was glad to have the distance of the phone call. My stomach churned and my eyes watered as I thought of my poor wife's inability to give her son happiness.

"I'm going back to sleep. I want to go to my mother's house tonight with you and Dan."

"Okay, Hon. But if you can't make it, that'll be all right."

The slow drive home ended with Daniel breathlessly greeting me by pushing open the storm door.

"Dad, guess what? Mom's feeling better! She's coming with us," Dan yelled before I could get in the door. "She's almost ready."

His excitement startled me. I looked past him and saw a Barbara I had not seen for three months. It seemed as if health had returned to her face. Her brilliant white teeth smiled for the first time in weeks. She stood straight, powered by an extraordinary determination, and gracefully scooped Dan into his winter coat. She playfully slapped his behind.

"Great, let's get going."

The road to Grandma's house wound through the wooded edges of the reservoir. Dan sat in the back seat, excitedly chattering about whatever came to his mind. The rising full moon shone through the bare, stark trees clearly showing the stubbed remnants of the fall's corn and tomato harvest. It was a textbook Christmas Eve, crisp and clear, that brought to mind roasting chestnuts and ringing sleigh bells.

"Ooh, they're here," Aunt Addie's high-pitched voice rang through the house. "They're here!"

As we lifted the presents from the car, we could see the bright expectant faces in the frost-edged window, backlit by the multicolored lights on the green Christmas tree.

Aunt Addie held the door for us. "Merry Christmas—C'mon in, the eggnog is spiked and ready for business."

The Italian-American Christmas Eve had lost its religious meaning for me, yet it never failed to give me a sense of a homecoming. No matter what deaths, births, tragedies, or blessings occurred during the year, Christmas Eve always had a comforting sameness. Petty jealousies were set aside. A Christmas Eve with good food, wine, and family meant the world was still a good and safe place.

We sat in the living room of Barbara's childhood home eating ice-cold shrimp. The pine scent of the Christmas tree melded with the light waxy smoke from the candles and the aroma of fragrant foods. For moments, I was nearly able to forget what else was going on in my life.

Across the table from me, Barbara teasingly tried to feed a shrimp appetizer to Dan. He allowed her to put the cold shrimp to his lips and then he mockingly shook his head no.

But his affirmative blue eyes, sparkling from the candlelight, longingly and lovingly looked at his mother. Her broad smile warmed Dan's fair face.

"You look beautiful, Papita." Aunt Anne used Barbara's childhood nickname. "Your cheeks are nice and rosy, and I love your new sweater."

"Let's open the presents!"

"Wait a minute. I hear someone in the den. Let's check it out."

A tall, thin Santa Claus wearing a cheap suit looked as if he was sneaking in through the window. Dan's widened eyes and gaping mouth gave witness to the miracle.

"Ho, ho, ho! You caught me. I'm just dropping by to give this little fella' an early present because he's been so great this year. Here you go, Dan."

Dan quickly retreated. He fit snugly between his mother's knees. Barbara's hand brushed back his hair and she smiled with all the love and affection a mother could express. The sparkle returned to Barbara's eyes. The heavens gave her this perfect moment as a gift. And I knew it was a farewell gift.

"Let's eat."

The next morning Dan woke me as he yelled, "Santa came!" I could hear the banging of three-year-old legs making their way up the stairs. "He left lots of good stuff, too. C'mon!"

"We'll be down in a minute," I replied. Turning to Barbara, I asked, "How are you feeling?"

"Tired. I'm not going to be able to make it to Christmas dinner."

"Okay, pal." I kissed her once beautiful hair, now graying and thinning, ruined by the medicine designed to save her life. "I'll go see how Dan's doing."

After Dan greeted all his toys and gifts, he hopped on the couch and cuddled with me. Silently, sadly, we watched the Christmas parade pass by on TV.

Long after the toys are broken, the candy eaten, and the gifts forgotten, I would like to think that Daniel will remember his mother with her beautiful thick dark hair, sparkling hazel eyes, and her warm engulfing smile. I hope he will remember his mother this way, laughing at the dinner table on Christmas Eve. For his life, I wish Dan this Christmas memory.

WITHOUT YOU

Carol Tufts

The perfect circles of your absence flow
outward from my proficient heart,
though who would know as you would
not know me, too many years beyond
you now, the future's fleshy ghost.
Those teasing nights we meet,
you are, mercifully, as you were
before the cancer leached it all away,
bleeding out the humdrum
trust we had in time, the lavish rooms
warm with bittersweet and windfall apples,
the burnished light pouring from our evening
windows into the darkening road
where our muffled children recede
like stillborn expectation
through all the fecund nights
we never had.
    And I've tried
to live as you had me promise,
to embrace contingency
for the whole green world it is,
as it was also once the unthought
order of that foreclosed life
where death sidled in,
his old reliable self.

ALTERED LANDSCAPES

Hazel C. King

The world as I knew it ended more than two years ago, during the frozen landscape of winter, when my forty-seven-year old husband slipped on a patch of ice and broke his leg.

Disturbing, but not disastrous, we thought. Some pain, dulled by medication; some time off work, compensable; some inconvenience in wearing a cast, the therapy to regain full use, we thought. Unfortunate, but not tragic. Or so it seemed, until an unsuspected blood clot broke loose from the injured leg and traveled to his lungs. And life as I knew it was over.

There are no words to express how the children and I felt. I functioned only because I didn't—couldn't—believe my husband was really gone. How do you plan a funeral for a man when you just cooked his breakfast? How do you comfort your children when their father is gone?

For months, the three of us slept together on the pull-out sofa bed in the living room, unable to bear the idea of going into separate rooms, alone—to sleep? We clung together, truly aware for the first time of how fragile life is, how precious each moment with those we love.

I kept going to work, and the children kept going to school. On the surface, life appeared normal. The reality was that we no longer knew what normal was. Normal was having a family of four, not three. Life with Daddy was normal, something we took for granted. Life without Daddy was like moving to a foreign country where we didn't speak the language, couldn't count the money. It was incomprehensible.

Each family has its own daily rituals that give life its rhythm and continuity. My husband's death ripped the fabric of our lives into fragments. While logic told me it was essential to develop new patterns to life, I found it all but impossible. It became routine for us to have no routine. Meals, as well as sleep, were disrupted. Putting food on the table required major effort; then, none of us wanted to sit at a table where Daddy's chair was empty. The familiar landscape of our lives was irrevocably altered.

Even now, after all this time, we still flounder. The dynamics of the family, as well as the details, are different now. My relationship to the children, and theirs to me, is not the same as it was when there were two parents in the home. Now, the lines between parent and child seem more horizontal than vertical. They depend on me; I depend on them. It is the three of us against the world.

Several months after the loss of my husband, I was diagnosed with breast cancer. That is another story in itself, but because of the timing, it is also an inextricable part of this story. Each event was a catastrophe in its own right; each made the other worse. If I hadn't had to deal with cancer, perhaps my grief would have been easier to bear. If I hadn't lost my husband, perhaps I could better have handled the cancer diagnosis.

My facade of control crumbled then. The anger I had been unable to express exploded in outrage that this was allowed to happen. Where was God when I needed Him? Could He be so cruel as to take me from my children as well? And why had He taken my husband, when I needed him now more than ever?

Predominant emotions were grief, rage, and terror in equal amounts. I grieved the loss of my husband, grieved for my children's loss, and grieved the loss of my health. The faith I had grown up with was tested as I walked through the valley of the shadow of death. I did, indeed, fear evil. There was no rod and staff to comfort me, no goodness and mercy. I walked through a bleak and lonely landscape, fearful that my children would lose both parents.

After surgery to remove the cancer, my body itself became unfamiliar. So much had changed in so short a time. I was no longer a wife; I was a widow. I was no longer just a mother, but a single parent. Now, I was also that most pitied of victims, a cancer patient. The future, if I had one, looked grim indeed.

The love and support of my family and friends helped carry me through the surgery and chemotherapy treatments. Yet it was my husband's support I craved. I needed his acceptance of me in order to accept myself. Would he—could he—have accepted the change in my body and love me still? It is something I shall never know for sure.

It was during that bad time that I asked my neighbors, gifted with landscaping, to "adopt" my yard. Instinct told me I needed to focus on something related to life and living, rather than cancer and death. The flowers and trees they planted were like an investment in the future, a promise that life would go on. I took comfort from the earth itself, the unending succession of seasons. Along with the flowers, my neighbors helped me plant seeds of hope for the future.

Fast forward a year or so past the end of chemotherapy. I am doing the spring cleaning for the first time in several springs. The magnitude of the task daunts me. How, why, did we manage to accumulate so many things? I clean and sort, deciding what to keep, give away, or discard.

My husband's clothes are put into boxes and placed in the storage building. When it was built, a few months before his death, we could not know that it would become a shrine to his memory, filled with the things that belonged to him. The children and I are selfish; we cannot bear to give away anything that was a part of him. Except for our memories, it is all we have left.

I keep a few things in the bedroom, a few shirts in the closet, small things in a drawer. An almost empty bottle of aftershave lotion is a pungent reminder. I open the lid and close my eyes, breathing my husband's aroma, imagining him near enough to hug.

Then I close the lid, trying to save what is left of the scent. It is all I have. I don't want it to disappear, as he did.

Once I am into the cleaning, I see other things that need to be done. A new hardwood floor is laid in the kitchen, bringing tears and self-doubt. Did I do the right thing? Why didn't I select the lighter finish to match the countertops my husband installed, rather than the darker finish? I weep nearly all day, convincing the floor installer and myself that I am an unstable woman, incapable of making a sound decision.

A call to my counselor helps. She points out that this is the first major change in the house since my husband died. My emotions sense it is a step farther away from him, from the time we were together. Besides, it is hard to make decisions alone.

"What do you think your husband would say about the floor?" the counselor asks.

I think a minute. "He would probably tell me to get a grip," I say, smiling despite my tears. "He was never one to agonize over decisions. If you don't like it, change it, he would say, but don't worry about it."

A few days later, the emotional storm is spent, and someone asks me how I like the new floor. I love it, I say, and it is the truth.

One thing leads to another. I decide to redecorate the kitchen in a southern-plantation theme, featuring the use of magnolias. When it is finished, I can visualize how well this new look will blend with Christmas decorations. It has been a long time since I felt anticipation, but I recognize it. It is a tiny step forward, toward emotional healing.

The new floors emphasize the need for repainting all the rooms. No interior painting has been done since before we moved in nearly thirteen years ago. Several years after that, my husband installed paneling and wallpaper in the living room and kitchen. The living room is fine, but the kitchen walls wear stains from the years of meals we shared together. The wallpaper needs to be replaced, but the children and I cannot bear to take it down. We compromise by painting over it.

I tell the children that Daddy's wallpaper is still there, beneath the paint, but we know it isn't the same. Nothing is the same. No longer can I ask my husband's advice on what to do. He is no longer here to validate my choices. It is up to me now. It is all up to me.

The half-bath off the bedroom is small, with no cabinet for storage. I buy a small lavatory and medicine cabinet, then add rugs, curtains, towels, and other accessories. The theme I have chosen is a flower garden, with birds and butterflies. I use things I have that fit the theme: a bird house music box, a grapevine wreath with a tiny bird, and small figurines. A final touch is a scene of country flower gardens so inviting I want to step right into the picture. I am pleased with the result and want to show it to my husband, then remember I can't. When will I stop looking for him in every room, stop wanting to share every detail of my life with him?

It occurs to me that I am not only redecorating the house, but redesigning my life. I am arranging my living space to suit my own tastes, without the need to consider another's opinion. Since the children aren't much interested in how the house looks, I am free to create an environment that will please my eye and nurture my spirit. Perhaps I hope that bringing new order and beauty to my surroundings will restore serenity to my soul.

I look at what I have done so far and realize that I cannot picture my husband in these surroundings. The decor is too feminine, too frilly, to accommodate his masculine stride that would leave bric-a-brac broken. He would have little patience with having to maneuver by the antique table placed in the hallway outside our bedroom door. The glassware collection it displays would not long survive his entrances and exits.

Somehow, the changes in the house emphasize the true finality of his death. Without the signs of his presence, I miss my husband anew, miss even the wet towels and dirty socks he always left for me to pick up. His absence is enormous, filling the house.

I look at this house and see I am a woman alone. It is a woman's house, filled with a woman's things. It is the landscape of my present, with little to indicate the past. It is where I must create a refuge for my children and where I must come to terms with being alone.

In spite of everything that has happened, life has moved on and so have I. In spite of everything, I am here to chart the growth of the trees and to watch the flowers bloom in another spring. I have struggled against adversity and grief and have lived to tell the story. With every new day, every small step forward, I am building the landscape of my future.

It is still a work in progress.

REARRANGEMENT

Maureen Cannon

After a "decent interval" (they'd checked
the calendar), they urged her to begin
To rearrange her life. How circumspect
They were, and kind. But every discipline
Eluded her until at last so did
The faces of her grief. He'd given shape
And substance to her days. As he would bid,
She'd lived, obedient. But now escape
From patterns was—she saw it—wise. Leave tears
To Sunday daughters, sorrowing. How dead
He was, beloved ghost, and she with years
Stretched, endless and mysterious, ahead.
She vowed to like her solitary bed,
To seek a need, to flee the bleak excess
Of empty hours and of idleness.
Eventually she'd learn to answer "Yes"
To widowhood, she thought. No longer wife,
But woman still, she—rearranged her life.

JOURNEY

Nancy B. Schmitt

Never are the complex, intimate spaces shared with a spouse more visible than when they are gone. And gone they were for me in a matter of four hours one August Saturday afternoon while our two youngest children and I went to a movie, shopped for school clothes, and picked up pictures from a daughter's wedding the week before. We would find out later, as we suspected, that a heart attack had taken his life in moments while we were gone—no warning, no preparation, no good-byes.

All the intervals from the arrival of the police, ambulance, neighbors, friends, in-laws, and priest through to the last good-bye five days later to out-of-town relatives were a blur of stunned emotions, decisions, and rituals. His death left a void in so many lives, especially for our his-mine-ours family (two plus two plus one). Day-to-day challenges for acceptance and healing were most immediate for me and our youngest children still at home; Amanda, fifteen, and Kelly, six.

DAY 5

Incredibly unbelievable that I could dissolve over a blank check in your wallet—a stupid blank check—a living, breathing thing to me, not a reminder of death. To my regret and horror I found a donation card for your eyes, a fact you never shared with me, nor did anyone ever ask, I might add.

Kelly is whimpering in her sleep. I have all kinds of reading materials explaining death to children, but nothing about the after-effects.

Although I am sleeping through the night pretty well, I am getting up with such emotional pain that it takes hours for it to subside. Only a week ago—one absolutely unbelievable week since you were alive one moment and then dead.

Kelly: "You're still wearing your marriage rings."
Me: "Yes, because I want to remember your daddy."
Kelly: "Will you get married again?"
Me: "No, it's going to be just you and me and Amanda here in the house."

Kelly: "Oh, I think I understand this. I just have one parent."

Kelly: "I think I know why my daddy died. God decided that he had lived long enough."

Kelly: "I wish we had been here the other day so we could have helped my daddy."

Kelly: "I'm lonely."

DAY 21
Today was full of the booby traps of little things that identified you: a coupon for your deodorant, your special shoe catalogue, the page ripped from the word calendar for your birthday this year.

Amanda seems angry and upset as I talk about changing things because it appears to her that I am totally removing you from the house. I must watch that I do not tread too hard on all that is here and familiar and comforting for the kids.

DAY 30
Today I placed the order for a grave marker and I talked a blue streak to the salesman because it helped just to talk about death and rituals and what gets one through the process.

DAY 34
Somehow I can't seem to shake the vision of your body here in the family room and the questions. Why did your body stop working that day? Why at home and not in your car or in the yard or some other place? Did you know you had a heart problem or did you keep thinking it was your stomach? Did you feel the heart attack or did you just pass out? Were you perhaps headed for the couch because you didn't feel well? Did you know we loved you very, very much?

DAY 98
Wednesday I go back in the hospital, as I did two years ago, for a biopsy and frightening wait for the results which could range from pre-cancerous cells, as before, to cancer as the pap smear indicates is probable. I hurt because you are not there to hold me and tease me and love me through this horror.

DAY 103
I saw no need to protest when the decision was made to have Thanksgiving dinner at a local inn because I understood the rationale.

But it was too stiff and artificial a way to avoid the pain of your absence. It was just too antiseptic not having leftovers and dirty dishes and people in easy chairs napping or watching football. No matter what happens next year, we are staying home.

DAY 120

I know you feel nothing, yet I think of how cold that cemetery must be, how chilled you would be if you were alive this wintry day. Oh, God, I miss you; all the good and bad and in-between. I trusted you enough to make dreams and ambitions come alive. You only saw beginnings. I cannot imagine what is ahead as those moments mature for all of us.

Feelings of abandonment creep in now and then, and they are tricky. In the beginning I had all kinds of people around to talk to, who expected and were willing to talk about how it happened, how the children and I felt. But what about the months down the line? The Wednesdays or Saturdays when I am crying my heart out because something on TV triggered a memory or a glance at a picture brings it all back? Now and then, I insert into conversations that I'm having a bad time, but I hate to burden people. In the end, even with caring children, friends, and relatives, there is a gap no one can fill.

DAY 193

Little things tear at me, like two cabbage cores in the sink from the first cabbage I've cut up since Greg died, cores I would have put on a paper towel for him to munch on. I cry when those things happen—not the gut-wrenching tears of six months ago, but tears of realized loss and fear and unanswerable questions, tears because so much disappears as the people in my life die. Sometimes my life seems stopped in piles of memories, photographs, and obituary clippings.

DAY 239

There was a time in my life when missing someone was so much a generality, but these days it is as specific as a grey cardigan or a very hairy chest or gentleness from a man who craved peace even when he was hurt or angry. I hurt because the taxes are mine and the laundry, the meals, the yard, everything. Funny, but I think I was able to be more self-centered married than I can be as a widow.

DAY 342

Lonely is taking my diabetic daughter to the hospital for the second time in one day and my best friend is away and my brother-in-law and sister-in-law are out for the evening and my mother's phone in California is covered by an answering machine.

Lonely is handling an emergency with a seven-and-a-half-year-old as my companion while my other daughter's doctor is on vacation causing me to deal with two unknown doctors in one day, and "Amazing Grace" plays on the radio in the wee hours of the morning, evoking the funeral once more.

DAY 365
One year—365 days, days I wasn't sure I could survive, but they are behind us now. I don't feel emotional at this particular moment, just tired, lonely, edgy.

DAY ONE YEAR + 20
It has been a weepy kind of week. I have cried a lot.

DAY ONE YEAR + 85
I am so aware of an aloneness hard to describe. Sometimes it is the peaceful recognition of the right to have a messy house along with children who breed as many or more messes. Sometimes it is the wrench of tears and the ache all over because a cat cannot talk to me at midnight.

Sometimes it's looking around at a group of friends who are married and content and whole, who would like to understand but can't. Sometimes it's the hours it takes to go to sleep because the bed is too big for me. Sometimes it's how the word "widow" still makes me wince in surprise and pain.

DAY ONE YEAR + 134
Is the grief work ever over? Sometimes I think the answer is an emphatic "No, never." Sometimes I think that nothing and no one can ever erase the pain my children and I have inside us.

Having had very little time as an adult without some significant connection to a man, I found it unsettling at times to be totally self-motivated and directed. I missed having a sounding board, supporter, critic, lover.

Probably the most vulnerable time was about a year after I became a widow. In the process of emerging from the deepest grief, I started to fantasize about the future. Perhaps because of the old patterns bred in the fifties and my widow's loneliness, my first full-blown thoughts were about being connected again with a man and that felt good.

To my surprise, however, other thoughts started to displace these romantic reveries. Moving ever so slightly away from a sense of panic at being alone, as in single woman/mother with no romantic male relationships, I began to pull out of moth balls a few dreams that still had merit and challenge. Shoved aside because they were rolling around in my head as real possibilities from the almost forgotten list of things I always wanted to do, if only . . . .

Evolution to renewed wholeness continues with each new day, each new risk, each memory. I loved well and hard and so have I grieved. I continue my journey.

NOVEMBER

Nancy Wambach

David would have wanted it this way. At least it seemed so at the time. Maybe I could preserve at least one tradition, show the kids we were still a family, only smaller now.

Every other Christmas since Peter and Nicole were toddlers, we'd driven to the mountain, slogged through the mud and needles, and chopped down our own tree.

On Thanksgiving morning, I awoke at 3:00 A.M., a regular occurrence since David's death. It had become my habit to lie there until dawn, concocting horrific scenarios regarding my fate and that of my fatherless children, now thirteen and eleven. This morning, however, I rose and began to stuff a twenty-pound turkey. I chopped celery and cried over onions to make my grandmother's special sausage dressing; I decorated myself with flour while blending in shortening for David's favorite pumpkin pie crust. Intermittently, when the nausea and fatigue that take residence in a grieving soul overtook me, I lay on the couch for a half hour or so. Then, with each new little burst of energy, I returned to the kitchen to peel potatoes and rutabagas, stir gravy, whip cream.

By 3:00 P.M., my face was flushed, my blouse was stained with the components of most of our menu, the table bore enough food for a Shriner's convention, and dinner was served. I hacked a few hunks off the turkey in the kitchen to avoid any awkward moments of realization that none of us had any idea how to carve.

We sat silent and grim, slicing and chewing dutifully, averting our eyes from the empty fourth chair. It seemed as good a time as any to broach the subject:

"What would you two think of going up on Sunday to get a tree?"

Nicole's fork made desultory swirls in her mashed potatoes. "Would we have to get up early? If we do, forget it."

Since her father's death six months earlier, she seemed to spend more hours each day asleep than awake. The circles under her eyes frightened me.

"No, not too early, hon. I just thought it would be nice, you know, something we could do together. What do you think, Peter?"

"I guess so, if you want to."

So it was settled. On a gray, drizzling Sunday morning after Thanksgiving, we piled into the family station wagon. I tested the windshield wipers to prepare for a torrent and couldn't help flinching a little at each assault of rain needles brailling the glass.

We started the long climb into the Santa Cruz Mountains. Nicole leaned against the door and stared out the window. Peter, upright and alert, watched for oncoming traffic, for any indication that the vulnerable family vehicle might be broadsided by a drunken maniac.

"Careful, Mom. Watch that guy on the right."

His fears about the wagon's frailty, at least, were probably groundless. It was a sturdy Ford, built and purchased in more optimistic days, and it rolled along the highway cradling its precious cargo, like a giant, surprisingly graceful beast. The steel-belted Michelin tires David had always insisted on carried it smoothly over bumps and ruts. ("Never, ever skimp where safety is concerned, honey. Remember that when you're on your own.")

I deliberately rested my tongue on my bottom lip to stop gritting my teeth.

"Uh, kids, does anyone remember how to get there?"

"Not me."

"Not me."

"There it is, Mom."

"No, I don't think so. It's further up."

"Wasn't it called Arrowhead Farms or something?"

"Loma Prieta, I think."

"That looks like it."

I'd always insisted that we return to the same farm year after year. Today they all looked identical to me, all peopled with happy, intact families.

Peter said, "Mom, I'm sure it was that one back there. I remember the little church across the street."

We pulled into a dirt driveway and emerged determined to complete our mission. We zipped up parkas and pulled gloves onto fingers already stiffening from the cold.

I'd always loved the scent of pine. Today it reminded me of the antiseptic cleaner used on the floor of David's hospital room.

"Your hat's in the box, Nicole."

"Oh, right, Mom. I'm really gonna wear a little kid's cap! Like that wouldn't be stupid beyond belief!"

"You always wear that cap, honey. You picked it out. You begged Daddy to buy it for you. Don't you remember?"

"How old was I? Six? Geez! That was like a million years ago! Anyway, my head's not cold. I'm not wearing it."

But she tucked the cap into her pocket anyway as she strode past me to catch up to her brother.

In stiff boots never worn more than once or twice a year, I tramped awkwardly through fudgy mud left by last night's rain.

A boy maybe sixteen years old squatted at the entrance, absently pulling sprigs of dead grass from the wet ground. He too sported a knit cap pulled over long, stringy hair; Peter nudged Nicole and whispered, "Hey, there's your twin. Dorky hat and all."

"Shut up, Buttface."

After grunting orders to cut only at the white line on any trunk, the seedy elf handed Peter a saw.

Rows and rows of trees and they all looked alike. Breathing hard, laboring to keep pace with my already-long-legged children, I began to doubt my memories of the not-so-distant past. Had I imagined it, that before my husband's illness, before the five years it took for him to die, I'd actually run two miles every day? Actually worried about cellulite and wrinkles? Did that really happen?

For a moment, I let my eyes linger upon the white line painted on each trunk. A whole forest of victims waiting to have their lives cut away just at the height of their beauty. They even made it easier for their murderers, directing, "Here! Cut here! Kill me here!"

It felt as if time had stopped for my little family.

In a couple of years, I'd actually be older than my husband ever would. If these present circumstances didn't kill me (a huge assumption, considering the way my heart lurched and kicked in my chest at times), perhaps someday I'd hold my grandchildren on my lap and show them the yellowed photos of a middle-aged man in outdated clothes and hairstyle.

I'd say, "This was your grandfather. I wish you could have known him. He would love you very much, as I do."

Maybe they'd play with the bulging veins on my wrinkled hands, stretch the folds of skin, look up at my white hair, at doting, filmy eyes, and try to imagine Grandma kissing this old-fashioned stranger.

"C'mon, Mom! We don't have forever!"

The children were now far ahead.

After a few cursory minutes of search and inspection, we agreed on a chubby fir with soft, tightly-clinging needles. Always before, I'd made a ceremony of encircling selected branches with my fingers and gliding them down the shaft—to check the tree for freshness.

At first, David balked at the logic of this. He'd say, "Honey, I can see how that might be important at a regular lot. After all, you don't know how long ago the tree was cut. But these are still growing! They're still alive. They have to be fresh!"

"I just like to do it. Am I hurting anyone?" I'd counter, and that would end it. I always had the final say about which tree we chose.

"Hey, Mom," Peter asked, "how tall is the living room ceiling?"

"I don't know. Why? You think the tree's too big?"

We stood on tiptoe next to it and tried to remember the height of the room. Why hadn't I thought of that before? Because David did.

We decided to risk it, and Peter set to work with the saw.

Nicole and I stood near, uncertain of our roles in this new circumstance, so we both touched the tree gingerly, in support.

Peter looked up, panting slightly from the unaccustomed exertion.

"Okay, Mom, about another quarter inch. Want to finish it?"

"Well, sure. All right." I'd never held a saw in my life before. But, by God, how hard could it be to slice a mere tree? I accepted the unwieldy, bow-like tool, with its arched wooden back and vicious steel points. In a determined frenzy, I pushed the saw back and forth against the solid trunk, feeling the teeth catch in the wood, watching the blade wobble.

Ping!

I straightened. "What the hell was that?"

"God, Mom, you broke the saw!" Nicole pressed her fingers to her forehead.

Peter sighed and shook his head in a mirror image of his father's familiar gesture.

"I knew it. I just knew it," I said to myself.

"Do I take a chance and let Mom use the saw, or do I just finish the job so we can get out of here?"

It seemed that, if I could just apply enough pressure on the little piece still gripping the trunk, I could separate it. I pushed my foot hard on the cut area. I tried to stand on it. Then I grabbed the top of the tree and tried to wrench it away. I ran in a slow, ungainly circle around the trunk, twisting the tree with me. I tried to cut some more, using just the maimed blade between two fingers. Finally I sliced an inch-long gash into my thumb.

"Goddamn son of a bitch!"

As I caught sight of my children's horrified faces, dizziness engulfed me again. I looked at the swinging broken blade, which by now resembled a fractured 1,000-year-old fossil of a shark's jaw, and carefully handed it to Nicole. Sliding down heavily on the muddy ground, I hugged my knees, lowered my head, and tried to take deep breaths. Droplets of blood stained my boot. I could smell sap bleeding from the tree.

People strode by, healthy saws in hand, inspecting with discriminating eyes the array of green merchandise. They gave wide birth to the row with the strange trio.

"C'mon, Mom, get up, okay? He was just being a butt," Nicole offered softly. She hissed at Peter, "Good one, idiot!"

Glaring at his sister, Peter said, "Look, Mom, it's no big deal. I'll just go ask the guy for another one. Try to get up, okay, Mom? C'mon. Please. People are looking."

He whispered to Nicole, "Take care of Mom. I'll be right back."

Nicole crouched beside me and inspected my finger.

"It's not too bad. You'll be okay."

She pulled the cap from her pocket.

"Here, hold this against it. He'll be back soon."

We sat in silence. Tentatively, she rubbed my arm.

Soon Peter arrived, triumphantly holding a new intact trophy aloft.

"I told him I broke it, Mom. He didn't even care. C'mon. Get up now. Okay?"

I wiped my nose on my sleeve and straightened my coat collar.

Clutching Nicole, I dragged myself up off the ground and wiped some mud off the seat of my pants. My finger wasn't bleeding much anymore.

Peter held out the new saw.

"Okay, Mom. Just put your hand on top of mine. We're gonna do this."

With two careful strokes, we sliced it clean and stood back as it softly, almost gracefully, fell. No snap or crash. What had been vibrant and healthy just minutes earlier now lay prone in the mud.

We dragged it to the pay booth and struggled together, ignored and unassisted by the entrance elf, to tie it to the car's roof with twine borrowed from the cashier.

Peter finally declared, "It'll hold as long as you take it easy, Mom. We can make it, I think. Let's go home."

That holiday season, the tree stood dark, heavy, and listing a bit to the right. Aside from opening gifts on Christmas morning, we rarely acknowledged its looming presence. We didn't show it off to friends who stopped by to see how the family was managing. Walking past the living room, I leveled my eyes forward and concentrated on my next step. But the three of us knew it was there. We'd put it there. And for that Christmas, the one we couldn't talk about for years, it would have to be enough.

SEASONS

Paula Porter

We buried you in the winter—
    Time frozen
    Emotions numb
    A chill settled on my heart.

Spring came—green and growing
    The ice jam thawed
    And pain gushed
    Flooding into my heart
    I mucked through living.

Summer brought a drought—shriveling up growth
    Scorching my tears
    A suffocating bitterness
    I sweltered in the intensity
    Of my oppressive loss.

And now autumn approaches
    I harvest my grief
    Gleaning a record yield
    My larder full
    Hoarding provisions because pain can't hibernate
During the long, lonely winter.

UNINVITED GUEST

Carol Malley

Susan had downed a Valium with two glasses of wine, grabbed a simplistic mystery that required no concentration, and headed into the living room. She needed help to do everything since he died.

She was staring at the blur of sentences on page eleven when the lights went out, the hum of the refrigerator stopped, and the hands of the clock froze at 3 A.M.

At first she thought it was a power outage, and took her time lighting a candle. The flicker of flame above her hand was the only light until she saw the beam of a flashlight glide across the kitchen floor. She heard something bump into the box of debris from her so-called life—five-year-old electric bills, old magazines and other mementos of daily existence—she planned to dump the next day.

"Damn." A male voice followed the clattering of the flashlight.

Only this morning, Susan had received a telephone call from a neighbor telling her of a resident three streets away who had been robbed while she slept. Susan had almost let the phone ring itself out. Now, she remembered the call.

"There's nothing you can take from me," Susan thought as she heard the burglar open a kitchen drawer.

"Who's there?" she demanded.

The absence of sound was the only answer. Susan paused until she heard captured breath being released by her intruder.

"I'm coming in there," she said loudly.

"No, don't!" was echoed back.

Susan entered the kitchen, and the light from her candle caught a skinny teenager in tattered jeans, clenching one of her butter knives in his left hand.

"What are you doing?" Susan demanded, sounding like the school teacher she used to be before taking leave from her job last year. She doubted she would be going back in September.

Susan didn't recognize the youth or his voice: "I was just looking for something." He wielded the butter knife at her.

"You don't have to threaten me. I don't care what you take."

"I wasn't threatening you," he said, a petulant child stamping his feet. "Who are you?"

"I asked first," Susan said.

"I'm a burglar, and you better step back." More waving of the butter knife.

"I'm Susan. My husband died eight months ago." Her autobiography in two sentences.

The boy carried an empty sack in his right hand.

"What did you do to my lights?"

"I turned them off. I didn't hurt your lights." He backed away toward the silent refrigerator.

Susan's uncombed hair stuck out at odd angles in the candlelight, making her look like a Halloween witch or a punk rock star, much older than thirty-seven. She reached out, her arm extended in silhouette as she grabbed the sleeve of the teenager's Patriots T-shirt.

"You're not going anywhere until you put the lights back on."

He dropped the sack onto the floor next to the flashlight, and pinched the blunt knife until it bit into his fingers.

"Let me go."

"Not until you put the lights back on. Pick up that flashlight, so we can see."

Susan marched the boy to the fuse box where she stood guard as he threw the switch. He jumped when the refrigerator hummed above.

"Who's there?" he whispered to her.

"It's just the refrigerator gobbling the electricity," she whispered back.

In the kitchen light once again, she noticed his fingers.

"You've cut yourself." She removed the knife from his hand and dropped it into the sink. He stood, wide-eyed, as she washed and patted his fingers dry with a paper towel.

"It's just a surface scratch," she said. "You'll live, but I think you need a new occupation."

"I gotta go now," he said, edging around her and running out the door.

"You forgot your sack," Susan called after him.

"You're crazy," carried in the breeze.

Putting away the sack, which would make a good book bag, Susan laughed for the first time in eight months.

TOMORROW AND TOMORROW AND TOMORROW

Phyllis Wax

Daughters, siblings, nephews, aunt,
we gather at the table
swallowing lumps
as someone else carves the turkey
  Hugged by your jacket while I shovel the driveway,
  I scatter salty drops which melt the ice
We lift our glasses for the kiddush
and start the Seder
straining to hear your voice
  Look, I want to say,
  a cardinal:
  listen
Flags fly on the greens
in Lake Park
but your clubs sit
cobwebbed in the garage
  A snatch of a Joplin rag,
  a phrase of Chopin,
  a soft suede cap,
  pizza, tapirs,
  songs around a campfire,

Herb's hospital room
   and I remember
  At commencement
  I must be proud
  enough for two
Each season I miss you
in a different way

LIVE AND LET LIVE
(Excerpted from *Grieving: A Love Story*)

Ruth Coughlin

There is to mourning a narcissism that borders on the pathological. At first, it is not as though you have a choice. It is not a question of whether to give in to it or not, for like an albatross with its beak pressed hard against your neck, this grief is just there. All-consuming, the desolation that hammers you can be perceived as wildly selfish and disrespectful of the world and people around you.

Someone calls to complain about his or her problems on the job, a glitch in a love affair, difficulty with a brother or sister, annoyance with the telephone company. It is true that whoever the someone is will recant, apologizing for griping "at a time like this," which is invariably what the someone always says. Just as invariably, I demur, assuring the beleaguered that there is no need for apology, that life goes on, that everything is relative, and that it's both important and maddening that the cable-television repairman didn't show up when he was supposed to.

I think about what "a time like this" means, and begin to realize that what I am doing is living with the ritual of everydayness and wondering how many people I am fooling. To imply that I am oblivious to the needs of others would be neither fair nor accurate, and it is true, too, that I often think how horrible it would be to see my friends go through this. But I am aware of how self-centered in this whirlpool of despair I have become. There are moments, for instance, when I would like to tell people that until you experience a loss this big, everything else is amateur night.

It is what I have come to call the dwarfing down of reality, the difference between an oak and a bonsai, the unassailable evidence that, compared to death and devastation, the rest of what passes for ordinary life is small change.

As off-track in my thinking as I may be, I try not, of course, to lash out at my friends and family; I am not that dumb. Without their love, I know that I would be in a padded room somewhere, mumbling to myself, telling my fellow inmates that I am Nefertiti or, maybe, Eleanor Roosevelt.

Instead, inanimate objects and strangers are occasionally treated to my outbursts.

Rage at the computer on which I work, Bill's computer, the one that never gave him a hint of trouble and is now in the habit of regularly devouring or scrambling my work. Fury at the copying machine that keeps jamming the paper; frustrated anger at the outside front door whose latch is broken.

Ten months after April 25, 1992, junk mail addressed to Bill continues to overflow the mailbox. I know about buying and selling mailing lists and about computers spewing forth old information; I know that most of this is unavoidable, but I would like not to be opening a "happy birthday" letter to Bill, printed in brightly colored ink, from life-and-accident insurance outfits.

It is the companies to whom I have, repeatedly, sent copies of the death certificate, along with detailed letters, that enrage me the most because they have not updated their information.

"Our records indicate that, even though you have a State Bar of Michigan credit card with $5,000 credit available," reads one form letter addressed to Bill from a purveyor of plastic, "if we do not hear from you by the end of next month, your credit card will expire and be closed. No replacement cards will be sent. We look forward to hearing from you. Yours sincerely."

Hell hath no fury like a widow, I say to myself, as I dial the 800 number, knowing, and not caring, that on the other end of the line will be some hapless clerk, the recipient of my wrath. I am trying to calm down as my thoughts short-circuit. What the hell do you know about expire? You think you can threaten a dead man? Go right ahead. You think you can threaten me? Just try it. Don't "yours sincerely" me with your stupid, money-grubbing solicitations. You want to know about closed, I'll tell you about closed.

I start out quietly and slowly, explaining that I have sent three copies of the death certificate and three accompanying letters to shut down Bill's account and that I have kept copies of my correspondence.

"We don't have any confirmation that your husband died," the woman tells me with authority and an infuriating dose of hostility. "But don't worry about it, the account's going to be closed anyway, since we haven't heard from anybody and it's past the deadline."

I can feel my body uncoil. I am a cobra about to strike, the venom in me throbbing to be released.

"Aren't you listening to me?" I begin to shout. "Believe me, I'm not worrying about it. The account was closed, it's been closed for ten months. Do you think it's any fun for me to keep getting these letters?"

"I'm sure it isn't, ma'am," responds the woman in her best bureau-cratese, using the one form of address I truly detest. "And it isn't my fault, either," she adds, an altogether unnecessary fillip.

I know it isn't, just as I know that I am sounding like a person calling from an asylum. This woman has to be wondering where I'm calling from, thinking they've locked me up and thrown away the keys, and that somehow I have escaped my cell to find a telephone booth.

"Just take his name out of the computer, okay?" I say through clenched teeth. I do not apologize, neither do I say good-bye. I simply place the receiver back in its cradle, amazed that I have managed to restrain myself from slamming down the phone.

I am ashamed of myself, and then I have an awful thought: my God, what if the woman I just hung up on is also a widow? Couldn't be, I reason. We widows understand one another; it's there in our eyes and in our voices. We are a community. We know the shame of being a widow, the person who survived, the one who couldn't save her husband, the woman who has to carry on alone but doesn't know why. Or how. A widow would never be pitiless to one of her kind.

I remember a party I attended not long ago when the hostess brought me across the room to meet another woman. "I have to introduce you two," she says, good intentions evident in her demeanor. "I just know you two have a lot in common and you'll have lots to talk about," she goes on, pausing for effect. "You're both young, recent widows." As soon as she says this, I can see she wishes she had never entertained the idea of introducing us, and my heart goes out to her. But the words are said, they have escaped her lips, and there they hang, floating in midair with nowhere to go.

For several moments this other woman and I are stunned into silence, able only to stare blankly, first at our hostess, then at each other, both of us frozen in time. There is no time to frame an answer.

Neither of us knows what to say, but somehow this painful silence has to be ended.

"How long?" I ask.

"Fourteen months," she answers. "You?"

"Nine."

We have exchanged six words, but each one is weighted with an absolute understanding. For the moment, there is nothing more to say; our six words and our eyes have said it all. Awkwardly we move away from each other to other parts of the house, other people, later to meet again. But for this small blip in time we have confirmed what we already know; in the fellowship of widows, shared experience is worth a thousand words.

"What about resentment and bitterness?" someone asks me. "Aren't you furious with Bill that he died, that he abandoned you, that he left you to pick up the pieces?"

Within me, I can feel something snap.

"Have you gone and lost your mind?" I ask, my voice high, squeaky, quavering, knowing that more than just a few people feel it is I who am losing my mind. "How can I be angry with him? I wasn't the one who was sick, I wasn't the one who was dying." I go on. "Nobody deserves to suffer like Bill did, except for maybe Ted Bundy, and even he didn't suffer like that. And, by the way, what are you implying? Do you think he chose to die and leave me?"

One night in a restaurant I see a couple seated across the room from me. They are both easily in their eighties, wrinkled as raisins, merrily downing Manhattans and smoking cigarette after cigarette after cigarette.

I cannot see what they have ordered for dinner, but I allow my imagination to picture that when their food arrives it will be a T-bone steak and a giant baked potato with butter and sour cream, and that when it comes time for dessert, each will no doubt ask for an artery-clogging confection, maybe a chocolate sundae with whipped cream and walnuts. Or maybe cheesecake.

My anger that they are alive and Bill is not is at first enormous. I cannot bring my attention back to the book I have brought along with me, but as my rage subsides somewhat, I remember Bill's description each time we'd find ourselves on our way to and from the Keys, in the Miami airport: "God's waiting room," he'd always say, not unkindly, as we watched middle-aged children help their parents with their walkers and wheelchairs. There was no malice in his observation, it was more a reflection of his fear of growing feeble and helpless.

"I guess it's about time for me to take hang-gliding lessons," he'd also say, right after his father and my father died, old men suffering the indignity of old men's deaths, again a not-so-subtle nod to the fact that becoming diminished and without control were two prospects he would rather not think about.

As it happened, he became both, though he managed to hang on to his dignity. He did not have the chance to grow old.

Now, as I regard this elderly couple in the restaurant, I admonish myself severely for being resentful about them. They are, actually, quite adorable, two people who seem to be having a grand old time.

Live and let live, I silently say to myself, repeating the phrase like a mantra.

Live and let live. I suppose at least I should try.

DEATH HURTS

Nancy B. Schmitt

The hurt begins inside
Where it twists all around
The memories of the moments
And days and weeks just before.
It moves on to the towels
And combs and shoes and sweaters
That belong to no one anymore.
It travels to the times you want
To hug or talk or eat together,
Remembering with a jolt
That your we is you alone.
It weaves into each new moment
Of living alone as you move about
Looking whole and feeling shattered.
It lingers with each birthday
And special song and evening alone.
It fades a little as you stop to look at
A glorious sunset or hug a special friend
Or think of loving someone again.

REFURNISHING

Diane Quintrall Lewis

This September day,
my day of sadness,

I don't want to go inside.
He's been gone one year.

I mourn him and
pieces of myself.

A friend brings books.
My eyes burn.

Others bring food, flowers, advice, touch.
Their fear.

These two line stanzas mean
yin and yang in everything.

Man and wife shall be as one
like the moon reflects the sun.

The unbelief of my husband's death
lingers though I eat and sleep alone.

Reading Lady Nijo taught me
to wipe my tears on my sleeves

but the weather is too warm for sleeves.
I put tissues in every room.

I drop rose petals in the corner
of the living room, mint

leaves in the bathroom sink,
grind lemon rind in the disposal.

I leave the bedroom window open for
sun, wind, bird song, rain.

Chapter Five
Composting

The same leaves over and over again!
They fall from giving shade above
To make one texture of faded brown
And fit the earth like a leather glove.

Before the leaves can mount again
To fill the trees with another shade,
They must go down past things coming up
They must go down into the dark decayed.

They must be pierced by flowers and put
Beneath the feet of dancing flowers.
However it is in some other world
I know that this is the way in ours.

—Robert Frost

There are so many layers to our grief. It is very much like the garden compost pile. Recycling in this way is vital to the healthy functioning of our garden. The compost pile is not meant to be the focus of attention. It is not the part of our garden we pridefully show the ladies of the local guild. But it is perhaps the most important part of our garden because it serves as the foundation from which all seeds grow. Our grief must also be composted.

Rich with nurturing materials—potassium, nitrogen, potash—the compost contains within its hot, deceptively active stillness the central ingredients for new life. Composting is a process of basic transformation of elements into a form that can be assimilated. Yet, look closer and you will see that microorganisms find a habitat there. Small life forms are born and die to further enrich the compost. New life is always coming and going within the compost pile even before the final product emerges.

This necessary work takes time. We keep it covered and dark so it can ferment. From time to time we turn it, and turn it again. We cover it. And let it be. It needs to sit. It creates its own heat. It breaks down. It transforms. It is active in a deeply dark and quiet way. This cycle is essential for new life.

Step outside the garden and you will find natural compost in the forest where leaves die, fall, mount up, and decay. If you dig down under the roots of the oak, you will find the moist, fertile, warm smell of earth, rich and thick, as leaves rot, break apart, decompose. This is essential for healthy growth in the cycle of the tree's life. Tiny pale sprouts work their way up and through the protective detritus to the light.

These stories then, as compost, speak of the many layers of our grief—uncomfortable things, painful things, things not displayed in the front of our garden. Most are not pretty or uplifting stories. They speak of much travail. They are often private. Composting stories reveal not our triumphs, but our stumbles. They describe hard, hurtful truths about the inner journey. But these stories also contain the ingredients of transformation that deep composting provide—the essential elements for new life. They tell how we break down, sift through all that has come until now, all that we must revisit as long as we need to work through it—the dying, the aches, the despair.

Read these stories, then, and understand their richness and beauty as a necessary compost. And perhaps in reading these stories you'll see how they are really hopeful. In them is the transformation from which sprout seedlings of new life, ever seeking the light.

OUT OF TIME

Bobbie Chalmers

Now that you are no longer to be seen,
to be touched and tasted,
my senses quiver.

In the clearing of the present
I raise my face to the air, to scents
of earth and wind.

It is not fear or memory that stirs
but moments out of time and space,
places where you live

that cannot be mapped or dated
but are marked by moisture,
qualities of light.

A scooter purrs on asphalt heat,
and I feel you in my thighs,
my cheek to your back.

Morning light, the clouds just so,
and we walk, we read to Mozart,
just hanging out.

It's the nothingness of our days together
that I miss the most, the simply doing nothing.

Soon the light, a smell, a glance, a sound
will pull me irresistibly. Shot
through the heart.

WIDOW BUSINESS

Victoria Sullivan

I live now in the heartland of the far north country.
Even my bones are chill. My heart is a stone.
In this place no one dies. But no one
is alive either. All the birds are black.
Sleep is only occasional and friends don't know
what to say. When they ask me how I'm doing,
they pause awkwardly, waiting for the lie
or the banal truth that I feel nothing much,
but that, yes, I'm eating and my belly has grown slack
with overly sweet foods and stillness.

It is summer and hot, even in the north country,
and the worst that I suffer here is
bad breath and a lack of meaning.
I never want to get up any more when morning
comes. The soft alarm chirp dins in a vacuum.
Get up for what? Another visit to the lawyer
in his neat suit and tie and plastic face?

More papers to sign? I remember signing for his ashes
at the funeral home. Heavy in the bag, they weighed
my heart like stone. I had to go directly to bed
—the day sultry like death—at five in the afternoon.

It's morning. I want to sleep and sleep in those sticky
meaningless hours, like all the meaningless hours,
only in these the bed actually beckons seductively:
sleep, sleep. Someone once said there was a bed
in all my poems. But that was back
when I had a husband.

AFRICAN MEDITATION

Jane-Ellen Tibbals

The time is now June 1996, two-and-a-half years after the senseless murder of my beloved. I sit, sweaty-palmed, on a rocky cliff 100 meters above the roaring rapids of the Victoria Falls gorge in Zimbabwe, a 150 million year old fault eroded into its present shape. Perhaps some things are timeless. Afraid of heights, looking into those depths below, I feel cold chills through me. But I have a mission to accomplish. I have come half a world away to mingle some remnants of my Donald's body with one of the mightiest natural forces in the world, a place he longed to see and never did. Truly an adventurer and lover of the natural world, he would get a chuckle out of this last freefall over these awesome cataracts.

I gather a handful of bone fragments (much chunkier than I expected) and fling them as far as I can, holding my breath, half expecting some force to carry me out and down as well. They disappear quickly into the clouds of spray billowing from below. "Fly away, o wondrous spirit, haunter of my dreams, fulfiller of my yearnings."

Donald didn't expect to die so young. Though he had made a will with cremation instructions, he indicated no burial sites or disbursal. That became my job, my choice, and my sorrowful mission. Some of his remains lie buried under a favorite redwood tree on our mountain property. Some have co-mingled with the stream that flows year-round beside the redwood path of our daily hikes. The ones I brought to Africa were for me as well. My years of longing to be here and to share this experience with him had to be in a different dimension. We had put off our dream too long.

And so, as I watch this finality of his material existence disperse into the elements, I think back on the many parts of my life—my ten wonderful, frustrating, joyful, and always interesting years with this man of my dreams. I think of that day such a short time ago, and yet so long, when a phone call exploded the world as I knew it. I think of my lifelong fascination with this continent and all the emotions that have pulled me here at last. And I think of death—how it has reshaped my own life and what it means in a world perspective.

I believe I was born wanting to go to Africa, and so in this summer of '96 as the 747 British Airways jet touched down at Harare International Airport in Zimbabwe, after twenty-two hours in the air, many thoughts went through my head. *What will I find here? Will*

Africa's call be satisfied by this one-month sojourn? Will I find answers to death, a frame for the unfinished picture of my life that was bludgeoned beyond recognition when my man, my life partner, died with eight bullets in his body two-and-a-half years ago? Will Donald be with me on this trip, delighting in the animals, the rugged outdoor camping, the gorilla trekking, that also had called to him? Some of these questions would be answered in the next four weeks. Some have remained to haunt me as I write, and continue to read and think about Africa.

This journey had actually started eight months before when I received a circular in the mail about an African adventure information night, sponsored by the local junior college. But to go to Africa alone . . . I had become used to short week trips by myself, but a whole month, without a buddy to share these experiences . . . But when I queried interest in my grief support group, my friend and fellow "widow" eagerly wished to accompany me. Eight months, and much research and logistical planning later, here we were, two women in mid-life, searching for answers and experiences that would give meaning to life once again and awaken a passion, a spark that seemed to have died with our mates.

What is this call of Africa to me? Is it just the exotic endangered animals we run the risk of losing forever, or is it the magnetism of a primitive, unpolished continent; a continent where the veneer of civilization has been stripped away, where death is a daily occurrence, where permanence doesn't exist, where the records of man are written in sand and in water, not as the stones and monuments of Europe and Asia. Man's marks are evanescent in Africa. Even the marks of death do not remain for long. Bodies are not counted. The names of deceased are not recorded except in the hearts and minds of those left behind.

I have lived closely with death for five years. I have experienced the aftermath of a life transformed by a single senseless act of violence and murder. How do people live with this on a daily basis? The scourges of Idi Amin, whose actions brought to international attention pictures of corpses lying in public places, mutilated, torn, dismembered. The Hutus and Tutsis tribal wars in tiny Rwanda left close to a million people dead in 1994. Only weeks before I arrived, a public transport ferry sank with 1500 people on board, overloaded beyond the legal limit and in spite of the captain's warning. Most drowned; they simply couldn't swim.

I saw Africa through eyes and a heart awakened to the horrors of murder, of loss. Africa is a continent where my single loss is magnified and multiplied exponentially every day. When death becomes commonplace, is it easier to put in perspective? Does it provide a certain freedom—freedom from the fear of death? Does one accept it as a normal part of everyday life? Is that how they survive? How else do these thousands of families, ripped apart by wars, famines, and displacement, go on? How do they manage such loss?

As I travel through Zimbabwe and East Africa, I watch and listen and hear the tales of a people whose consciousness is attuned to survival, the here and now, food on the table today. There may be no tomorrow. It is only today that matters. The Buddhists teach us this as well. It is only what we do and are and experience now, in the moment, that has meaning. All parts of life are accepted, even death because it is part of a whole; of a never-ending process. We hear stories of the native who is put in jail and dies because he has no concept of tomorrow's freedom and life today is intolerable.

At home ruminating on this month of exposure to other cultures so diverse, I try to find the perspective that leads to meaning and understanding. My own experiences with death made it a deeper, richer, more sensitive journey; a journey into the depths of my being as well as a journey of sights, sounds, smells, and tastes. Donald was with me in many moments; in dreams, in meditations on the deck of a Lake Victoria ferry overnight ride, and in a tented camp on the outskirts of the Serengeti, listening to night sounds of the baboon, elephant, and lion. I could hear his hearty, ready laugh; I could see his childlike enthusiasm as we crawled on hands and knees through the jungle growth to find the gentle gorillas, much as he had teased and laughed at me over my apprehension at meeting with wild boar on our hikes in Hawaii.

Many times each day, in Africa, as in my home in America, my thoughts turn to this man who has left me. Life is truly tenuous no matter where you live on the planet. Don and I learned that the hard way and too soon in life. We truly believed we had decades to love and to explore the world together. When in fact, we had only that day; that time; that moment, to choose a life of love and reverence and joy. This is what remains for me today; this choice, though now alone, is still mine.

SOMEWHERE LESS ALONE

Nancy B. Schmitt

Twenty-five people
Are seated around me
In this chic fast food place
And all I feel
Is the need to
Cry gut-wrenching
Tears and be held
Against the pain
I feel now that
Time is my own
And I really know
You are dead,
And the people
Around me eat and
Talk and laugh
And I must find
Somewhere less alone.

MISSING

Phyllis Wax

They've all been thrown away,
the clothes you wouldn't replace,
foreseeing the future as a locked door
you'd never be able to open

I didn't have the heart to buy anything either.
It seemed indelicate. Even now
as I keep losing earrings
I trace and retrace my steps,
looking. It feels unfaithful
to think about new ones

I sit in semidarkness
in a house where each night
lights flash and burn out
one by one

Finally I rise and walk from room to room
screwing in new bulbs,
half expecting the light to help me find you

IN THE MOMENT
(excerpted from *Geography of the Heart*)

Fenton Johnson

I love better now, more wholly and completely, not because I have learned some exotic technique but because I know death.

I am in France, driving Larry south and west from Tours, along the banks of the Loire. Two days later he will be dead, impossible to believe then or now, but in this moment we are driving, we are fleeing south and west, to Nantes, the Atlantic, the Gironde, the Pyrenees, Spain, Morocco, we will run as far as we can, as far as it takes. The Loire flows on our left, a broad, silvered ribbon reflecting the towering pastels of this Fragonard sky. On our right yellowing poplars shiver behind limestone-walled villages and ornate chateaux.

I drive until I am blinded by tears—Larry is so quiet, so ill. Under the crenellated medieval towers of Langeais I stop the car and turn to him.

"Are you in pain?"

"No."

"We could turn back."

He presses his finger to my lips. "I'm happy being quiet here with you."

This is what I am trying to learn, the lesson Larry was teaching: the sufficiency and necessity of being quiet here with you.

But we have no choice but to cross that river, to turn and head back. Life takes the shape of an hourglass: focusing down, past and future falling away until there is nothing but this moment, this present place, the two of us amid this ancient, pastoral, autumnal countryside. Surely this is as close as I will get—surely it is as close as anyone could bear—to love pure as sunlight; to our reason for being alive.

And the sun sinks lower in the sky, the light fails, time is running out; a day, a life is racing to its end. The sunlight slants across the reed-choked Indre, shining white on the raked and graveled paths of Azay-le-Rideau, this fantasy castle. A swan sinks on extended wings, his double rising to meet him from the depths of the lake's emerald mirror. He lands, and the chateau's slate-sheathed towers shatter, ripple, then reassemble their inverted perfection. Stark, sharp shadows of osiers, black rapiers against green water, Larry and I set out to walk the symmetrical paths except that he cannot lift his swollen feet, shoes scrape gravel and so he turns back to the car. I turn to follow, then crouch to take up a handful of pebbles, to lodge in memory the feel of this place that I will surely never touch again in the presence of this man, this friend of my youth. The rough and raked stoniness grates against my palms, the gravel runs through my fingers, but it is the thin, serpentine-flecked dirt of San Francisco, and I am standing on the hill above the apartment where I now live, where I have lived alone since Larry died. The bright white bowl of the city spreads out below. To the north the copper-red towers of the Golden Gate Bridge rise against the tawny Marin headlands.

I am in California, not in France. It is years later, I am here and he is not but love goes on, this is the lesson that I have taken, for a comfort that must and will suffice. In grief there is renewal, of love and so of life.

WINGSPAN

Amber Coverdale Sumrall

Fog blankets the forest.
Wrapped in the dark quilt of my dreaming
your spirit fades, leaves no trace of you
So much unspoken, a silence of deep piercings.

Two owls call to one another
as they did after your death,
their voices sharpening the stillness.
I stood then, in the dry creekbed
behind our home,
gathering stones, pellets of gristled fur
cast down from their perch.
In the violet dusk they kept watch
as I formed a circle:
a language of symbols to span
this new distance between us.

sunlight claws through layers of grey.
I want to tear open thin tissue,
expose what refuses to heal.
Bone-white fragments collect in my bed,
memories soft as the down beneath wings.

THE WAY IT IS

Peg Rashid

It's the same old street, the same old windows, the same old spider plant behind the two old caned rockers.

Of course, it is not the same. It will never be the same. She sits on the old couch looking out the windows as she has for fifty years. In darkness she had rocked her babies as she gazed out at the trees and shadows under the dim lights. She had rubbed the collie's ears with her foot as she hummed to her infants one after another until there were six. And she had sat weary-eyed in the first light of morning looking out at snow-covered cars as she sipped coffee while they dressed for school, promising herself that when they no longer needed her to drive them she would just sit here, relish her coffee and look out these windows, just sit and look and dream.

And then it had happened. It had taken only a second, the snap of her fingers. All too soon they were grown and gone.

The same old house, the same old windows. She had watched the changes. Trees died and were replaced by small trees that grew tall and were replaced again. As she watched, kids grew up walking to and from school, disappeared, and more kids appeared, grew up, and disappeared. But it is still the same old street through the same old windows.

Mr. Jones saunters slowly into view, smoking a cigar. Mrs. Jones does not allow Mr. Jones to smoke in the house. Every morning he passes in his snap-brimmed hat, puffing and squinting, checking out the block. One of their dogs had bitten Mr. Jones when he first moved into the neighborhood and she had had to take him to emergency. She had feared that Mr. Jones would never be a friendly neighbor. She had sensed that he suspected their collie of more than just an instinct to protect the kids as she had tried to explain. He was young then. Now he is retired and strolls confidently as though he owns the block. He pauses to talk with neighbors who are mowing their lawns or walking home from the bus stop.

He will not be stopping here today. It is not the same here anymore. There is no one to greet him, no Fandy parking while Mr. Jones waits for him to leave his car.

"Jonesy got you again, eh?" she'd say when eventually he came in.

He'd have the paper under his arm and perhaps be carrying a bag from the market, which he would put down carefully, grinning, as he shook his head slowly back and forth. He did that, hesitated before he spoke. She'd wait. Sometimes impatient people filled that space with a question, another remark. She knew to wait.

"He says that blue '87 Escort has been parked in front of Harrington's for a week. Hasn't moved. He thinks someone should call the police." They'd laugh together. Jonesy always suggested someone else should call the police.

At night they sat here on this old couch, he at the end under the big lamp, reading. She recalled how he would slowly put his book on his lap, thinking. After a time he would turn to her.

"We didn't hear from Frank today."

"Yes. Yes, he called. I told you. Remember? Joey has a cold."

He'd nod. And then he would ask about the others in turn. They would talk about them quietly, sometimes perplexed, sometimes chuckling, remembering. He was a quiet man, a comfortable man. At peace with himself. He accepted life's blows with silent resignation.

"That's the way it is," he'd say. "What's done is done."

Now, she watches Mr. Jones from her window. He pauses, his cigar held in the air, and looks at the house.

"What is he thinking?" she wonders. "Is he remembering his talks with Fandy? Is he meditating on life and how quickly it can be over? On the passing of time? Can he be aware of the void behind these windows?"

Slowly he places the cigar between his teeth and moves on.

In recent years Fandy liked to putter in the kitchen. Late at night she'd awaken to smell bacon frying or cornbread baking or onions, and she'd think, "The kitchen will be a mess in the morning."

Now she wakes in the night imagining those smells, imagining that he is painstakingly building a bacon and onion sandwich. She hears him opening a bottle of beer, his footsteps moving back toward the couch. He is settling down with his book of old poems in his corner under the lamp. The kitchen is neat and stark and lonely now when she rises to brew her coffee.

A terrible cold envelops her. She clutches her faded old robe about her and goes to the bedroom to find his warm slippers. The room is dark. The shades are drawn. She crosses quickly and flips them up, flooding the room with morning sunlight. Beyond the windows the red brick wall of the Williams' house seems to sparkle in the glare. She brings a plant from the kitchen and puts it on the window sill. The greenery against the brick wall is a pleasing sight. She busies herself fluffing the pillows and straightening the bedspread. Then she stands, looking out the window.

A cardinal, followed by his mate, darts between the houses, followed after a short interval by a small flock of multicolored pigeons.

"That's the way it is," she says, and sinks her chilled feet into his fur-lined slippers.

VENUS

Carol Malley

She holds the world in her hands,
that winged Goddess.
Caressing it with her warmth,
opening her fingers, she admits
skies of cold wind blowing through
the plains of my heart.
The goddess of lovers,
does she know what it's like
to lose her mate?
Or does she blow storms upon us
merely for amusement?
Gentle one minute, harsh
the next, unpredictable.
Does she know what it's like
to lose her mate?
Is that why she cries
torrential rains?
Rivers streaming down
her face and mine.
She turns the Globe
from morning to night
to mourning night.

HOPE

Grace Brumett

JULY 20, 1996

I was 36 when that shattering phone call came and dying became my teacher. With three little kids and a husband I adored, we were living an idyllic life in the Sierra Nevada foothills. Leisurely dreaming of the whole life stretching endlessly before us. Feeling only the minor ups and downs of a normal young family's life. A future.

"Honey, sit down. Just got the results of the biopsy. The doctor says it's cancer. Lymphoma. Looks bad. Don't tell the kids until I get there. We should do that together."

Everything inside me screamed, *NO! This isn't real. I cannot go through this. This is too hard.*

So began a year of encounters with the medical establishment, of quickly educating ourselves about a disease of which very little was known, of making choices under the pressures that a delay could be deadly, of being pushed by the medical establishment in one direction and by well-meaning alternative-thinking friends toward another. There was no time to prepare ourselves emotionally. We were thrust into the unknown.

And the news got worse. The prognosis was slim from that initial diagnosis. Our chances were gloomy. Thirty percent survival with immediate surgery. *I cannot do this. It's overwhelming.*

As Michael and I frantically stumbled through the illness, I soon realized that somehow I must find my own source of strength so that I could continue to support my husband and my children emotionally. Those moments of fear were the worst. Like waves of utter unreasoning terror, the fear would at odd moments engulf me. In my intense need for help I went off alone, so long ago now, to a special spot in the forest. I sat down, not knowing what else to do. I just sat and I just sat and I just sat. Fear arrived as a mighty demonic presence. Panic. A tremendous pressure on my chest. Overwhelmed, I could neither fight nor resist. So I fell right into that fear. I went right through the convulsions.

This is fear. This is terror. This is the unknown.

Breathe. Breathe. Heart pounding right on through. No sense of time. An eternity. Riding on wave after tumultuous wave of hot terror. Until at last the fury was spent and there I was safe on the other side— a place of surprising calm. A beautiful vision came to me. The warm fall breeze gently stirred the pine boughs against the azure sky high above me. Within a ray of sunlight filtering through the sparkling Ponderosa pines I saw the form of Michael, his body transparent and radiantly glowing with life. He was perfectly whole, luminously beautiful. At that moment I knew, from that instinctual intuitive place that resides deep inside, that Michael would be okay, no matter what the path chosen or what the outcome. And I knew that I would be okay as well. Nothing could harm his essence, or mine.

Thank you. If this then is truth, give me a tangible sign. Even still went my small doubting mind. As my eyes looked down to the forest floor, there before me crouched a most magnificent mountain lion. We gazed clearly and directly into one another's eyes with an undeniable recognition for one timeless moment before he leaped off into the forest, the embodiment of power and strength. I knew this was a sign that my vision was a clear one—the mountain lion was a witness to it. I went home. Whenever thereafter the fear arrived—and often it did—I called on my vision for strength and support.

At every point in the journey when the cancer returned years later and continuing on throughout my grieving, my reaction always began with, "NO, I cannot do this. It's too hard. It's not fair." Yet I always did. Waking from nightmarish dreams to the stark dream of day, I would voice again, "NO, I cannot do this. I don't know how I can do this."

But it's like childbirth. There really is no choice but to see it through. Life is not a fairy tale with a happy ending. It's not like that. There is also the dark, scary shadowy stuff of life—the part no one ever wants, the part called suffering, loss, death, grief. And there is no simple formula to move through this part. There are moments of terrible doubt. I have often felt like I was being yanked unwillingly along by the very roots of my hair, kicking and fighting every step. But somehow I have also found my way with some measure of lightness, peace, and even laughter.

So a summer after Michael died, I recorded this in my journal:

AUGUST 8, 1995

I just hung up the phone this Tuesday evening. My friend Pam leaves Saturday for Auschwitz to accompany some art pieces to a world conference, "Healing: Perpetrator and Victims of the Holocaust." She still has no travel money. It was an anxious conversation. Because my family endured and survived its own personal holocaust in a six-year battle fighting the cancer in my husband's body, she asked me to write some words about hope to send along.

He died just a summer ago. We are all still reeling, perhaps because the dying took so long and was so devastating for each one of us. Truly a cancer belongs to the whole family. Its impact is severe for the surviving members as well as for the one who is dying. As I slowly emerge from this long year of grief, I have no wise thoughts about hope or any of those other big-word concepts we fling around so casually as if we understand them. I don't know what they mean anymore—hope, faith, suffering—nor the whys. I recall, mythologically, that the one redeeming quality found at the bottom of Pandora's box, when all the evil and ugliness of the world spilled out, was hope.

I do not know about hope and about no hope. All I know is I don't think it was ever hope that kept us laughing together in death's face. It wasn't hope that gave us our moments of utter ecstasy together and alone those last few months when the doctors declared Michael terminal. It was in the face of no hope when we became truly awake to each precious moment.

So, Pam, here is a very short poem about hope.

HOPE

Cancer in my dear husband's body—NO!
95 percent chance for a total cure.
We draw our line of hope.
Back again.
Now hope for remission
More time together with our children.
Back yet again!
With the same fervor we hope now for new treatment.
Search frantically following every remote obscure lead
of healer, diet, therapy, special waters, prayers,
every New Age alternative promise
each one offering a thread of hope.
To no avail.
We redraw our line of hope.
Now hope for a day of no nausea with the current
chemotherapy treatment.
Hope to make it through this night without heavy
drenching bed sweats soaking blankets through
five times a night
leaving us exhausted and sobbing in one another's arms.

Hope for morphine-release no pain for an hour
long enough to celebrate our son's eighth-grade graduation.
Hope for a miracle.
Hope the tumor wrapped about the spinal cord
will respond to radiation zaps and shrink
long enough for another less paralyzing tumor to "take him."
Finally, hope for it all to be over.
Always hope dangling before us the promise
that it be other than it is.

I don't know about hope.
All I know is it wasn't hope that brought
such exquisite pleasure to Michael the last week
as he selected and arranged with slow meticulous
care and delight that bouquet of summer flowers
to surprise us and grace our table.
It wasn't hope that brought him the peace to tell us
"I'm ready to go"
and he really meant it
because three days later
he died.

I don't know about hope.
With all hope over, why is it
that I take such deep pleasure now
this next lonely summer without him
to pick and arrange the flowers
he will not see
to grace my table.
But I do.

SEAOATS

J. F. West

Even minus the mood born of association,
seaoats rippling on a lonely beach
evoke within the average watcher a nostalgia
unrelated to those dead days when youth's blood
gorged his arteries, scalding his heart's walls;
when I suddenly round a turn today and happen
upon such a scene, a lone gull wheeling
below a cloud, scudding, to shroud the sun briefly,
my heart is wrenched, and a pang sears
my sinews like lightning's slash
down a tall quaking aspen's bole
as I visualize one special April day
when we lay in the warm sun at summer's start,
our bodies quaking from the first mere touching,
a knowledge later to grow familiar and bland
after long seasoning in the snug bedrooms of becoming
and three new lives coming from the cleavage.
Oh, but that was years before the April night
when death as indifferent as lightning's flash
incidentally intervened, leaving one alone.
Therefore, when I see such ripe growth rippling
on a reaching strand, the world appears
little more than a reach of rolling dunes
where seasoned seaoats brush the scudding sun.

ON DEFINING GRIEF

Mary H. Ber

Call it
a block of paper
scrolling into your computer's Delphic maw,
It will emerge
and emerge and emerge,
a stream interminable as Styx,
murmuring by itself
long after your fingers have left to
peel apples for dinner.

Call it
a hydra made of water
surging up
through any body outlet—
wet eyes,
hot breath,
bursting bowel.
It's a beast
rising within you,
a monster spilling suddenly
over any moment's peace.

"Nothing lives forever,"
you always said;
and to prove it,
you died.

You were a whirlwind
in life.
My solid, steady steps
could never keep up,
but you would double back,
take my hand,
fill me with your own
lightness.

You surged through life.
Remember when we built our home,
rooted it with fruit trees and the birch
we carried, on a lark, from north Wisconsin

Well, we made mistakes.
The slim, white birch is dying—
too far south.
The peach trees and the cherries—
too far north—
bleed sap and bow their leaves.

Only
in myself
your roots remain
as you whirl round and round my thoughts,
holding me to you,
holding the hands of my heart.

You sit in my mouth now
like a piece of peppermint.
Thoughts of you melt across my tongue
cleansing and moistening dry lips,
leaving sweetness
along with the sting.

GRIEF'S RAGE

Marna Hauk

1. If my life is hair, grief is the ribbon
that binds all the strands. Grief is the
braidwork that nets the fine fibrils. Grief is
the buncher and twister of dread(s).

2. Rage then is ripper. Rage is
Medusa, uncoiling snakes freely. Rage is
destroyer, relentless remover. Rage then is
scissors: the tearer (terror) at root and at
end.

3. Grief and rage are fine stylists. Soon I'll
be bound, bald, skull-scarred at their hands.

CLOCKWISE

Nancy Wambach

Yesterday a friend showed me his new toy, a "Personal Life Clock." For only $99, he purchased the illusion that he could monitor the future. An imposing gray granite monolith, pyramid-shaped, it sports green digital numerals that count backward to "display the actual hours, minutes, and seconds remaining in your statistical lifetime."

After my husband's cancer surgery, after three feet of his colon was sliced away, he wore a long red scar in an arc beneath his navel. Like a lurid, lipsticked grin, it mocked me, mocked our plans, youth's presumptuous conviction that we could design our own tomorrows.

It became my habit to rub my lover's belly in long, languid circles. Sometimes it seemed like our belly, our cancer. Always clockwise I rubbed. I included the scar, which eventually whitened.

A scientific journal, perused in a doctor's office years earlier, had described how a slow, clockwise massage of the abdomen would aid digestion, improve peristalsis, move stomach contents quickly through the treacherous gauntlet of the bowel. After the diagnosis, I envisioned stubborn carcinogenic bullets of food lurking for years in secret pockets of Bill's guts. Maybe one of them was the culprit, the very one responsible. Affixing blame was important in those early days.

So I rubbed the scar and it calmed me, too, as people pet their animals during the most brutal family quarrels, hug themselves and stroke their own arms while awaiting bad news. It comforted us both, the touching, moving in the right direction.

At night before surrendering to sleep, my head tucked in the familiar fleshy nook between his chest and arm, I rubbed. His fingers fanned above my ear as he kissed my forehead, my temple, my eyes.

I reached around his sleeping form to hug him from behind and hold his middle in the morning, before the shrill alarm made urgent demands. Now. Get up now. Do it now. Groggy, perhaps half dreaming still, he turned and pulled me to him. The chest I burrowed my face into was furry, sweet and warm, sleep-creased.

Always I rubbed, clockwise.

I loved to press my mouth to the scar; its ridge, like a trail of hardened candle wax, tickled my lips.

A committed non-believer in all I could not see, hear, or document, still I often visualized the remaining, abbreviated tube of colon beneath his fatty flesh: clean and milky it was, virginal, pure.

In my way, I prayed over the scar and the precious belly, was eager to sacrifice, to appease the wrath of a vengeful god I could not see, hadn't meant to offend.

Often I worried that my poor, unfocused prayers, insubstantial and inadequate, might lose direction, lose thrust, evaporate into the ether.

Then the cancer returned, metastasized.

Bent and reeling, we sat facing a desk and empty chair in a office on the fifteenth floor. My thighs squished on a slick leather seat as I rocked back and forth. Silent, mostly from shock, partly from reverence, we awaited the coming of the oncologist, alias God. I gripped the worn arms of the chair to refrain from diving headlong out the large, clean picture window.

An ornate German clock on the wall ticked militarily. Its sharp, gold hands pierced the carved Roman numerals equidistantly circling its marble face. At each corner, the head of a stern, bearded, elderly male frowned at me. Was this the trinity? If so, who was the fourth member? Had I failed to placate him, too?

The chime rang once, then again.

Our last hope entered, wearing a white lab coat. He shook Bill's hand, nodded at me, displayed the X-rays, furrowed his brow, decreed, "As you can see, there are significant lesions on the liver and left lung" (we couldn't, but pretended to). "Clearly, the cancer is well advanced, inoperable. I'm afraid the prognosis is grim. Curious, though . . . do you see this part down here? This is the colon, the original site." He pointed. We nodded dully. "For some inexplicable reason, really it defies logic, the entire area is clean. I see no trace of disease here, not even a shadow."

Nights now, sleep is an elusive, reluctant, unreliable lover. Alone, keeping to my side of the bed, I rub my chest and watch the second hand sweep around the illuminated face of my tiny alarm clock. Over and over it wends its dependable clockwise route.

I think about designing my own Personal Life Clock. I guess it would have a giant round face, frowning. A single hand would lurch backward. As the hours, minutes, seconds ran down, at times the hand might race, spin in a dizzying frenzy toward no real goal. *Tempus fugit*, a warning. Sometimes it would inch imperceptibly. Its arc, speed, pattern would be random and matter not anyway.

Granted another chance, I would love sloppy. I would rub all over, less circular, less precise, less right.

LITTLE DEATHS

Maureen Cannon

Always it is the sudden dark surprise
That stops the breath. Oh, I have clearly learned
This death of yours by heart. I have grown wise
Among the lines of that long poem, returned
Again, again to find that deep within
The puzzle answers hide, the little cores
Of comfort, even peace. I can begin
To breathe you into all the open pores
Of my own body now, not shattering.
You would be proud, I think. And strong? Dear love,
They are synonymous—survivals bring
Such strengths as shake a world! And, thinking of
The way you teased, remembering your eyes,
I call out "Miracles! Look, love, how sane
I am, how brave . . ."
                              until the dark surprise
Kills every word and stops the heart and pain
Is what the world's about, the awful breadths
Of pain. There are so many little deaths.

Chapter Six
Metamorphosis

"Tell me, O older and wiser sister," I wrote, "how long will this grief last?" Old and wiser, she wrote back: "Grief is never over. The time will come when you control your grief rather than the other way around. You'll draw upon those memories when you need and want them, rather than having them show up uninvited. But your grief will never go away, which is the way it should be. It is part of who you are."
—Fenton Johnson, Excerpted from *Geography of the Heart*

For the survivor, the death of a lifemate is many things. It is an ending of our past and dreams. It is a time when our vision is narrow; where we see only the endings.

But it is also the beginning of a metamorphosis—a propulsion into a cocoon of transformation. Yet, as with all new starts, it is not without difficulty. It can be like falling into an abyss so deep and endless it may take years or even decades to draw oneself upward where, with open eyes of wonder, we may catch a ray of light and hope encouraging us to carry on. We all travel this way at a different pace and break open our cocoons at different times.

When we do come to this new place, we discover gifts: new meanings, new awakenings, and new possibilities born from a pain so exquisite and so profound we will never see the world with the same eyes of innocence. Hopefully, this new vision will be full of extraordinary wisdom and courage. And hope.

The stories and poems you will find in this chapter capture the essence of many steps and stops along this path. You will find tentative reachings for new relationships, memories that bring solace, hearts moving forward, yet always looking backward. You will feel the comfort and timelessness in the silent language of nature. The voices echo our losses, and bridge many planes of consciousness to reveal a communion not bound by earth's time and substance.

All are the voices of hope and images of the splendid new butterfly that has emerged, filled with potential, and soaring high in a metamorphosis of life.

. . . The end precedes the beginning.
And the end and the beginning
Were always there
Before the beginning and after the end.
And all is always now . . .

—T. S. Eliot

A REMEMBERED LIFE

Robert Vasquez-Pacheco

A decade has passed since he died. We move swiftly to the close of the century. With each advancing year, his myth grows stronger and brighter as his reality slowly fades and darkens, a transformation not unlike those experienced by Jesus and Elvis. Such is the life cycle of all myths. There seems to be some equation of inverse proportions at work here, for the less I remember of him, the more I create him. He now exists totally in my memory, alive only along the neural pathways in my brain. Like some caterpillar, his body disappeared into a black rubber chrysalis that morning in February, only to emerge as a rare and beautiful butterfly now fluttering behind my eyes. The Jeff I knew no longer exists. The Jeff I know will live as long as I do. He shares, in fact, a charmed existence with all the relatives and friends who inhabit the amber mansions of memory within.

The remembered life brings a kind of growth, unanticipated by the living or the dead. For as time passes, Jeff develops attributes and has experiences that he didn't have in his real life. Memory is never exact, which is why history is always a work of fantasy. Jeffrey is covered with the accretions of my recollections, like the various objects nailed and hung upon the wooden body of an African fetish figure. I remember incidents, hear conversations that may, objectively, have happened to someone else, but in the remembered life, they are now attached to him. So through my recollections, his life changes and grows, having new experiences which produce not the Jeff who was, but the Jeff whom I remember. Perhaps death is not the end as has been predicted, for like a seemingly dead tree stump in the eternal spring of memory, it will always send out tiny green shoots of a new life. So Jeff lives, in a manner of speaking.

At this point in time, I have mourned Jeff for longer than we were together; in fact, for longer than I knew him, although I will always know him.

I keep a photograph of him on my desk. It keeps me mindful of the grace that he brought into my life. It also reminds me of a time before the scourge, a time now romanticized into the proverbial golden age of innocence. It was our time in the garden before the plague, when, like the serpent, AIDS transformed our ignorance into a painful knowledge. The photo was taken during the summer of '82 at an outdoor concert in

Central Park. We are standing together, smiling at the camera, two happy, healthy, and very much in love gay men. Although smiling, my mouth is open as if I am saying something to the photographer, probably some snide comment. Jeff is laughing, probably at my typically snide comment. The Jeff I see in the photograph has not changed. Even in later photographs of him, as the illness spread through his body, he remained the same. It is important to me that he remain the same.

For a long time, after he died, I was desolate at the thought that he was no longer with me. But as the years pass, I realize that he has not gone. His body has decayed in the ground of that cemetery in New Jersey but his essence, at least the essence that I have constructed in the decade after his death, remains alive and vital. He is with me all the time, as much a part of me as my love of writing.

My Jeff, whether the man I knew or the man that he has become in my memory, will always be with me. Everything, both the light and the darkness that I have known or will know, becomes a part of him, like Krishna in the *Bhavadgita* and like Arjuna, I am perpetually awed by his presence.

IT WAS ONLY A KISS

Joseph F. Sweet

"It was only a kiss," said John.

"Only a kiss, only a kiss," replied Victoria. "Be careful, John. Don't think with your hormones. You're not a kid anymore."

"Look, it's been almost two years. If you don't want to share me, you shouldn't have left me." John let his anger rise toward Victoria for the first time since she died. "I know it has been hard for you—I mean, I don't know what the heck it's been like for you. You know I'll never forget you. I don't want to forget you. You'll always be with me. But, geez, it was only a kiss."

"Only a kiss . . . only a kiss . . ." she mimicked.

The first long, pervasive wave of grief had ebbed. John had conquered most of the details of living in the wake of Victoria's death. He had learned to iron, use the washing machine (although he had yet to master the subtleties of the various cycles), and be a mother to their five-year-old son, Nathaniel. The rash of dinner invitations and consoling phone calls had died away. His friends and relatives had returned to life among the living. The tears of grief became more difficult to rouse. With their departure, a sense of routine returned to John's life. The routine seemed comforting, but in his darker, more fearful moments, loneliness tinged by hopelessness crept into his soul.

John sat in his darkened living room. With Aretha Franklin's voice slowly seeping out from the stereo and a Cabernet Sauvignon settling in his glass, he projected a silhouette of Victoria on the white wall. She resembled a protected witness testifying behind a screen at a Mafia trial.

"Well, what do you think of Sybbie? Is she someone to pursue?" the ghostly Victoria asked.

"I don't know, Vic. She's just a friend. I'm just getting used to you not being here."

"Not good enough, John. Take a good look at her before you find yourself in a comfortable relationship that you will regret. Make sure you are not settling."

"At this point I just want the pain to end. I ache every time I see your empty chair at the dinner table. I grieve each time I think of the waves breaking on the beach this summer without you, and I cry each time Marvin Gaye tells me you will no longer be mine. But at least I can stand it now. My body has recovered from the shock. I can get through the day; that's all I need," said John.

"But now what? You get through the day, but what do you do with your day? You do your job. You take care of Nathaniel. You cry. Where do you go from here? You provide Nathaniel with love and security, but where is he going to get his joy of life? Where is he going to learn that he can make his world rather than wait for the world to do it for him?" said Victoria.

"You always could make me feel guilty. I know I should do it for Nathaniel, but something is missing. Something that will make me do it for myself. You left me with a gaping hole, and you are not around helping me fill it."

John sipped his wine, turned up the stereo, and closed his eyes. Jackson Browne sang about the death of a dancer friend.

Sybbie appeared early at work the morning after the office Christmas party. She knew her best friend Jude would arrive shortly to get the news. Syb excitedly reviewed the clients she would see that day. She kept busy, always moving forward personally and professionally. To Sybbie, complacency was death.

"Well, how'd it go?" Jude asked before she could remove her coat.

"Wonderful, just wonderful," Sybbie said.

"Details, details, please," said Jude.

"Well, he kissed me," Sybbie said.

"He did? Finally old molasses lips made his move. How far did you let him go?"

"I didn't have to let him go anywhere. That's all he did; one long kiss and a couple of short, little ones."

"What was it like?"

"It was great for me, like we are finally getting somewhere. But for him, I don't know. He seemed scared, like a little boy kissing his first girlfriend."

"Did you tell him you don't bite on the first date?"

"Oh, my God, Jude, don't call it a date. If he heard you he'd become apoplectic. Besides, dating is dangerous at forty. We've only met weirdos and leeches that way. Today, to meet a trustworthy guy, you need to watch him over time, like at work, like watching moss grow on a tree."

"Now for The Question: is it love or is John another social work project? Will you sour on him the way you turned away from David when he didn't become the man you wanted him to be?"

"John isn't David. They are very different. David was depressed, void of ambition. His idea of a great Friday night was pizza, beer, a burp and in bed by ten."

"Interesting, and just what does John do now on Friday nights?"

"That's different, Jude. John has something to be depressed about."

Jude interrupted, "And you are just the gal to get him out of it."

John walked into the office, gave an upbeat, "hello," then quickly continued down the hall to his own office. As he settled into his chair, his fears crept over him again.

"Shoot. What am I going to do now? I should never have kissed her. Vic was right, my hormones got me into trouble. How can I face Sybbie now?" he thought.

Jude appeared in the doorway. John focused on that big "I knew it" grin of hers.

"Jude, get in here quick and lose the smile. I need help. Did Sybbie tell you what happened last night?"

"Hey, loverboy, the whole office is talking about what happened last night, or at least a sexier version of it."

"Shoot!" John seemed stuck.

"What's wrong? You like Syb, don't you? You have spent enough time with her over the last few months. You guys get along great."

"It's not that I don't like her. I just don't want things to change. Syb's nice. But she's not Victoria. She is not at all like Victoria. It's confusing."

"What are your choices here? You could continue your one-man living shrine to Vicky with her picture plastered all over your office, or you could take up with Syb who is wise, wonderful, beautiful, and—"

"And," John interrupted, "your best friend, and, evidently, you are her agent, too."

"But it's true, John. It's been two years; everyone knows how much you loved Victoria, but you deserve that love again. And so does Nate."

"But Sybbie," John continued, "is so different from Victoria it scares me. This may be hard to believe, but I don't remember Victoria ever making a mistake. She enjoyed perfecting what she had. We had a toaster for the eighteen years of our marriage that shined every day as if it were new. I was proud of how Victoria took care of our house, our son, and me. Victoria clearly understood what she wanted in life and what she didn't want. Others opinions were just that to her—opinions. Victoria taught me more about being an adult than my mother did. She taught me about boundaries, values, and self-respect."

"If you learned your lesson well, you don't need another teacher," Jude said.

"Yeah, I guess, but Sybbie is so different. For her, whatever she has isn't enough—not enough experiences, trips, degrees, knowledge, or material goods. It's not that she's superficial. Sybbie extracts deep joy from her experiences and possessions. She needs excitement the way Victoria needed perfection. But if I go with Sybbie, I don't know where I'll end up."

"Who the hell does? You may be looking for more security than life has to offer," Jude said.

"Victoria and I fit well together. We had a beautiful house and a beautiful son. We had a beautiful life. We loved the Beatle's song 'When I'm 64.' I may be odd, but I looked forward to retirement. I'd fall asleep dreaming about growing old with Victoria and tending our home and garden together. Falling asleep, we fit each other perfectly. We knew each other well. We moved as a team."

"Then she left," she said kindly in a soft voice.

"Yeah, then she left," he said, wiping the tears from his eyes.

John tried to avoid Sybbie for the rest of the morning. He stayed in his office at the end of the hall writing reports and making phone calls. In the late morning, when Sybbie could not tolerate the silence any longer, she called him on the interoffice phone. John apologized for his forward behavior the previous night and repelled her efforts to discuss the matter. He told her he needed time to think.

But, in truth, he could not think at all. He stared a lot and rearranged the papers on his desk. He responded to a few phone calls, but otherwise could not bring himself to do much of anything. He felt stuck. As he was preparing to leave for the day, he heard the dreaded footsteps race forcefully down the hall.

"Oh, shoot," John wanted to hide.

"Johnny, we need to talk," Sybbie said.

"I told you, I need to think first."

"I don't have enough time to let you think it through yourself. Look, it was only a kiss . . . ."

"Yeah, where have I heard that before?" John interrupted.

"Well, it was only a kiss, not a marriage proposal. I don't know what you think about it, about us, but I liked it. I like you, and I want to get to know you better. I even want to date you, but hold off calling the minister."

"I know," said John, fidgeting and unable to make eye contact.

"We're both single and you seemed to like me, at least before you kissed me. I know how much Vicky meant to you, and how much she still does. I'm not trying to replace her, but perhaps you might have room for me, too."

"I just don't know what to do. It just doesn't feel right, not yet," said John.

"You're putting the cart before the horse. It'll never feel right until you move your behind," Sybbie said.

"That's your opinion." John's confusion lost out to his anger.

"You think that you are playing it safe, wanting to do your grieving business right, but a time comes to live instead of thinking about living. You are trying to follow all the rules, but that's just a lame excuse to wallow in your neat little house with your wine and your songs. Sometimes I get angry watching you. You have a lot of potential or I wouldn't be hanging around you so much," said Sybbie.

"Potential!" John finally had something to say. "Potential! What about who I am? If you only care for what I might become after I finish my grieving business, then you haven't learned anything from the problems of your first marriage. To have a relationship, you have to accept the person as he is. That's love."

"Who said anything about love? I only want to date you. The choice is up to you. C'mon over to my house for dinner tonight and we can discuss us some more."

"No, thanks," John felt trapped. "I gotta go, bye." He managed to move by her without a touch. Sybbie fumed; John raced away.

After work, John drove to St. Ann's cemetery to visit Victoria's grave. At first, such visits were an eerie experience for him. In the grief group he attended for the first three months after Victoria's death, he always listened with interest to others graveside experiences. One woman, even into the second year, visited three or four times a week, tending the gravesite as one would a favored garden spot. She fertilized, weeded, and even raked and hoed with a scaled-down garden set. She needed to care for her husband in death as she did in life. A man in the group, whose wife had been dead for two years, used the cemetery as a hot spot to meet women. Cemeteries were cheaper than bars, and most of the women were single and a bit vulnerable. For most others, grave visits presented the opportunity to purge, confess, cry, or just catch up on the family news.

Mainly, John just watched. With disbelief, he saw his fingers outline Victoria's name on the gravestone. He witnessed the blades of grass slowly erase the seams of incision that outlined her coffin. He noticed how the sun would vainly attempt to warm the cold ground before the shade would reclaim its territory. In bleaker moments, he would catch a mental glimpse of the effects of disease and death on the once proud body of his Victoria. Sadly, he bemoaned the countless hours of loving care which Victoria spent maintaining her regal body and beautiful, thick black hair. He thought of the money her father had spent on braces that carefully straightened her white teeth. Teeth that no longer gleamed with her smile. On these visits he just watched and thought; but today's visit would be different. He entered the gates with a purpose.

John took the first left after the gates of the cemetery and stopped the car at the third gravesite. He sat on the hard stone base of the small monument looking at the barest outline of Victoria's grave. The outline was more memory than reality.

"Vic," John called softly, "I could have been married to you forever. It was great. I loved our life. I loved you."

Victoria did not respond.

"But your death has made me a very different person. I had to become you. I had to do all those things you did; I had to become all those people you were. I had to clean our beloved house; I had to acquire your discipline. I could no longer rely on your integrity, your strength, or your intuitive knowledge of right and wrong. I had to do all of this, and more, alone."

"Jude was right, Vic. You taught me well. I survived your death because of you. I'm sad, tearfully, painfully sad, but I also feel free. Today, for the first time, I can see a future with Sybbie. It's different, confusingly different from my dreams of life with you. But I'll be all right. I love you. I'll always love you."

He kissed the stone and drove out through the gates. He picked up Nathaniel at school and drove to Sybbie's house, hoping the dinner offer was still open.

"After all, it's only dinner," he thought to himself.

SUMMONS

Amber Coverdale Sumrall

How can I sleep
remembering the pleasure
that radiated from your hands?
Your eyes reversed the flow
of rivers and fish leaped
out of shallow water
to spawn in the slick wet
of our bodies. Sinking slowly
sweetly, we learned to breathe
in the absence of air:
mouths open, oblivious
to the deadly hooks
buried in silted beds.

Outside, in bone-chilling cold
your breath frosts the bedroom window;
your long, slender fingers press
against the moon-streaked pane
as if you were still alive
still wanting me.

Slowmoving currents
in another's hands
bring me to the surface
but it is your voice
that calls to me
across the silvered husk
of night.

COUPLES

Karen D'Amato

The things couples do,
crazy of me to want to build
that house again so badly
that my mouth is always full of salt,
flooded from inside.

Open it and, Magic, all the words
I wish I never said to you
spill out so I won't forget
the things couples do,

but better next time,
to build that house again
because I have to,
in streaked clothes
with my quivering chin.

I never made a sound
like the sob of when you died,
never heard its racked
animal before, but there it was.
It stirred the air for days,
like the things couples say
because each one is broken.

Forgive me. There cannot always be
silence of eyes drinking in
or words as jewelled as a night city.

But I pray a lighted window
in the next house I build with someone
is all he'll know of my tongue's
stinging as he stands
expatriated in the rain.
Minutes of piercing only walls
and I'll come out changed,
with an umbrella of words he can answer.

We loved each other.
For the things couples say
because they're true and not-
saying hammers at the heart,
I forgive you. Crazy of me to feel
I have to, when there is nothing to forgive.

RECUERDO

David Garnes

JUNE 28, 1992: MANCHESTER

Luis died at 6:30 this morning, peacefully, in our bed. His hand was still warm when I went back into the bedroom just before the funeral people came. We had to move some furniture so they could get the stretcher in and out. These are the two things I keep thinking about.

DECEMBER 3, 1990: HARTFORD

Today Luis was given the State Commissioner's AIDS Leadership Award. He's a cynic regarding public recognition, particularly in a political context, but he's also a performer and somewhat of a ham. I know this pleased him. There were a lot of cheers and whistles from the audience when he walked to the front of the room.

NOVEMBER 26, 1992: SAN JUAN

I am spending Thanksgiving here, my first trip to Puerto Rico since Luis died. I'm staying in Isla Verde, near Santurce, where Dona Mery lives, and Carolina, where Luisa and her family have a house. Luisa is eight years older than Luis and lived in the apartment upstairs when they were growing up. Luis always called her his sister, and her two boys once stayed with us in Connecticut for a few weeks when they were little. It is all wrong that I am here without Luis. I remember the first time he showed me around the island. This is his country, not mine.

JULY 1, 1992: MANCHESTER

I asked Catina if she would help plan the memorial service. I think she is glad to do this, but I also need to remember that this is a hard time for a lot of people. I've never known anyone who engendered more intense affection in his friends than Luis. It used to bother me that I had to share him with so many people, but that was a long time ago.

OCTOBER 24, 1981: STORRS

I've been at my job in the library for a couple of months. I think I'm going to like it here in Connecticut. The other day I just happened to be working at a colleague's desk during her lunch break. A quiet voice above me said, "Excuse me, I'm the grad assistant working with the bilingual program, and I have some books for you to order." I looked up and saw the smile. What is it about this man's smile? It's gentle, confident, open. It's the first thing I noticed about him. His name is Luis Felipe. His family calls him Willie.

MAY 16, 1986: HARTFORD
Yesterday the doctor asked me to wait outside while she spoke to Luis. About five minutes later he called me in and I knew right away what she had told him. We didn't say much, just held each other. Today we had a long—and good—talk. He is off the oxygen and recovering quickly, and I just want to get him out of the hospital.

SEPTEMBER 25, 1982: MANSFIELD CENTER
"Hi, I'm home," I shouted as I closed the door one night last week. From downstairs I heard footsteps running, and then I saw Luis' head as he turned the corner on the landing. He still couldn't see me from that angle, but I will always remember the joyous, expectant look on his face. Can I really be making someone this happy? Me?

NOVEMBER 26, 1992: SANTURCE
When I opened the black iron gate to Dona Mery's patio, I thought of all the times Luis must have walked these steps and greeted the cats who are forever waiting to be fed. How many of the cats I saw today did he know? In the back bedroom of the apartment—Luis' old room—I noticed some textbooks, neatly arranged on a high shelf, from his days at the University of Rio Piedras. It's noisy all the time around here, and Dona Mery told me that Luis used to study every night at the library, a long ride away, to escape the boom boxes and the neighbors shouting and the kids playing in the street.

APRIL 12, 1992: BOSTON
Luis sang "Gracias a la Vida" at Jose and Larry's service of union. I was a little concerned that he hadn't recovered from the pneumonia completely, and he is still really thin. But his voice was strong and true, and everyone came up to him at the reception and told him how beautiful his song was. It's been almost eleven years since we met.

MARCH 24, 1989: HARTFORD
Luis was on television again. He's been interviewed so many times as an AIDS educator that it's not such a big deal anymore, but I recorded this so he can see it later on. I'm always amazed at how at ease he is and how perfectly he speaks English. Maybe that's why my Spanish is still so

lousy. I am so proud when I see him in public, and I always think, yes, and after the show he's mine!

JUNE 22, 1992: MANCHESTER
The Hospice staff who come to the house are good people. I really like Liz, the nurse, and I know that she and Luis have taken to each other. A lot of friends want to visit and I am trying to balance what is good for Luis, for me, and for them. I admit that I lean more to those who were there for him always. Yesterday he played cards with Mary, and won. We've gone for a few rides in the car. Today I asked him if he was glad to be getting out in the fresh air. He looked at me with that sweet smile and just said, "Oh, yes!" His hand holding mine felt so strong and warm.

FEBRUARY 8, 1993: SANTURCE
Today I met Luisa at her office and we walked for ten or fifteen minutes through the crowded streets to visit Dona Mery. Luisa pointed out two empty movie theaters where she and Luis used to see Saturday matinees, and a pizza house where they ate afterward. "Willie was always talking, talking, talking when we were little," she said. "He was always looking up when we were walking and asking me questions about this, about that."

JULY 12, 1992: WILLIMANTIC
The Hispanic Church was the right setting for the service. Luis' heart was really in this community. I turned around at one point and it was a shock to see so many people. I am glad I wrote in the program instead of speaking. We ended with a tape of Luis singing "Gracias a la Vida." I tried not to feel the irony.

JANUARY 17, 1994: MANCHESTER
Today Dan and I were talking about Luis, and I said I felt that he had been my partner, my friend, and maybe even a bit of my child, inevitable I think, where there is a fourteen-year age difference. I wonder where I feel the greatest loss. He was first of all my partner—my life companion and lover. But I think I also understand the helplessness a grieving parent must feel. I would have done anything to make him live. This pain never goes away.

FEBRUARY 1, 1993: MANCHESTER
I have hundreds of photos from the trips we took: Luis entering the main gate at Disneyworld. Luis, a tiny figure in front of the Queen

Mary in Long Beach. Luis laughing next to a guard at Buckingham Palace. Luis in New Orleans, leaning on the Bourbon Street sign. Luis barely visible in a sea of grass on Block Island. Luis standing in front of a steamboat in Nashville. On that trip, I had met him after an AIDS conference, and he was wearing the white and yellow tee-shirt that says "Remember Their Names."

JULY 11, 1992: WILLIMANTIC

From the program notes of "A Celebration of the Life of Luis Felipe Pereira": I am honored as Luis' partner to be able to share with you in this celebration of his life. To have known Luis in any capacity is to have experienced a warmth and love we all look for, but do not often find. When you were with Luis, you knew that he was there for you, at that moment, with all his humor and honesty and caring. Whatever I was able to do for Luis was returned to me many, many times over. Rest in peace, Love, and know that you have given me a lifetime of joy.

NOVEMBER 30, 1993: MANCHESTER

I'm back from my fourth trip to Puerto Rico since Luis died. Why have I gone running down there so many times this year? This morning in San Juan, as the plane taxied for the takeoff, I had a sudden and overwhelming image of the cemetery in Bayamon. I felt the sun beating down on the bronze plaque, and I heard the constant buzz and drone of the cicadas in the burnt grass. I will go about the business of my life, such as it is, and the sun in Bayamon will keep scorching the ground, the rains will come and go, drenching the artificial flowers, and still Luis will remain in that marked plot, locked in time. I am beginning to know that what I am looking for is really in my heart. There he sings and laughs and holds my hand. There he is always smiling, running up the stairs to greet me when I come home.

MELANCHOLYMUSIC

Gloria Rovder Healy

Standing alone
beneath a pale daymoon,
listening to the ocean's
melancholymusic,
I want to waltz in your arms,
feel salt spray splashing
our bare feet.
"Come dance with me,"
I cry,

"Can you hear me?
Do you see me?
Is where you are as
magical as this?
Are you waiting for me?"
I wonder,
and wait too,
waltzing alone in three-quarter time
on slowly shifting sand.

GOING IN CIRCLES

Susan Heinlein

A REST TOO SHORT

Blow Wind so warm
You, who touch the open wounds within
Who quells the bleeding
And soothes the pain.
Hurry winds of life
And heal thy battered soul
For soon I must return to battle
With mind as spear and soul as armor

—Merrill Gerdts (1941–1994)

He is everywhere. He is nowhere.

He is even on the wall. Standing in the doorway of his office, I re-read the poem that hangs between two windows. Even though it was written years before we met, its words reach out and touch my aching heart.

Yes, hurry winds of life and heal thy battered soul.

My stomach is another matter. It is in knots. The entire floor of his office is covered in piles and heaps, dozens of boxes, stacks and bunches, every surface covered—the chaos of things no longer used. I am intimidated by these things from the dead, even the beloved dead. So all I do is stare at this monument of disorder, mute, paralyzed. Minutes pass. But I need to stay focused. *It is time,* I chant to myself, once twice, three times. Remember what I know: his possessions no longer comfort me. It is only the memories I can keep.

So today I will begin to release Merrill's memory to the safekeeping of my heart, rather than the floors, closets, drawers, boxes, and bookcases of this room where he had spent so much time.

At least that is the plan.

After two years of protecting each and every thing—the mechanical pencils, ancient slide rules, and reams of mathematical formulae; the bookcases filled with college texts and other obscure titles; the pilot manuals salvaged from his days of flight; every tool used to create his inventions and art, build his designs, or repair the broken ones; each scrap of paper where he wrote notes in his large, loopy script; letters he'd saved since childhood and written to people I'll never know—I tell myself that I must let go of these things that he never could. I can let them be stored safely and securely in boxes or given away to family members or the usable donated to people who will never know his name. Some will be thrown in the trash. Forever gone.

At least that is the plan.

For a long time, I didn't know if I would ever let go of his things, much less go through this process. Our possessions, I cherish. Many call forth precious memories of days I thought would never end. But others were from that time before. Ours was a mature relationship. When we met, he was in his forties; I was thirty-four.

I look around at this vast accumulation. The responsibility is overwhelming. Where do I start? How does one place value on this or that? Choose what to keep and what to let go? Of course, I'll keep our shared treasures, but much of his things are truly unmemorable to me—holiday cards dating back thirty years and written by people even he could not remember (I once asked); antiquated technical manuals of products he had designed but no one will again use; electronic parts to unknown machines; photos of strangers and places unidentifiable; all the receipts and bills he had ever paid; decades-old tax information preserved just in case of an audit that he never had. Or ever will.

Then there are his clothes. He kept them all through weight gains and losses, fads and aging. Letting go was hard for him as well. Even when we moved in together and space was at a premium, he resisted a downsizing of the past. It took him months to come to terms with the disposal of a polyester leisure suit, patiently kept it in his closet for twenty-five years. He was convinced of a fashion comeback. It still might. But he won't be here to wear it.

For a long time after he died, I would make a daily pilgrimage to the closet to breathe the fragrance of his clothes. The olfactory implosion filled me with memories. Loving moments. I would bury my face in a jacket, a sweater, a shirt; they were all I had. But now I can no longer call forth memories stimulated by fabric. His smell is gone, replaced with a stale, mildewy odor of disuse and time.

No, I remind myself as I lean against the door frame inhaling the memories. *If I don't do it now, I may never again have the courage. Besides,* I remind myself, *to get through this, all I have to do is remember.*

I recall the moment when I realized that I did have the strength to begin this process. It wasn't the passage of time—it's been over two years—or some hidden strength-of-self. No, it wasn't even anything practical. It was about feeling safe. It was about acceptance. It was about love. I needed his permission. And I know exactly when he gave it to me.

Here then, is my story.

It was a balmy night on a boat prodding slowly across Lake Victoria. The African air was filled with rotting fish smells, lake breezes, peeling, moldy paint, and the indefatigable lake flies that held an uncanny resemblance to the common moth. These small, winged stow-aways either filled the air in competition with oxygen, or lay fallen on the deck in a two-inch carpet of insect bodies. It made the deck nearly impossible to walk. You skated, holding tightly to whatever structure was nearby. It gave a whole new meaning to the nautical wisdom, steady-as-she-goes.

We had just left Uganda bound for Tanzania. I was excited with the moment, but I also needed sleep. So with no other space available on the deck where we were camping, I swept clean an area with my feet and laid my sleeping bag beneath the misfiring fluorescent light. A bad choice. My senses were blasted with the blinking, buzzing cacophony of electricity, and thousands of lake flies jockeying into position to fling their tiny bodies helplessly into the light and eventually down upon me.

Since it was hot and humid even with the gentle lake breeze, I lay on top of the bag, mesmerized by the boat's foamy vee-shaped wake on the blue-black lake surface. But with the loud hum of the diesel engines below and the suicidal bugs above, I found sleep impossible. I wandered off from my dozing companions to the huge forward hole to watch the night's activities. It was nearly 2:00 A.M. and other than the ebony-skinned Tanzanians shouting as they worked, I was alone. This was a real banana boat, and I wanted to see the men arrange the edible yellows wrapped in gunny sacks to protect them from bruising, and the hearty, green ones used only for cooking, and requiring no gentle handling. Women and sleeping children perched on the top of the highest moun-tains of bananas, some piled fifteen feet in the air. Other men, perhaps the bosses, stood in the background and lazily chain-smoked, talking and gesturing with one another. Every so often, they'd yell something in Swahili to one of the workers. The men would laugh and gesture. Commerce in Africa is not always profitable, but it is filled with expec-tation and energy.

For over an hour I watched, on occasion wondering about their lives. Were these workers happy? What were their dreams? What did they know of beyond this lake? What did they know of death? I wanted to talk to them, but I was invisible from my perch above.

I left behind the raucous happenings only when the moment's expe-rience was overwhelmed by fatigue. Heading back to the area loosely called "First Class," I knew that if I was going to get any rest, it had to be right then. The next day would be grueling, with hours of driving over, around, and into pothole after rock, more resembling the pockmarked terrain of a military siege than the country's main cross-country highway. From the port city of Bokoba, where we would debark in just four hours, to the Serengeti's Western Corridor—only sixty miles—it would take eight hours of jostling that would make our bones ache. Driveable roads are not a priority in East Africa.

Now, as I crawled into my sleeping bag, I knew sleep would be easy, despite the winged assault, the spectacular audiovisual display of the fluorescent lights, and cacophonous brotherhood of those who would work through the night as they arranged their precious cargo. I was asleep in minutes, but not before I made my nightly plea for a dream, a Merrill-dream, as if there were someone, somewhere who was taking orders for dreams.

I missed him terribly. Although muted by time, my grief had a lot to do with why I was sleeping on the crickety, insect-infested deck of an African banana boat. It had a lot to do with everything I had done since the day he died in July 1994.

Those few hours as I slept and as the boat made its way slowly across Lake Victoria will always remain unforgettable. I have dreamed my dreams before, but this was something quite different. Yes it was.

I was in an antique store with a woman I had briefly met in Nairobi. When I glanced out the window, I saw a group of women dressed in gauzy, ethereal gowns and sitting in a circle. In the middle sat a lone man. I could see when he stood up that he was quite tall. Behind me, my companion continued to talk, but my attention was riveted on this man. When he turned toward me, I saw it was Merrill. As he stepped out of the circle I ran out the door and into his arms.

I remember thinking: this is not a dream.

For hours, or perhaps only minutes, I could not tell, we held each other and moved in small circles. He told me that this is the cycle, these circles, that there is no beginning and no end. He told me that I must remember that, no matter how hard it is to understand. He said that he was okay and that I would be, as well. I can let go of my pain by just keeping the memories in my heart.

For a long time he held me and whispered in that beloved baritone. I cannot remember what words he said, only their intention. I told him that he looked serene, so peaceful. He hugged me and said, yes, he was.

For awhile longer we made our slow circles. Then he said he had to go. He touched me on the cheek, smiled gently, and walked back to the group. Bereft, I turned to follow, but he put his hand out.

No, *he said softly, his eyes gentle and loving. It was not yet my time. And then he was gone.*

It has been several months since that night on Lake Victoria. To this day, I carry with me some of the images and words, all the joy of having met him again, a profound sense of peace, and the strength I need to stand in this doorway, trash bag in hand, resolve in heart. I know that my most important job is to hold safe the memories; to keep his voice alive by re-telling his stories. Our stories. It is an easy responsibility.

Nonetheless, I hesitate; afraid of failure; afraid of success. The job is daunting and I don't know how I'll respond. If I have learned anything from Merrill's death, it is that nothing is for certain, most of all emotions.

So, I breathe deeply, close my eyes and let his winds of life blow gently over me. I visualize the bananas, the boat, the flies, the shouting Africans. And the circles.

Yes, remember the circles, I remind myself as I move toward the first box.

GRATITUDE

Bobbie Chalmers

She dusts the weeping buddha, wipes marble,
        shines lamps. In broad light, sweet sorrow,
        she handles an everyday picture of him.

At once, no warning, there he is. Taking up space.
        Weighing in. She had forgotten, living so long
        with scents in flight, images framed.

And then this remembering, untinged by grace.
        Not unlike the kisses that sometimes startle her awake
        in a sweat and gasping, in gratitude and disbelief.

I THEE WED

Nancy B. Schmitt

My memories are of
The home-made fabric
Of our marriage with
Its uneven tension and
Flawed threads in
So many places, yet
Beautiful in its whole.
What I hesitate to do yet
Is take the finished piece
Off the loom and
Put it away.

TIME TAKES ALL

Karen Klussman Lewis

One morning shortly after my husband George died, our four-year-old son Willy led me into the garden. He showed me the treasures that he and his daddy had put there during the recent Easter week.

There were blown glass balls used to float fishing nets from distant lands; a massive anchor salvaged from the deep, some chain from another shipwreck; and a brass sundial glinting under its cover of blooming lavender. Willy asked me to read the sundial.

The sundial was like so many things, people, and places that George collected during his lifetime—another thing that he never shared with me. The inscription reads: *Time takes all but memories.*

And in that moment, I felt a wealth of memories in the wake of his absence. I wondered, *Did George know that he was close to death? Was his death even self-inflicted, a careless reaction to our marriage's emotional tornadoes? What were his last thoughts, feelings? As he was diving in cold swells, searching the rocky bottom for sea urchins to harvest, did he know? Did he reach for two small children? Did he even reach for me? What was he thinking when he left "Time takes all but memories" in my garden?*

I remember a hazy Monday afternoon, the day of the phone call. The call telling me about George's accident. A whir of Coast Guard helicopter and apologies from medical technicians. A blur, drifting, drifting in ocean swells of shock and sadness. Somehow I was grounded with two children holding on tightly.

I remember taking Willy to retrieve the body. It was important for him to know, to feel, to see his father. To experience the reality of his father's death, for it may be the shaping incident of Willy's life. Just as George was forever shaped by his own parent's early death when he was a teenager.

I will never forget the cold, stiff effigy of the man who, at forty-four, had just hours earlier been so full of life. It took months before we realized George's truck would not turn into our driveway again.

Today, five years have elapsed since George's passing. I heed the sundial's wisdom. I mull over memories of George with the children. It is a cool, gray morning at the wild Northern California seashore, where lichen-encrusted boulders plunge into white water and the sea churns beneath a family of gulls. I walk hand-in-hand with Will, now nine, and our daughter, Carrie, nearly six.

Gull cries surge through my heart as mournful as a solo oboe echoing in deserted alleys. Each gull flies its solitary destiny, at times mated, at times alone.

Mornings like this bring to mind the day we scattered my husband's ashes in these waters. The gulls cried then. The memories come without invitation.

It was a fog-gray afternoon when friends and family gathered at our apple farm to create George's memorial service. Willy had not fully understood that one shoe-sized box weighing like bricks actually contained the remains of his father. Carrie was so new to this world, her spirit was probably closer to her father's in the after-realm than to any of ours rooted to this life-realm.

People near me at the time of George's passing saw a slender, quiet woman of thirty-five years with garden-calloused hands, a perpetual suntan, and two angelic children, one a nursing infant girl with the sapphire blue eyes of her father.

Our home was so recently constructed and inhabited that my husband's memorial became our housewarming party, where more than one hundred souls gathered to grieve, to honor, and perhaps even curse the man who had died.

Nobody could comprehend the mixture of emotions that twirled within me like cloud cover swirling around latitudes of our planet Earth.

Fortunately, friends and family stood by me in silence, in sharing, in sorrow, or even in laughter as the situation warranted. Friends stood solid and I leaned. I leaned and learned to lean some more. Friends and family were there, and are there. For this I am deeply and forever thankful.

I began to realize on that day, for many reasons, that George's death was a blessing rather than a curse. We created an elaborate ritual of fire, banners, prayers, and offerings to spirits above. His death seemed connected somehow to our daughter's recent birth. Are not death and birth equally honored parts of the same life continuum?

George shunned old age and would have been a miserable invalid. He died in the ocean, his chosen element, performing the work he loved.

George's death was also an affirmation to each survivor about the gift of life. A gift to be savored, celebrated, and endured moment-by-moment. Each of us gathered that day sensed a reality that death may call at any instant. Death has, like the ocean, some unfathomable, non-negotiable claim upon each of us.

His death bestowed an obscure blessing on me. It released me from pain, pain and a sense of doom that had wrapped itself like an octopus around our married life. No one except myself and four-year-old Willy had any idea of the arguments that left permanent soul-inscribed scars. The bruises of emotional and verbal abuse.

Emotional healing takes time, and the moments, weeks, months, and finally years following the death of my husband have taught me lessons about sorrow, forgiveness, terror, gratitude, and ultimately, joy.

I felt sorrow when George died. An empty, weightless sense that not only was he gone, but also that I was suddenly not the same person as I had been while married to him.

Stripped of the man who united us, the children and I were left to create new lives. Possibility is the strand, thin as a spider's web, to which I clung so desperately.

Sorrow, which most permeated my soul, is the sense of loss of my children's father. Gone are the days-to-be-shared. Kindergarten graduations never-to-be-shared with their dad, the first-time-riding-a-two-wheeler days, the I-can-swim-by-myself-in-the-ocean days. Gone. But as we grieve, so do we celebrate.

One moment of life is falling-down-funny. One moment I'm so mad I'm getting the hiccups. One moment the giant pumpkin seeds are sprouting and poppies are growing again in daddy's spirit garden.

When George died, it was springtime. Signs of natural renewal abounded: in the garden, in the woodland forest, in the path of the sun seeking summer equinox and sending flashes of light into our home. The children and I together discovered signs of an eternal spirit. An eternal spirit connected to him.

Sorrow gave way to terror that grasped at my intestines with chilly fingers for months after the memorial service. I was afraid about raising two children alone. Would I be able to teach them all that they need to learn? Would I live long enough to usher them into adulthood? Could I shoulder the burdens of business and household?

I was suddenly terrified of dark shadows during long nights. Noises, especially a strange and plaintive howling of a feral cat or fox in the woods, set my nerves tingling.

When the phone rang, I sometimes felt panic, even if it wasn't a Monday. As if the phone could ring again with dreaded death-news.

The sight of an ambulance could set me on edge, suddenly fearful for children at school, for other loved ones, wondering for whom the siren sounded in the quiet afternoon?

The shadows and noises in the night—did they scare me because they might be George's spirit come to claim me? Or was it dread that his spirit was forever gone, unavailable for guidance, lost in the void of the unknown hereafter?

Face to face with apprehensive nights, I came to realize that I do not want to find George or his soul again in the afterlife. I even pray that whatever drama we were meant to share, has been finished. If we were to meet again, I fear he would be dangerous to me.

On some of the long, dark, lonely nights after George died, I found companionship with my infant daughter. She cried from a different set of needs than mine and yet we would find the rocking chair and comfort each other beneath vast arrays of firestar.

The stars have a way of letting us know that there is a plan for life here, even if we cannot understand all of life's nuances.

Terror moved out of the center of my soul to make room for me to embrace forgiveness.

I began to forgive on the day that George died. This process continued for days, weeks, months, and is happening now even five years after his death. I would never have believed that one man's death could teach so much compassion.

I forgave George for dying. I forgave him for leaving the children. I forgave George for abandoning me, a process that began spiritually at least a year before he died. I acknowledged friends who chose not to be present for his memorial.

I began to reconcile mixed emotions about the long days and nights of separation and anxiety while George toiled on his fishing vessels. I forgave the boats and his work companions for demanding so much of his time and energy.

I even have come to pardon the government for creating conflict in Vietnam, for sending George as an innocent youth to fight there, and for bringing home men trained to kill, trained to hurt, trained to endure, and for causing young men like George to be so damaged that they were not able to settle into peaceful family lives ever again.

I have made allowances for my "old" self who spent over ten years of life with the "wrong" man.

I forgave George for leaving me one night on the verge of miscarriage. A night when my parents helped transport me to the hospital in puddles of blood because my husband thought it was urgent to catch a ride back to his out-of-state job.

I have forgiven George the letter from one of his clandestine lovers that I discovered while our daughter was in neonatal intensive care and my every energy was devoted to our baby's survival.

I have come to forgive that particular woman and any other women who were physically intimate with my husband while we were married. I forgave them for enjoying him in a way I never could, while I was taking care of his home and business; doing his laundry; rearing our children; working my fingers and muscles and soul to new dimensions of strength in fulfillment of my husband's dreams.

All is forgiven. All so suddenly simple.

In fact, I wish that my former husband had run off to Argentina or anywhere with that woman, instead of dying. The children would then at least have a daddy somewhere that they could talk with, write to, and possibly visit.

I do regret that George did not live long enough so that Willy and Carrie would know, in absolute truth, that they were his most precious treasures and how very much he loved them.

And as the memories come to the surface, we share. I affirm to the children the goodness of their father. I hope that the scar of "that night" of our most awful family argument, will fade from Willy's memory.

Forgiveness is in some ways like love, it touches all of our senses in random and miraculous ways.

I never felt so naked nor vulnerable as when George died. My life became transparent like a dragonfly, so that anyone could see right into my soul. Suddenly, I realized there was not a moment to squander in emotional pretense or costume.

So much has happened since my husband died. I fell cataclysmically in love the year after George died with one of our casual friends, a married man. I betrayed their marriage and entered a wild canyon of many-colored layers of distrust and sorrow that had stained my own marriage. I forgave myself for this trespass and wondered if I would ever be forgiven.

It seems like a search for compassion within the self leads automatically to discovery of gratitude.

The time after George's death has been full of gratitude. I praise God for blessing me with more tender moments of life.

As each of us gathered in memory of George, I remember fog and smoke mingled in the tree tops. Mist beaded into pearls on May's new green grass. Each dewy pearl is like a seed of possible life moments. The seeds swell, within each of us, evolving into gardens and deserts and jungles and oceans of experience.

Friends gathered at the memorial that day have since faced death, cancer, heart attacks, incarceration, birth, divorce, marriage, job loss, and so many other intense life experiences. They have each been touched with the courage to face their lives, moment by moment.

I give thanks to George for gracing me with two treasured children and a home in which to live. I give thanks to George's family, who love me and the children unconditionally as friends and as family.

I feel gratitude to God for letting me love again. For allowing me to discover my lifemate, my new husband. For revealing to me the challenges, powers, and possibility of the true marriage of loving, open hearts.

As I have walked the widow's path, I can affirm that time does heal. But time also brings new sorrows. Time is the dimension that unites memory, healing, sorrow, love, and the other realms of human experience.

For one long moment of retreating tide, pulling at me like part of a heart muscle, I notice a tide pool of water glistening clear as a sapphire. Cold, blue, pacific, like Carrie's eyes, suddenly turbulent like her father's.

There is a rough-furred gray sea lion body tangled with bull kelp in the sand where vultures feed. The sea lion is cold, gone, as surely as George. And the tides keep rolling, the sun shines, burning layers of black and gray from my heart. I am suddenly swimming in a perfect day without memory, without expectation, without any sense of time cascading all around, like little waterfalls onto the beach.

ASHES TO ASHES

Joanne Calkins

When I picked up the box from Newton's Family Funeral Home I was surprised that it was so small; then, that it was so heavy. I had always heard that the human body was mostly water. Without liquid, it was only several pounds of ashes, packed inside a brown plastic box four by six by ten inches. The label read: "This urn contains the remains of James Lyle Chapman, inurned by Whitman Cemetery and Crematory, 5/25/94."

When I got home, sitting alone in our dark living room, I opened the box. Silent and gray in a clear plastic bag, the ashes were heavy like gold, but looked more like sand.

"This is my love. This is Jim," I said, trying to convince myself. I felt them. They were as dry as dust and gritty with a few chalky chunks. I smelled them. No odor at all. I closed the bag and put it back in the box.

I wanted to get close to him but when I hugged the hard box, hopelessness flooded through me.

Is this what's left of the body that I had wanted so much in the beginning, even though I wasn't sure it was love? Is this the man who loved me "madly," whose hug was like a whole body massage?

I remembered his strong arms and shoulders, his handsome profile and bald head, his funny bowed legs, his hands that went instinctively to the places in my body that ached. Now I ached all over, and where was he?

I wanted to see the wild, wiry beard that shone in the sunlight like copper. It gave off sparks of yellow, green, and purple, especially through tears and eyes out of focus when I buried my face in it. I never got a good photograph of his beard, although I tried many times.

Now it was nothing but several pounds of ash. The ashes were all I had, so I kept them on the mantle in the living room next to a collection of his photographs. I would sit there and look at them and remember, sometimes smiling, sometimes crying, sometimes both. Eventually, I felt reverence for the ashes, as I had felt reverence, love, and wonder for his body in life.

Thankfully, I had the pictures. I had photographed Jim many times. When I admired some part of his body too much he would be embarrassed and say, "Okay, I'll leave it to you when I die." I would grimace at the thought, and he would laugh. Now that the ashes were on my mantle, I didn't care that I had signed a paper at the funeral home saying I wouldn't scatter them around.

"Whoever made that law can go to hell! I'll put them wherever I want," I often said to myself. "He left them to me."

But I knew it was too soon to let go of the ashes—if I ever could. For the time being, I was content to leave them safely on the mantle, waiting.

Of course, I knew that Jim was more than his body, so I was surprised at what happened about six weeks after he died. At the time, I was still nervous about being alone at night. One night, I suddenly awoke from a deep sleep. I heard a bang and the sound of footsteps on the wood floor in the living room, then on the linoleum in the kitchen and as they got closer, on the carpet in the hall. I was terrified. I had nothing with which to defend myself. It was too late to get under the bed or into the closet. I was paralyzed in fear and didn't dare open my eyes.

Then something breezed through the door without opening it. A gentle wind marvelously lifted my hair and caressed my head and face. My chest vibrated as though something had entered it. Relief, love, and joy filled me. Suddenly, I felt he was okay; he was watching out for me, telling me, "You're not alone. I'm here."

Shortly after that, I began to think more about the contact we still had. I bought a wind chime and hung it in the apple tree in the backyard.

"If he can make air move, we can communicate that way," I reasoned.

Sometimes I would hear it ringing and run to the window and call out, "Hi, love." When I was working in the garden I would walk by and jingle the bells, flirtatiously, not unlike the way he had twirled my telephoto lens as the camera hung on its strap on my chest. Sometimes, when I missed him painfully, I would actually hug the chimes. They would go crazy.

I realized that I felt much better talking to his spirit than to his ashes. Also, I began to sense that some people who came over were nervous with my prominent display of ashes in the living room.

I began to think more and more about what to do with the ashes. The memorial service had happened months ago. Since Jim loved nature, I began to take the ashes out to his favorite places.

At first I got friends to go with me. Then relatives. We cried, even as we made jokes about the "sacred" Styrofoam cup used to transport his ashes. But after their first outing with me and my ashes, most of my friends began to feel too sad, so I went alone.

For me, each time was a ceremony—a fond, usually cheerful remembering, a grieving, and a letting go. I needed a lot of ceremonies. I believed that Jim was more of a free spirit than ever and could be wherever he wanted to be, and was in these special places.

I put some of his ashes where we had picnicked or camped or scuba dived along the coast of California. I threw them into the waves and sometimes the wind flung them playfully back at me. I sprinkled them in waterfalls and springs and on the top of mountains overlooking the Sierra Nevada. I always tried to photograph the spot where I left some ashes.

"Enjoy the view, Jim," I would say, or "Goodbye, I love you," or "Now you are a part of this place you love."

I left some in the desert near a bizarre cactus, which I know he would have photographed if he could. Friends and I placed them under the old oaks in the local park. His Mom and Grandma and I put some at the foot of El Capitan in Yosemite right in the place he had photographed in a wonderful black and white so long ago. I put a little pile on a rock in the San Joaquin River so that when the spring rains came the ashes would be washed out into California's Central Valley where he was born.

Jim was a Vietnam veteran. Agent Orange had caused the cancer that killed him. I felt deeply resentful, but I knew that although he had suffered greatly because of the war in many ways, it was not a completely negative experience for him. So I searched for a place to put his ashes at the new veterans' cemetery. I didn't put them in a plot or near the straight rows of flat, white stones—they were too much like ranks of anonymous soldiers.

I sprinkled them next to the sign at the gate that said: *We are trying to preserve this place as a home for wildlife including the coyote, bobcat, foxes, gophers, mice, snakes, and locusts. Please stay out of the high grass.*

I threw some into the high grass.

I dropped a handful of ashes from a bridge into the rushing water of the Wyndot-Mendotta Canal and then photographed the white spot as they dissipated into the current on their way to Southern California. Once I offered his ashes to the fire on a mountain in New Mexico because I knew he would love going up in smoke to be part of the thunderheads, scrambling to obscure the moon.

I fertilized the apple tree in the backyard with his ashes and watered it with my tears, remembering when we planted it on Valentine's Day. I carried some of his ashes with me all the time. I didn't mind that some of him ended up in the bottom of my purse or in the trunk of the car. He had a right to be there.

At first, I used up a cup or so at each favorite spot. Later, I had to decrease the amount or I would have run out before I was ready. I needed to save some for Mexico and Central America where we had traveled. I still want to get some to Vietnam and the home of the Montagnard people. In some places that I liked, but wasn't sure he would—such as cities—I only put a teaspoonful. Much later, I took him places he had never been: to the peaks of Machu Picchu and the blue water of Tobago.

Jim's mother finally decided to put the ashes in the cemetery in her town. I had no objection. It would give her and other relatives a place to visit, but there weren't many ashes left. It was a very light plastic box that went legally into the crypt. But it was another beautiful memorial service.

I saved some for myself. I bought a blown-glass vase with swirling blue currents and waves and put a cup of ashes in it, and glued a perfect sand dollar on top as a lid. I'll keep these, of course, until the next wonderful opportunity for remembering comes along.

CONVERSATION IN THE DARK

Barbara Adams

The phone is ringing. 2:30 A.M. The dial tone buzzes. No one, again. "Why do you keep calling me if you have nothing to say? It's been two years. You should have accepted reality by now. I know it's you. I called the phone company to check my line. The supervisor said there was no record of any incoming calls at 2:30 A.M. Maybe I was dreaming," she said. "What do they know? My hearing is as good as a cat's."

"Either say something, or leave me alone!" she says into the phone. Then tells him the rest:

"For two years, I've looked for you in all your favorite haunts. Just once, I caught a glimpse of you—at sunset, last fall. You were standing on the hill in back of our house, you and Allan. You had fish poles over your shoulders and brook trout hanging from a string. You looked so happy.

"I'll never forget the first time you cooked trout for me. I was hooked. 'They have no scales,' you said, gutting them, cutting off their heads. You washed them in the stream, rolled them in flour, then dropped the red-dotted silvery blue fillets into bacon fat sizzling over hot coals. I knew, then, you would always take care of me."

The phone is ringing. 2:30 A.M.

"Hello, Little Squaw . . . ."

"Oh! It is you!"

"You're not angry anymore, are you?"

"No, dearest, I'm not angry anymore. Please talk to me—tell me how you are."

"I was so tired—you have no idea how tired I was. I've been catching up on sleep. Two years already! Allan came by one day and said, 'Let's go fishing.' The day you saw me. We sure caught a lot of fish that day. I never could have caught that many alone.

"Allan always knew where the best places were to find trout. He kept them secret from everyone, except me.

"I've been calling you, darling, because I'm getting sick of sleeping and fishing as much as I want. I'm sorry if I've been keeping you awake. We were so close, I don't want to let you go. You've been having a good time without me, I see—I've been watching you. I expected you would, eventually. At first, I was really pissed that you didn't come with me. I was so jealous of your vitality, your enjoyment of everything.

"God, I was tired. Please forgive me for leaving you. I still—will always—love you. Anyway, you deserve time to yourself. You took such good care of me, you never took care enough of yourself. But those guys you've been seeing—good God! Are you trying to prove that women are just as stupid as men? At least you came to your senses and dumped the first two. This guy Jack, now, is the best so far—you may just make it with him. I wasn't so bad after all, was I?

"Goodnight, dear, I'll be here, waiting, when you want me."

"Wait! Please, don't go again! Talk to me! Where can I find you? Darling, I miss you so much."

The phone is ringing. It's 2:30 A.M.

"Why won't you talk to me anymore?"

Because you're not listening anymore.

PHOENIX

Linda Ribordy

I see my body rising through the smoke of the fire, twisting, spiraling upward out of the heat. I have crashed. I have been reborn.

A few weeks after the love of my life died unexpectedly, someone said to me that this tragedy was a tremendous growth opportunity for me. She suggested that I had a choice to wallow in my grief or I could choose to grow from this heartbreaking experience. From the depths of my despair, centered only in my pain, I very clearly told this person that she was full of shit. Please get out of my house, my life, my line of vision. My life was over. I wanted to die. I did not to want to live without him. I certainly did not want to grow and become more.

When the center went out of my life, my whole being imploded, collapsing inward. There was no core to my being. There was no substance. Every organ quaked, my stomach ceased to digest, my throat ceased to swallow, my lungs ceased breathing. Grief apnea is pervasive. Interrupted breathing, interrupted sleep, interrupted life.

My desire to simply lie down and die with my loved one battled with the innate human will to survive. The survival instinct won. And so I go on. Walking through the pain, waiting impatiently for the next wave of grief to roll over me. Choices to be made: I sink into the pain even as I begin to look at sunrises as the very depiction of the glory of life. I start to move forward.

I found movement to be healing—not random movement, but movement with a purpose. My particular form of intense therapy was to walk. Strap on the tape player, with his favorite tape, and walk until no coherent thought was left and the body was tired enough for sleep and brief episodes of peace. As my body tightened in response to the unfamiliar level of exercise, my personal approval rating thermometer began to rise. And so I walked. And walked. I cried vats. I healed.

I did not court healing. In fact, I actively resisted it. Healing meant letting go of the love of my life. No way was that going to happen. What if I feel better? Won't I forget him? To pay adequate homage to him, I must keep crying. He won't believe how much I love him if I stop crying. If I pause to enjoy, I am betraying his love.

I know now that I will never stop crying for my mate. But the intensity and frequency does lessen. The pain has receded from the very beat of my heart to a soft murmur as the blood flows through my veins.

And one day I realized that I have created a new person—a single person with an outrageous zest for life. A single person—with an attitude.

"No, I am neither married nor single," I told the census taker. "I am a fucking widow . . . . I will always be married to him. He just happens to be dead. Get a clue." And I watched their collective jaws drop, and celebrated—for one moment, in one place, someone felt my disease with life and shared it.

The phoenix has a new image, a new view of life: Live right now because it could all be gone in the blink of an eye. Forget the future. I can't control it so why worry about it. A lesson I've learned well. The future that I envisioned is gone. Now I know what will be, will be, and let it be, let it be. The phoenix has risen. A new life emerges, built on a foundation of love and memories. I am invulnerable to other people's demands, needs, and expectations. I do what I want, when I want, and I do what feels light and right. I ignore the unreasonableness of other's lives and live my life my way. I have been liberated. I frequently check the pulse of my needs and wants. And I listen to what I hear from my heart.

While I would never have chosen this path, I am on it and I am in charge. Just for me. I check with no one at decision time: I am it. And you know what? It's okay. I can do this. I am alive. I love life again. I don't intend to miss a minute of it.

THE WISH

Gayle Elen Harvey

Weeks since leaves fell, August outlived,
lick of flame becoming conflagration, charred
text spreading through October.
Mountain after mountain keening silence.
Months thin to winter when the padlocked sky
is heavier, with-holding, as it sometimes does,
the answers.

Death's raucous-winged. It nests in swamps
like loneliness and even now is lying wait
in backyard thickets, keeping scheduled,
unscheduled appointments.

Grief is recent as a phone call
but we cannot stay where you have left us.
Even now, the fishing streams you loved,
tug all around us, warming to your wish
for memories wonderful as summer when the wind's
hand spills a million fireflies, like stars,
to bless us, when even night, itself, relinquishes
its dark cloth.

A QUESTIONS OF NAMING

Rondi Lightmark

Dear Jim,

Six months ago last Monday, you stepped out of your body. The next day, the eye of the moon eclipsed and later, it rained. The following weekend, as we all gathered to celebrate your life in the darkening November light, you threw a rainbow down to tell us you were okay.

The day we passed the sixth-month mark, I was down in New York with the book you inspired in me to prove that out of the shattering fall unexpected gifts. The next day, the sun, like the November moon, blinked once in remembrance. In the center of town people danced, not knowing some of the dance was for you.

The week passed and Friday brought a great wind and cold, a reminder of the bitter endless winter days. The pond glazed out of habit. As I got ready to leave for the weekend, the stovepipe rattled and banged and the house shook in the gale. I pounded on the pipe to make sure that it would not fall out of the wall, since there was still a bit of fire in the stove from the frosty morning. It was so wild outside, it almost made the pipe sound inhabited.

The stovepipe rattled and banged all night. The next day, Marcus and Terry, visiting in my absence, remarked on the noise, but knowledge did not dawn until the body of the stove itself took up the sound and soot began to rhythmically puff out of the cracks. "There's something in there," said Terry, and left for home. Marcus got around to checking that evening and opened the door. A long, sharpish beak. A beady eye. My stove had birthed a full-grown female Merganser duck!

When Marcus finally came to terms with the reality of the situation (not quite comprehending how my stove, accessible only by four right angles of pipe and chimney and one three-inch wide baffle, could do such a thing), he called Mom, wise woman of the forest, for help and subsequently was able to reach in and lift her (not Mom, the duck), light feathery, decidedly sooty and exhausted from the ashes, and place her in a box for the night. In the morning, he showed her the pond. She quacked for joy and took a swim and then a serious nap on the shore.

When I arrived home later in the day and heard this story and witnessed the duck's composed departure down river, I marveled at this singular event that had graced my home, my stove, my life.

I know that you are gone—and yet not gone. A mirror is turned in a strange and different way and I look for refractions from the cosmos all the time, trying, always trying to learn how to speak this new language we have between us. I immediately began asking, "What does this mean?" No, I do not think you paid your former home a visit in duck form, although remembering your sense of humor, I wouldn't put it past you. No, it's taken me until this moment, three o'clock in the morning to figure it out. It may have looked like a duck, but it was really a phoenix! It was you and the heavens in another translation, like the moon and the sun and the rainbow.

Out in the yard, all the daffodils the children planted for you last autumn are up and leaping and trumpeting on the riverbank. The river melted gently this year, no torrents and chunks of ice on the edges and now its round-the-clock work is to remind me about flow. "Be a duck," it murmurs now, outside in the remnants of night, wanting to share in the mystery or reclaim one of its symbols.

Everywhere I go these days, I meet or hear about someone struggling with or dying of cancer. There is a battle waged, but I remember well that point when the battle metamorphoses and the terrain becomes pregnant with stillness, peace, and possibility. Love emerged, both in the warrior and in those companions who have helped hold the sword. Those who find some key to unlock a door into new life here, find they have acquired a brimming, transformative energy that comes from the conquering of fear: energy which cannot be held, but must be shared. And you, Jim, for whom the other door opened, still find so many tender and magnificent ways to send that energy back.

These days, if I meet someone new to the kind of pain and process I have been through, there is always an element of excitement in me, strange to say.

"Wait," I want to say. "Watch and stay open because amazing things will come your way. More love and grace than you ever would have dreamed possible. Light a candle every night and cry if you need to, but don't forget to ask for help. Write down your dreams and they will teach you. Do at least one thing you have been talking all your life about doing because you will find much is possible."

You've been given a life with a big bump in it. Use it to get up really high so you can see far, then jump off and fly. Something wonderful will hold you. And if, by chance, a big wind gets too full of itself and throws you down, say, a chimney and you have to spend lifetimes flopping and crawling through smoke and soot in the dark, know this: someone will open the door.

Welcome the light, and remember who you are: it's all a question of naming.

WHERE TUNNELS END

Maureen Cannon

What shall I tell you? That you will survive?
You will (there are so many of us), and
You'll wonder why. But pain keeps one alive
As much as joy does. Let me take your hand,
And I will say no word beyond what we
Can bear who know so well what hell can be.

Now it is time. Perhaps your grief's become
As much a part of any Monday as
Your daily bread. It's Tuesday's tea. On some
Sweet Thursday you—surprised—have laughed. Ah, has
The world grown round again, and is the night
Less long? Grief is a tunnel, but there's light
Where tunnels end. I promise, life is meant
To savor still. It's simply—different.

STORIES
(Excerpted from *Geography of the Heart*)

Fenton Johnson

This is what the ill and the dead have given me: An appreciation of the soul, an understanding of the spirit, how pure these words are, how absent from our culture, how great is our particular responsibility to restore them—as artists, as writers, as vessels for the stories of our dead.

As I have participated in the deaths of so many of my peers, I have come to believe passionately in the ways in which words—in this case the names and stories of our dead—have the power to invoke among us the presence of those who, as Orthodox Jews would have it, have traded the world of appearance for the world of truth. This is why remembering and speaking out are so important. Through remembering—through invoking the names and stories of those I have loved—I engage my most essentially human quality. Human beings are animals who remember and tell stories—as much as any other, this characteristic distinguishes us from our fellow creatures. The dead have given me an awareness of the mystery of life and death. I have a responsibility to remember them by living out that gift.

I think about all this; then I remember a story of someone or some place gone from my life and tell it to somebody else, and in the telling of that story take my proper and necessary place in the chain of being.

Since my house
burned down
I now have
a better view
of the rising
moon

—Masahida

ACKNOWLEDGMENTS

With gratitude and endless love to my beloved Donald whose sudden, untimely death taught me so much about life. Your integrity, grace, and guiding spirit carried me through ten years of adventure, love, and personal growth. I thank you, wherever you are. You left me in good hands—my daughter Elizabeth and my brother John, who held me together through this great tragedy and through five years of family losses. We're a small family, but powerful. My daughter's in-laws who took me into their family as one of them. My grief support group who, weekly, shared my tears and the laughter which can come only from the most profound pain. All my friends who were there if I needed them but allowed me to take my own lonely path on this journey, knowing they would be there at the end of the tunnel. My beautiful, darling Nanook who daily makes me laugh and love again. My endless appreciation for the wondrous place I live—its majestic redwood forests and beautiful beaches have been a haven of peace and solace for creating the balance necessary to keep onward in my life's journey, no matter what it brings. Lastly, to Grace and Susan, my forever friends. We found one another in pain; we continue together in laughter and love. —Janie

Living so close with the long and intimate dying of a beloved, I find I have received many gifts. One is a profound sense of gratitude which permeates my life now. I learned the importance of actively thanking those who cross our path and whom we even briefly touch. Many have touched me throughout Michael's death, my grief, and the creation of this healing book. I extend my deepest thanks to all of these sentient beings.

First I must thank my three wonderful children—Kia, Mike, and Eric—for your love and belief in me. You have shared the journey with all its peaks and valleys. Thanks to our wilderness land in the dusty Sierra foothills—always my refuge. Thanks to the Yuba River. Your clear green waters bring peace I find nowhere else. Thanks, mountain lion, for crossing my path and lending me your totem of strength. Thank you, feathers, for keeping me connected to the Great Mystery. Thanks, Mom, you and I widowed within the same year know both the courage and surprising new pleasures to be found. Jack for being there. Susie, my absolute very favorite Keeker and "husband." Andy for keeping the songs and friendship alive. Karla for protecting the door. Janie and Susan, who understand. All my second-grade students who hugged my tears away. All my friends and colleagues at Gateway School for amazing support—

Peter, Kathleen, Patricia, Rima, and Kim. Lorraine, Pam, and Lisa for feeding me. All the drunken sailors who laughed me back to life. My dear comrades who showed me endless compassion and encouragement—Serge, Michael K., Pam, Pat, Merle, Paul, Steve S., Tony, Cindy, and Vicki, our nurse. All the hands and hearts that have held me, too numerous to list. Meta and Earl for bringing Michael, the love of my life, into the world. Lastly, thank you, Michael, my soulmate. I get it, honey. It's all just a flash, like you said, and we are together. —Grace

This must begin with Merrill, who helped me soar with confidence. Your love, support, and belief in me then, is what keeps me going now. Thank you for our beautiful redwood sanctuary. I feel you everywhere beneath those branches. My gratitude is forever. And thank you to all who opened their hearts to me throughout this unimaginable passage. To Carola, my lifeline for three decades. You help keep me centered with wisdom and humor. My love and gratitude to Merrill's family for always including me. Most especially, to Sharon who stands by me as her brother's other memory. To my nieces and nephews: Stephanie, Jason, Sarena, Renato, Kelly, Mike, and little Matthew. To Vicki, the greatest of all big sisters, who dropped everything to be with me on July 26, 1994, and of course, to both Carolyns. To those of you who cared for Merrill before me—Dave, Harvey, Antoine, Jarda—and those who joined me as death approached and then, as I stood alone: Bev, Trev, Jean, Pat, Birgit, Judy, Minnesota Linda, Judith, Dr. Rick, Lou, Earl, Victoria, Steve, Don, Bev C., Nanette, and anyone else I've forgotten. To Ga Ne Na, who taught me how to let go, and Janie and Grace, how to hang on. And finally, to my son David, who supports all my odd choices, but regularly hugs me anyway. Thank you for being in my life and for giving me the only gift that could soften my loss: Taylor, my granddaughter, born seven months too late—he would have loved you so. —Susan

We would like to thank all the contributors—many of whom we were unable to include—for your extraordinary patience and for openly sharing from your hearts in the hope it will help others. It will.

Our gratitude is great. Thank you all. To the Hospice Caring Project of Santa Cruz County, especially Scott and Connie, for bringing us together. Deep affection to our "group" for keeping safe our stories and giving unwavering support throughout this project: Dale, Juliana, Joanne, Bob, Sheila, Jeannie, and Linda. To Juliana for your editing. To Dale and Carola for your supreme skill and patience. To the National Writers Union for its resources and Steve for your eleventh-hour editing and ever-present literary advice. To Linda and Sheila for your legal expertise. To Judith for your cyber-smarts. To Dena and Amber for your knowledge of anthologies. To Carol and Thomas for your words. —The Editors

BIOGRAPHIES OF THE EDITORS

Susan Heinlein is a freelance writer living in the Santa Cruz mountains, who survives by writing newspaper and magazine articles and marketing copy. She has worked as a stringer/staff writer for newspapers and was the San Francisco Bay Area's first female sports writer in the mid-1970s. Her lifemate and dearest friend, Merrill, an engineer and inventor, died of cancer in 1994 at the age of 54. She has a son and a granddaughter.

Jane-Ellen Tibbals has a B.A. in Literature and an M.L.S. in Library Science. Currently she is a manufacturer's rep for a women's athletic apparel line. She lives with her wolf hybrid, Nanook, in Ben Lomond, California, and has a married daughter in Philadelphia. Her mate, Donald deRenne, was a well-known entrepreneurial consultant to start-up companies in Silicon Valley. He was murdered by his brother in December 1993.

Grace Brumett is a teacher, writer, musician, and mother of three: Kia, Mike, and Eric. She lives in Santa Cruz and was married to Michael for twenty-five years. Michael was a builder, artisan, musician, and devoted father/husband. He battled Hodgkins Lymphoma for six years and died at home on June 18, 1994, age 48.

BIOGRAPHIES OF THE CONTRIBUTORS

Barbara Adams has published two books of poems (*Hapax Legomena* and *Double Solitaire),* a book of literary criticism, poems and stories in numerous journals, and essays. She is a professor of English at Pace University, New York City. Her husband, Elwood, a bricklayer, taught people with learning disabilities and wrote children's poems in the last years of his life. In 1993, he died of a stroke caused by chemotherapy.

Mary H. Ber has spent most of her life in the Chicago area. She taught high school English for over thirty years and now teaches at Roosevelt

University, co-edits a fledgling literary magazine, and has begun earning a master's degree in women's studies. She has published short stories, poems, and essays.

Margaret Blaker and Carl Blaker were married in 1948 in Washington, D.C., where they worked for many years, Carl at the Department of Agriculture and Margaret at the Smithsonian Institution. Margaret lives in Winter Haven, Florida; Carl died there in 1989.

Karen Calcaterra, a 47-year-old widow and mother of two, currently resides in Butte, Montana. For the past twenty-seven years her love of children has kept her teaching elementary school. Karen enjoys traveling, reading, and spending time with her offspring. Her husband, Carl, was killed at age 45 in a mining accident.

Joanne Calkins was a teacher for many years in Watsonville, California. After the death of her husband, she began to write for personal healing, and finished two adventure travel photo books that they had been writing together. She is now a writer-photographer, concentrating on peace and justice, nature, and personal essays. Her husband, Jim, died in 1994 of cancer brought on by Agent Orange.

Maureen Cannon has been widowed for almost twenty years. Her contributions were written out of "despair and desperation during what seems a long time ago." Today she is "'making it" solo and is profoundly grateful. Her husband, Jim, was a sales engineer, who built up his own company and ran it successfully for twenty-five years. A disciplined man, the only thing in his life he couldn't control were his brain tumors.

Marsh Cassady is the author of forty-four published books. A former actor/director and professor, he has a Ph.D. in theater and is fiction/drama editor of *Crazyquilt Quarterly*. Pat Cassady, also a poet, was most of all a mother to two biological and three adopted, biracial children. She died in 1978.

Roberta Chalmers lives in Laguna Beach, California, where she grew up and later shared a home with her husband Douglas. She was 47 when he died in 1993. She has two children and recently became a grandmother. Douglas was a psychology professor at the University of California, Irvine.

Ruth Coughlin is an award-winning feature writer and author of *Grieving: A Love Story,* who has been the book editor for *The Detroit News* since 1985. She lives in Grosse Pointe, Michigan. Her husband, William J. Coughlin, was a senior U.S. administrative law judge and author of fifteen novels. He died in 1992 from cancer.

Karen D'Amato has an M.A. in English from the University of Massachusetts, Boston. Currently she is working toward her M.Ed. and teacher certification and teaching poetry writing to second and fourth grade students. Her husband, Alan Daly, died in 1991 from a recurrence of testicular cancer.

S. K. Duff's poems have appeared in many magazines, journals, and books. His mate, Richard Holman, an accountant, gardener, and animal lover, died in 1993, in his mid-thirties, of AIDS.

Penelope Dugan lives in Willsboro, New York, and teaches at Richard Stockton College of New Jersey. Ingie Lafleur (1941–1993), her mate, was an historian of Eastern Europe and passionate fighter for social justice.

Ida Fasel is a Professor Emerita of English, University of Colorado at Denver. She is published widely, conducts poetry workshops, and is the author of *On the Meanings of Cleave* and seven chapbooks. She has won many prizes. Her husband, also a university professor, was born in Danzig and came to this country after World War II and completed his Ph.D. at Columbia. He died of cancer in 1973.

Miriam Finkelstein is the author of a novel, *Domestic Affairs* (1982). Her stories have appeared in magazines such as *Ascent, Arizona Quarterly, Kayak,* and *Kalliope.* She began writing poetry in 1990, shortly after the death of her husband. Her poems have appeared in *Commonweal* and *Women and Death.* She resides in New York City, where she is a learning specialist. Her husband, James, a psychiatrist, died in 1989.

David Garnes is a reference librarian and health sciences bibliographer at the University of Connecticut. In addition to writing essays for numerous reference books, he is a recent contributor to *Answers: The Magazine for Adult Children of Aging Parents* and the anthology *Connecticut Poets on AIDS.* His mate, Luis Felipe Pereira, died in 1992 and received many awards for his counseling work with the Hispanic community and for his statewide leadership in AIDS education.

Fanny Elisabeth Garvey is a student of theater, English, and history at Georgia State University. Her area of interest is contemporary Black and Irish literature. Her career goal is to teach at the college level, as well as write fiction and plays. She is the mother of two children, with whom she resides in Atlanta. Her Irish husband taught English until his death in 1982 at the age of 34.

Nancy Gotter Gates has had nearly two dozen short stories published, as well as many poems and articles. She is currently working on a novel set in Florida. She lives with her cats, Puff and Lovey, in Greensboro, North Carolina. Her husband, George, an employee of Goodyear Tire and Rubber Company, was one of the top ten salesmen in the country. He died in 1986 at 55 years of age.

Diana Goldman is currently working toward an M.A. in writing at Manhattanville College. Her short stories and poetry have appeared in literary journals nationwide and she is working on her first novel. She married her childhood sweetheart, Joe Velie, who died in 1985, less than a year after starting his own business.

Gayle Elen Harvey was the recipient of the 1989–90 New York Foundation for the Arts award and has published in *Sojourner, Atlanta Review, International Quarterly,* and *Plainsong.* Her most recent chapbook won the 1995 Permafrost Poetry Contest. Her husband, Patrick Moccaldi, died in 1986 at the age of 57. He was a beloved math teacher as well as a pianist, cook, reader, and fisherman.

Marna Hauk is a dyke, published poet, permaculture ecological systems designer, and earthern home and sacred-site builder flourishing in the Pacific Northwest. Open to connection with other sentients thriving on Mama Earth, in radical trust of the benevolent mysteries. Her mate, Anne Marie Seeber Ravenstone, died from leukemia in 1993 at the age of 25.

Gloria Rovder Healy was widowed on an April afternoon in 1976, leaving her with two beautiful children and wonderful memories. To heal, she began writing poetry and has won national contests; her work has appeared in literary journals. Newly remarried, she and her family live on the Jersey shore. Alexander Rovder, a Rutgers grad and a procurement analyst, died at the age of 52 while gardening.

Fenton Johnson is the author of two award-winning novels: *Crossing the River* and *Scissors, Paper, Rock.* He has received fellowships in literature from the National Endowment for the Arts for both fiction and non-fiction writing. His most recent book is *Geography of the Heart,* a memoir of his own upbringing in Kentucky and that of Larry Rose, an only child of German Jewish survivors of the Holocaust. Larry Rose, his mate, died of AIDS-related illness in 1990.

Nancy Kassell began writing poetry after twenty-five years of teaching Greek and Latin literature. Her poems have appeared in *Feminist Review, Southern Poetry Review,* and *River Poetry Review.* She has also written a nonfiction book, *The Phythia on Ellis Island: Rethinking the Greco-Roman Legacy in America.* Her husband, Saul Moskowitz, worked as a space engineer in celestial navigation and guidance.

Hazel King, widow of Raymond King, Jr., is the mother of Melissa and Steven. She is a homemaker, freelance writer, and retired North Carolina state employee who enjoys reading, travel, photography, and community theater, as well as church and family activities. Raymond died in 1994 at the age of 48. A natural comic, he is remembered for his legacy of love and laughter.

Christopher Koch became a licensed clinical social worker after his wife's suicide in 1990. Part of his work is with suicidal children and their families. He has turned a "bomb" into a resource to assist others. He shares his life with a sweetheart and precious friends. Debra's grandfather, father, and brother all committed suicide.

Eva Kolosvary is a visual artist, working in a broad spectrum of media, from printmaking to assemblage. Following the death of her husband and creative partner, she was unable to even enter her studio. Writing down her pain and emptiness became part of her slow healing process. Her husband, Paul, died in 1995 of cancer.

Diane Quintrall Lewis is a poet and artist. Four years after her husband died, she bought two-and-a-half acres of avocado trees. She has published work in several anthologies and journals and is the editor of *Magee Park*

Poets. Her husband, Warren, was a chemical engineer by occupation but other loves included his children, gardening, cooking, and karate.

Karen Klussman Lewis studied at Mount Holyoke College and graduated from Stanford University. She writes, gardens, and teaches with California Poets in the Schools. Karen is the mom of Will and Carrie and is happily remarried to the sculptor Will Lewis. They live in rural Mendocino County. The life of her husband, George Tomlinson, was claimed by the ocean, his lifelong passion, at the age of 44.

Rondi Lightmark is a freelance writer who also has over thirty years experience as a teacher of arts, music, and philosophy. She has written for V*ermont Magazine, Parenting, First for Women, Baby,* and *The Brattleboro Reformer.* She is currently writing a garden book with a spiritual focus. In her husband's last years, they shared the teaching of a kindergarten group of twenty children. James Robert Chapman died in 1993 at the age of 47.

Carol Mahler works as a humanities scholar for the Florida Humanities Council, a creative writing teacher in a Punta Gorda bookstore and in the Bartow Public Library, and an inventor/presenter of the DeSoto County Library Summer Youth Program. A mother of four, she is also a treefarm owner in Arcadia, Florida. Her husband, Roger Lewis Renne, died in 1990 at the age of 53.

Carol Malley is a reporter for the *Springfield Union News* and *Sunday Republican* in Massachusetts. She is a member of Amherst Writers and Artists, and a participant in its Irish and American writers exchange program. She on the staff of *Peregrine,* a literary journal, and leads a writing workshop for Latino teens. Edward Malley, Jr., a photo editor for a metropolitan newspaper, was 44 when he died in 1982.

Dale Matlock, printer and artist, owns a screenprinting business in Santa Cruz, California, serving local and regional clientele. He grew up in Texas and Oklahoma, earning a B.A. in art at the University of Tulsa. His wife, Nancy, well-known in education and political circles in Santa Cruz, died in 1994 of ovarian cancer at the age of 46, after surviving two heart operations and breast cancer during her short life.

Maude Meehan is the author of *Washing the Stones,* a collection including her first two books (now out of print). She is internationally published in literary journals, reviews, magazines, textbooks, and anthologies. Co-author of "Wheels of Summer" (a film script), she teaches poetry workshops through University of California at Santa Cruz. Don "Ace" Meehan, compleat Renaissance Man, so loved, so missed by family and friends, died suddenly in 1992.

Greggory Moore is a former arts critic for a local newspaper and an editorial assistant of a nationally-distributed literary journal. He earned a M.A. in English from California State University in Fullerton and his work has been published internationally. His wife, Sylvia Faith, died on her birthday in 1994 at the age of 31 of coronary thrombosis.

Thomas Moore is a writer and lecturer who lives in New England with his wife and two children. He was a monk in a Catholic religious order for twelve years and has degrees in theology, musicology, and philosophy. A former professor of religion and psychology, he is the author of *Care of the Soul, Soulmates, Meditations, The Re-Enchantment of Everyday Life,* and *The Education of the Heart.*

Shirley Ohrenstein is a clergyman's widow, a native Californian, and a writer of fiction and poetry centered in the San Francisco Bay Area and Northern California. She has a B.A. in Social Sciences and an M.A. in English Literature from Humboldt State University. Her husband, Dr. Edward Ohrenstein, was a liberal Protestant clergyperson with a background in law. Together they reared four children.

Sheenagh M. O'Rourke grew up in Northern Ireland and emigrated to the United States in 1983. She met her husband, Manny, in September 1986; it was love at first sight. They married three months later. Manny died of liver cancer in 1990. He was an ardent sports fan and health fanatic. Before he died, he wrote a poem.

Betty Peckinpah is a poet, printmaker, and matriarch of a large wonderful family. She was married for fifty-nine years to Denver Peckinpah (1917–1996), jurist, photographer, raconteur, and wit.

Paula Porter received her M.A. in Creative Writing from Iowa State University in 1993 with a poetry thesis titled "Transplant," about a bone marrow transplant ward. She resides in Massachusetts and is a Internet editor. Jim Porter was a championship roller skater and a journeyman steam fitter for an electrical utility. He died on Christmas Day 1987 of Hodgkin's and non-Hodgkin's lymphomas from Agent Orange.

Jeanne Quinn has worked as a buyer for a chain of bookstores and recently has been writing for a local newspaper. She is a published poet and photographer, having had several one-woman photo shows. She has five grown children and ten grandchildren. She makes her home in the Pocono Mountains with her dog Lady and cat Tasha. Her husband Jack, died at the age of 47 of coronary thrombosis.

Peg Rashid divides her time between Detroit's inner city and northern Michigan, places central to her writing. She works as a volunteer in a center for Detroit's homeless and for a hospice. Fandy Rashid died at 84, the proud possessor of the friendship of countless ordinary people of all races and backgrounds, with whom he had shared his love of language and humanity.

Linda Ribordy was born and raised in Southern California. She and her husband, Jerry, married at age 20, lived all over the country and raised three children together. Two years after the youngest child graduated from college, Jerry died unexpectedly of a rare lung inflammation. He was 51 years of age. Linda is a family lawyer practicing in Santa Cruz, California.

Nancy B. Schmitt began writing as a teenager. As a professional and volunteer she has worked as a weekly newspaper journalist/photographer, public school community relations specialist, a public relations manager, and researcher-editor-production supervisor of *Malvern*, Pennsylvania's centennial book. Her husband, Gregory Schmitt, worked for General Electric and died in 1985.

Mary Schultz completed a B.A. in Honors English at California State University, Northridge in 1979 and has supported her family as a full-time writer since. She was married in 1990 to a Montana widower. They travel extensively, investigating the planet and enjoying their passel of children and grandchildren. Her husband, Harold Stone, a truck driver, died in 1973 in a work-related accident. He was 29 years old.

Layle Silbert has published close to a hundred stories in literary magazines, a book of poems, and three collections of stories. As a photographer she has photographed numerous writers, both American and foreign. Her husband, Abraham Aidenoff, was Deputy Director of the Statistical Office at the United Nations Secretariat.

Cassandra Smith writes fiction, nonfiction, and poetry and has published in *Triquarterly, The Crescent Review, Nommo 3,* and *Obsidian II.* A doll artist, she has been a museum curator, university professor, director of marketing, and security guard. She now works odd jobs to support her writing habit. Her mate, Richard McCoy, died in Vietnam.

Carl Stancil, a former engineering teacher, is now a consultant on a veterans project in Vietnam, providing economic benefits to homeless children and older people. Rosmarie Greiner, his mate, was born in 1939 in Bern, Switzerland. After completing her education in Switzerland, she came to the United States, working and studying in the East. Her life work as an activist took her to Peru, Nicaragua, Cuba, and Southeast Asia. Her work as a children's advocate culminated in the nationally acclaimed Children's Peace Bibliography.

Ginny Stanford is a nationally known artist whose paintings are represented in many private and public collections. Stanford's paintings have graced the covers of many books including *The Light the Dead See,* a collection of her late husband's poetry. Her prose was first published by *The New Orleans Review* in 1995. Her husband, Frank Stanford, was a well known poet who took his own life in June of 1978. He had published seven books of poetry.

Carol Staudacher is a grief consultant and author in the fields of mental health and education. Personal experiences have led her to a continuing exploration of all facets of the bereavement process. She is the author of four books: *Time to Grieve, Men and Grief, Beyond Grief,* and *Hypnosis for Change.* Ms. Staudacher lives in Santa Cruz, California.

Joelle Steefel's life, Part II, is set in San Francisco and includes a new mate. The legacy of losing a mate is that in addition to writing, she is involved in a variety of social issues including the support of cancer research. Her husband died at the age of 44 from lymphoma, after fighting valiantly through chemotherapy, surgery, and radiation. He died six months short of their twenty-fifth wedding anniversary.

Mari Stitt, originally from Ohio, finished college with a degree in music education. After raising a daughter and son, she returned to school for an M.A. in human relations. She taught sociology for seventeen years before retiring to the mountains of southern California to live in voluntary simplicity. Her husband, R. Dean Stitt, was supervising psychologist for San Diego's City Schools. He retired at age 55, dedicating his life to wildlife preservation on twenty-four acres in the Cuyamaca Mountains. He died in 1990.

Victoria Sullivan, playwright, poet, and essayist, lives in Manhattan and teaches English at Saint Peter's College in Jersey City. She reads her poetry in clubs and on television, has had Off-Off Broadway Equity productions of her plays, and co-edited *Plays By and About Women.* When her husband, Steve Rosen, was alive, they collaborated on works involving his jazz piano playing and composition and her poetry. He died in 1995 at the age of 51 of pancreatic cancer.

Amber Coverdale Sumrall has edited or co-edited twelve anthologies. She is co-director of WomenCARE, a women's cancer resource center in Santa Cruz, California. Writing has been her spiritual practice for twenty-five years. Her mate, Les Breeze, died at age 29 from injuries incurred in a motorcycle accident. "Les was my mate and became, after his death, my muse."

Joseph F. Sweet has been a probation counselor, supervisor, and administrator for the state of Rhode Island for twenty-five years. He also has held a private counseling practice for twelve years. He has written over twenty articles, including personal essays and articles on history and geneology. His wife, Barbara, was a social worker who died from lymphoma in 1988.

Carol Tufts teaches in the English Department of Oberlin College. Her poems have appeared in a number of journals, as well as the recent Beacon Press anthology, *Claiming the Spirit Within: A Sourcebook of Women's Poetry.* She is also completing a first collection of poems.

Robert Vazquez-Pacheco is a gay Puerto Rican writer living with AIDS. His poetry and essays have been published in various anthologies and journals. Recently he returned to New York City and is currently working on his first novel. His mate, Jeffrey Leibowitz, died from AIDS-related complications in 1986. He was 34 years old.

Nancy Wambach lives in San Jose, California. Her children are in college and when not working or writing, she swims, gardens, reads, and does volunteer work. She has not remarried. Her husband, William, died two weeks after his forty-third birthday. By profession he was a microwave engineer, but his life's passion was producing and nurturing children with his wife Nancy.

Phyllis Wax lives in Milwaukee on a bluff overlooking Lake Michigan. Her poetry has appeared in *Wisconsin Academy Review, Plainsongs, Windfall, and Wisconsin Poets' Calendar,* as well as in an award-winning poetry video, *Drive.* Phillip Wax was a lawyer and an accomplished pianist who died of lung cancer in 1993.

J. F. West, the son of sharecropper parents, was born in 1918 in the Appalachian Mountains. He graduated with an A.B. in journalism from the University of North Carolina, and earned an M.A. in English. Now he is professor emeritus of English at Appalachian State University and author of seven books, three of them collections of poetry. He was endowed the John Foster West creative writing prize at Appalachian State University. His wife, Nan Love West, drowned when her car went over a bridge on the way home from work. She was 42.